LAST
CHANCE
FOR
JUSTICE

LAST CHANCE FOR JUSTICE

**How Relentless
Investigators
Uncovered New
Evidence Convicting
the Birmingham
Church Bombers**

T. K. Thorne

Lawrence Hill Books

Chicago

Copyright © 2013, 2018 by T. K. Thorne
All rights reserved
First hardcover edition published 2013
First paperback edition published 2018
Published by Lawrence Hill Books, an imprint of
Chicago Review Press, Incorporated
814 North Franklin Street
Chicago, Illinois 60610
ISBN 978-1-61374-864-0 (hardcover)
ISBN 978-1-64160-019-4 (paperback)

The Library of Congress has cataloged the hardcover edition as follows:

Thorne, T. K.
  Last chance for justice : how relentless investigators uncovered new evidence convicting the Birmingham church bombers / T.K. Thorne. — First edition.
        pages cm
  Includes bibliographical references and index.
  ISBN 978-1-61374-864-0 (cloth)
  1. Murder investigation—Alabama—Birmingham—History—Case studies. 2. Murder—Alabama—Birmingham—History—20th century 3. Bombings—Alabama—Birmingham—History—20th century. 4. African Americans—Crimes against—Alabama—Birmingham—History—20th century. 5. Hate crimes—Alabama—Birmingham—History—20th century. 6. Birmingham (Ala.)—Race relations—History—20th century. I. Title.
  HV6534.B5T46 2013
  364.152'309761781—dc23

                            2013014307

Cover design: Joan Sommers Design
Cover photo: 16th Street Baptist Church's damaged facade, Birmingham
    Public Library; Inset © Brian Cahn/ZUMA Press/Corbis
Interior design: PerfecType, Nashville, TN

Printed in the United States of America

To Granny,
Who stood up for principles of justice and taught me
to love words and the places they could take me

CONTENTS

AUTHOR'S NOTE

◆

IT WAS A GREAT surprise to my family when I became the first Jewish
police officer in the Birmingham Police Department. It was a surprise to
me as well, as my chosen path was social work, in which I had recently
completed my masters at the University of Alabama. At that time, women
and blacks were the exception in the police department, and affirmative
action policies were only being discussed.

The experience was totally outside anything my background could
have prepared me for; but I managed to survive, and I retired as a captain. Although the department had the mixed bag of personalities that
one would expect in any community, it was a fulfilling and interesting
career. Most of the officers I worked with were dedicated professionals
who put their lives at risk every day to serve their community.

My intention in writing this book was to tell the story of the 1963 Sixteenth Street Baptist Church bombing primarily from the perspective of
the investigators. I was a child in Montgomery, Alabama, when the bombing
occurred, and have only a vague memory of watching with confusion the
resulting riots and chaos on television. At the time, I was unaware that my
mother and grandmother were quiet supporters of the civil rights movement
or that the Ku Klux Klan had burned a cross in my grandparents' yard. Virginia and Clifford Durr, leaders in the civil rights struggle, were close family
friends. Their country home in Wetumpka was my favorite retreat, and one
of their daughters was my regular babysitter. We were childhood friends of
Aubrey and Anita Williams's grandchildren. Robert Graetz—whose first job
as a white Lutheran minister was to serve in a black church in Montgomery
and whose home was bombed during the 1960s—quips that my siblings and
I were the first to integrate in Montgomery, playing with black children in a
small plastic pool in his backyard.

My primary sources for this book were my interviews with the investigators who handled the case and others involved in the investigation; FBI

summary reports and reports from FBI interviews and informant sources; teletypes and internal FBI memos; transcripts of covert recordings; and trial transcripts. I also called on historical material. Quoted material from the suspects was taken from official FBI documents and from the investigators' notes. All of the quotes from persons other than the suspects were taken from documents, transcripts, or my interviews. I did, however, rely heavily on Frank Sikora's book *Until Justice Rolls Down* to help understand the attorneys' summations in the Blanton case, for which I only had an audio recording as source material. In some cases regarding personal exchanges between investigators Ben Herren and Bill Fleming, when they had no memory of exactly when the discussion took place, I took the liberty of "placing" the conversation in the story, but the material came from taped interviews with them.

A selected bibliography provides resources and further reading suggestions. My apologies in advance for the numerous names encountered in the book. It couldn't be helped. There is a list to assist the reader. I have been careful with the facts as I was told them, giving priority to verifiable documentation, but I take responsibility for any errors.

It was a privilege to spend many hours in interviews and communications with investigators Ben Herren, Bill Fleming, and Bob Eddy. Both Herren and Fleming constantly gave credit to the prosecutors, fellow FBI agents, and staff that supported their efforts. Bob Eddy told me several times he was not a hero, just a member of a team. It was indeed teamwork that brought this case to trial and convicted the perpetrators of this heinous crime. In no way does that diminish the investigators' incredible effort and commitment. I do agree the true heroes are the witnesses who risked their lives to see justice done. That is a debt we can never repay.

This was a story that needed to be preserved for its own sake. Having spent over two decades in the Birmingham Police Department, however, it also has been my desire to do something positive in furthering the tarnished relationship between the African American community and law enforcement. Despite all the progress made, resentment and distrust still sometimes fester from the wrongs of the past. The Sixteenth Street Church bombing and the death of four innocent girls can never be righted. Those children cannot be brought back to life by the efforts of any human being, but seeking justice is what law enforcement does . . . at its best. It is my hope telling the story of finding that justice and the dedication of those who sought it might be a step in the healing.

LIST OF NAMES

◆

David Barber Jefferson County district attorney (1980s–2000s)

Bill Baxley Alabama attorney general (1990s)

Bobby Birdwell Childhood friend of Tommy Frank Cherry

Thomas E. Blanton Member of Eastview #13 Klavern

Albert Boutwell Mayor of Birmingham, 1963

Jack William Brown Klansman from Chattanooga, Tennessee (1960s)

Mitch Burns Klansman who worked undercover for the FBI

Ralph Butler FBI special agent (1960s)

Charles Arnie Cagle Member of Eastview #13 Klavern

Herman Frank Cash Member of Eastview #13 Klavern

Flora "Tee" Chambliss Robert Chambliss's wife (1960s)

Robert "Dynamite Bob" Chambliss Convicted of Birmingham Church bombing in 1977

Bobby Frank Cherry Member of Eastview #13 Klavern

Marsha Gail Cherry Tommy Frank Cherry's wife

Tommy Frank Cherry Son of Bobby Frank Cherry

Tommy Frank Cherry Jr. Son of Tommy Frank Cherry; grandson of Bobby Frank Cherry

Willadean Brogdon Cherry Bobby Frank Cherry's third wife

Elizabeth Cobbs Niece of Robert Chambliss (later a.k.a. Petric Smith)

Don Cochran US assistant attorney for Northern District of Alabama (1990s)

Addie Mae Collins Victim of church bombing

Sarah Collins Survivor of the church bombing

John Colvin Electronic technician with FBI (1960s)

John Cross Pastor of Sixteenth Street Baptist Church (1960s)

Mary Frances Cunningham Sister of Flora "Tee" Chambliss

Bob Eddy Investigator for Bill Baxley, Alabama's attorney general (1970s)

Edward Fields National States Rights Party, editor of *Thunderbolt* magazine

William "Bill" Fleming FBI special agent (1990s)

Bob Gafford Owner of an auto parts store in Chambliss's neighborhood, and an Alabama state legislator

Gertrude Glenn or Kirthus Glenn Witness from Detroit (1960s and 1970s)

Mike Gowins Terminally ill man who remembered Bobby Frank Cherry

Chris Hamlin Pastor of Sixteenth Street Baptist Church (1990s)

James Hancock Jefferson County deputy sheriff (1960s)

Art Hanes Commissioner of Birmingham in 1963

Ben Herren Birmingham Police Department sergeant and FBI analyst (1990s)

Troy Ingram Member of Eastview #13 Klavern

William "Bill" Jackson Catholic barber associated with Klan

Johnny Johnson Chief of the Birmingham Police Department (1990s)

Doug Jones US attorney for Northern District of Alabama (1990s)

Gloria LaDow Bobby Frank Cherry's stepdaughter; Willadean Cherry's daughter

Robert "Rob" Langford Special agent in charge of Birmingham FBI (1993–1996)

Wyman Lee Member of Eastview #13 Klavern

Joseph R. Lewis Special agent in charge of Birmingham FBI (1996–2004)

Don Luna Member of Eastview #13 Klavern

Pershing Mayfield   Member of Eastview #13 Klavern

Denise McNair   Victim of church bombing

Jack Nelson   Bureau chief for *Los Angeles Times* (1970s)

John Ott   US assistant attorney for Northern District of Alabama (1990s)

Robert Posey   US assistant attorney for Northern District of Alabama (1990s)

Carol Robertson   Victim of church bombing

Gary Thomas Rowe   Controversial FBI informant (1960s and 1970s)

Robert Shelton   Klan Imperial Wizard

Arthur Shores   African American Birmingham civil rights attorney (1960s)

Jack Shows   Chief investigator for Bill Baxley (1970s)

Fred Shuttlesworth   African American minister of Bethel Baptist Church; founder of Alabama Christian Movement for Human Rights

Teresa Stacy   Cherry's granddaughter

J. B. Stoner   National State's Rights Party chairman

Petric Smith   Elizabeth Cobbs (after gender reassignment)

Robert Sidney Thomas   Grand Cyclops of Eastview #13 Klavern

Gary L. Tucker   Patient at Bryce Hospital claiming to have made the bomb

Waylene Vaughn   Girlfriend of Thomas Blanton

Jabo Waggoner Sr.   Commissioner of Birmingham (1963)

Jeff Wallace   Deputy district attorney for Jefferson County (1990s)

Tom Ward   Investigator for Bill Baxley (1970s)

Macon Weaver   US attorney for Northern District of Alabama (1990s)

Cynthia Wesley   Victim of church bombing

Levie S. "Quick Draw" Yarbrough   Member of Eastview #13 Klavern

John Yung   Assistant attorney general (1970s)

PROLOGUE

◆

ON JULY 9, 1997, in a room at the sheriff's office in Athens, Texas, waited a man whose name could still evoke an array of emotions: anger, grief, . . . fear. Sergeant Ben Herren felt none of these, but his heart hammered with the familiar mix of anticipation and anxiety he'd experienced often in his career, particularly on a burglary or a domestic violence call, or when poised to kick in a door on a drug raid. You only thought you knew what was on the other side of that door, and once it was opened, it couldn't be closed again.

The man on the other side of this door was Bobby Frank Cherry.

In the darkest hours before dawn in September 1963, he and his companions drove down a deserted alley in Birmingham, Alabama, and placed dynamite in some brush beneath the side stairs outside an African American church—a bomb that exploded Sunday morning, killing four young girls and changing the world. The girls were in the church basement in their white dresses, getting ready for Youth Day services when the east wall imploded. A single searing moment erased whatever the future may have held for them.

It happened decades ago, but only one of the four suspects was convicted. For many, the case festered, a wound that persisted because only justice could begin to heal it. In their minds, justice had not been done. And a worse question lingered—had justice ever really been sought?

A different kind of doubt loomed before Herren. He'd flown to Texas from Birmingham to interview this man about a crime that had happened over thirty years earlier. Many witnesses had died or disappeared; physical evidence didn't even exist anymore. The case had already been investigated twice—in the 1960s and 1970s. Why was he here now, in 1997?

In an unprecedented move, the Birmingham Police Department had loaned Sergeant Ben Herren to the FBI to take one last shot at the

Sixteenth Street case. Herren and his FBI partner, Bill Fleming, spent fifteen months working in secrecy toward this moment, poring over every piece of the massive collection of accumulated documents—ninety-one volumes on the case alone, not counting the hundreds of intelligence volumes on the Ku Klux Klan and other groups—literally thousands of pages. They had devoted long hours to discussing strategies for this moment, their best chance at getting evidence they could use.

In planning for the interview, they hoped having a local boy show up, in the person of Sergeant Herren, instead of a hated Yankee FBI agent, would encourage Cherry to talk. They also hoped the canker of guilt and the shock of seeing Bob Eddy, the investigator from the 1977 investigation, would shake Cherry enough to rattle out what had never passed his lips: a confession of his participation in the bombing.

Bill Fleming was the Birmingham special agent assigned to the case. Herren was glad not to be in his partner's position, waiting on an outcome without any power to influence it, but Fleming was interviewing other people, including Cherry's grandson.

The responsibility for this critical interview was Herren's. He took a deep breath. Who would have dreamed that the man about to walk through this door was the same man who, as a short, scrawny twenty-four-year-old two decades ago, taped quarters to his legs to make the weight requirement for a Birmingham police officer?

Today, no weight dragged at his legs, but one bore down on his shoulders. If this didn't work—if they couldn't get Cherry to confess or give them a good lead—the Sixteenth Street Church bombing case would die a final death.

Those little girls deserved better.

1 | THE MANTRAP

BIRMINGHAM POLICE DETECTIVE SERGEANT Ben Herren couldn't think of a reason he would be in trouble—recently anyway—but when his beeper went off with a message to return to the office and see the lieutenant, he acknowledged it with the enthusiasm of a student called to the principal's office. It was two years prior to the interview with Bobby Frank Cherry, and the bombing of a church thirty-two years ago was hardly on his mind. Herren wrapped up his interview with a burglary victim and headed back to the police administration building without a clue that his life was about to change.

His new boss, Lieutenant Diane Cribbs, had started out on the wrong foot with her detectives. From the minute she hit the door, she made it her mission to change everything. She rearranged the office, the paperwork, and the assignments. Everyone was grumbling behind her back. As senior detective, Herren felt he should do something. On the third day, he told her, "Lieutenant, have you got any idea what my responsibilities are here?"

"Yes," she said, puzzled. "You're the South and the West Precinct sergeant over the detectives."

Herren shook his head. "No, I've got three responsibilities, and only three. First responsibility is I gotta get them guys out there to do what you want them to do. Second, I gotta keep them from killing you. Third, I gotta keep you from making stupid mistakes"—he took a deep breath— "and you're making my job hard."

1

To his surprise, she had taken this well, and they developed an understanding, discussing issues and working them out together. Still, he didn't like being called to her office without a clue as to what it was about. Police are paranoid by nature; it tends to keep them alive.

"Ben, I've got an assignment for you," she said when he stepped through the doorway of her small glass cubicle at police headquarters. Space was a rare commodity in the aging building, which had once been the Birmingham jail—the very one from which Martin Luther King Jr. wrote his famous letter in April 1963 (written on the edges of a newspaper and bits of paper supplied by a jail trustee and smuggled out through his lawyers) declaring that citizens have a moral duty to challenge unjust laws.

"An assignment? More cases than the ones I've got?" Herren protested.

She shook her head. "The chief called down and asked me who my best detective was, and I said you."

He blinked, instantly suspicious. "What am I getting into?"

"He wants you to go over and talk to the FBI. They're thinking about reopening the Sixteenth Street bombing case."

Herren was stunned. Birmingham's chief was Johnny Johnson, the first black chief in the history of the city, so he wasn't surprised Johnson would be interested in the civil rights struggle. But the church bombing happened in 1963. This was 1995. Herren finally got his wits together enough to say, "Well, you know, that's an old case," an understatement if he had ever uttered one.

"Yeah, I know; they're just looking at it. We're not even sure we're going to commit manpower to it, but the chief wants you to go over there part-time and see what you think about it."

That was how it began for him.

The real beginning took place several months earlier when Robert "Rob" Langford, the FBI special agent in charge (SAC) invited several black community leaders to the FBI offices to talk. At first none of them responded. Langford went out to meet some of then, enlisting their support in calling a meeting. His intent was simply to talk with them about the FBI and to try to break the ice in the frigid relationship between the Bureau and the Birmingham African American community. When the meeting was finally held, Reverend Abraham Woods blurted out, "Why didn't the FBI investigate the bombing of the church? The FBI never did do anything."

The comment surprised Langford, who had come to the Birmingham office in 1993, thirty years after the bombing of the church. He replied that he was sure the Bureau had investigated it extensively. Woods was not persuaded, "Well, they never did anything about it." Langford promised to look into it.

FBI Special Agent in Charge Robert "Rob" Langford.

Tony Nichols

Near the conversation's end, Woods fired a parting shot; Langford wasn't sure whether it was meant to be serious or in jest—"By the way, none of us want to eat your donuts because we're afraid they're poisoned."

Langford called for the case files to look into the matter, and about thirty files were brought to him. The FBI had definitely investigated the case, but closed it after a decade with no prosecutions. Several years later, in 1977, the state of Alabama had tried and convicted one of the suspects, Robert "Dynamite Bob" Chambliss.

Langford was a good friend of Reverend Chris Hamlin, the pastor of the Sixteenth Street Baptist Church at that time. Hamlin introduced him to Petric Smith, the witness who had broken open the case at the Chambliss trial. With Reverend Hamlin's assurance that the FBI SAC really wanted to reopen the investigation, Petric Smith agreed to an interview with Langford at Smith's home.

Langford then floated the idea of reopening the investigation to one of the assistant US attorneys and received a "lukewarm reception," so he turned to David Barber, the district attorney for Jefferson County, who was very receptive and supportive. Langford talked Barber into driving with him to Montgomery to speak to a man Langford thought could answer the question that had burned in his mind since Abraham Woods's comment. The man was Lieutenant Colonel Bob Eddy of the Alabama Department of Public Safety, the primary investigator in Chambliss's trial eighteen years earlier.

"In your opinion, Bob, can we solve this case?" Langford asked Eddy.

Eddy's answer was, "I believe you can, if there are some witnesses still alive."

Langford asked Eddy to come to Birmingham for a meeting in the FBI's office. This was the first meeting Herren attended. When Eddy began to talk, Herren snatched out his fountain pen to take notes. Eddy, a quiet, intense man, looked over and nodded in appreciation, "Nice writing instrument." That small connection was the beginning of a relationship of mutual respect and friendship tying together Eddy, Herren, and Special Agent Bill Fleming, the civil rights investigator for the Birmingham FBI office.

Others present at the meeting included BPD's Chief Johnny Johnson; District Attorney David Barber, and Assistant District Attorney Roger Brown; as well as a representative from the Alabama Bureau of

Investigations and Alcohol, Tobacco, and Firearms (due to the involvement of dynamite in the case).

FBI staff had already worked for several months compiling a list of witnesses, marking those who were dead and those who were still alive. It wasn't pretty. One hundred and fifteen people on the list were dead. Of the approximately forty witnesses left, what was the chance any would testify? Of the original prime suspects, only two were still alive: Bobby Frank Cherry and Thomas E. Blanton.

Herren did not hold any illusions. No one in the FBI thought they had the evidence to go to trial with the remaining suspects. Their only hope was that witnesses, mostly Klansmen and their relatives, were older, closer to meeting their Maker, and would perhaps want to clear their conscience and "get things right." It was a slender strand on which to initiate a major investigation. Still, Langford pointed out, there was no way to know without pursuing it.

After the meeting, Herren went back to his usual responsibilities at the police department. Time passed, and he figured the whole thing was dead. Then another meeting was called. And another. It seemed the FBI followed a pattern he was familiar with in law enforcement—having meetings about having meetings.

One afternoon in 1996, when he had been on the case only on a part-time basis, splitting his time between his police detective duties and the FBI building, Chief Johnson called him into his office. The chief didn't waste time. "Tell me what you've got, sergeant."

"Well," Herren said, "we do have two of the main suspects—Bobby Frank Cherry and Thomas Blanton—and a few witnesses still alive. But Cherry is sixty-five years old and not in great health."

The chief considered him. "You're the one with the information. What do you think? Is it worth committing manpower to it?"

Herren had been chewing on this question, figuring it was coming. This was his chance to back out. If he said the whole thing was a wild-goose chase, he could go back to the Burglary Unit, returning his life to its status before his lieutenant had called him into her office.

He felt divided on what to say. On the one hand, for him personally, it wouldn't be a bad assignment this close to retirement. It was something different and interesting, and surely they would allow him a take-home car. On the other hand, he didn't believe they had any chance of getting a conviction, and he didn't want to be involved in a losing proposition.

A mountain of files lay in wait, information the FBI had collected during the reign of Director J. Edgar Hoover and the unrest of the 1950s and '60s. A thorough investigation would involve a lot of grunt work, poring over all that paperwork, and it probably wouldn't amount to a hill of beans.

Chief Johnson waited for his answer.

Herren had been ten years old when the bomb ripped through the basement of the church—almost as old as Denise McNair and only four years younger than Addie Mae Collins, Carole Robertson, and Cynthia Wesley. He knew what the case meant. The legacy of Birmingham, Alabama, was Eugene "Bull" Connor, the racist public safety commissioner of that era. For the nation, time had stopped in 1963, and the word "Birmingham" evoked pictures of dogs and hoses turned on children. That wasn't his police department, and it wasn't who he was. All the pros and cons Herren had weighed back and forth settled on one fact: regardless of the outcome, this was clearly the last chance for an investigation.

He met Chief Johnson's eyes. He believed this was just going to be an exercise, and they were never going to get a conviction. But if it fell to him to do it, he wanted people to know the Birmingham Police Department had given its best effort.

"Chief," he said, "if we're going to do it, let's do it right. Full-time, not part-time. Let me go over there and see what we can come up with. If we can make a case, we'll make it. If we can't, we'll close it out, but it'll be put to rest one way or the other for the final time."

———————

That was how, in October 1996, he ended up in the "mantrap."

The small interview room lay between the public area and the secured inner sanctum of the FBI offices, an attempt at security on the fourteenth floor of the old 2121 Building in downtown Birmingham,

Alabama. Never meant to be an office—one steel desk, three chairs, and no windows—the room had nonetheless been assigned to Herren. Isolated between two locked doors, he could not have felt more like an outsider . . . until he learned he was not allowed inside the actual FBI offices. He had to ask for a key and use the public restroom.

At first, several federal and local agencies had been interested in forming a task force, but by the time Langford let DC headquarters know he'd reopened the case with a teletype in April 1996, the investigation had fallen to just the FBI and Birmingham PD, that is, Special Agent Bill Fleming and Sergeant Ben Herren. That was a good thing, as far as Herren was concerned. Too many cooks can spoil the soup—or screw up a case.

The next step was to review all the old files, which needed to be done in secret. If word got out they were opening the 1963 bombing case—and the media would be hot for such a story—it would alert the suspects, robbing the investigators of any advantage surprise might grant them. If they ended up with no case, the expectations and hope built by a premature release would crumble into disappointment and increase community cynicism toward law enforcement.

Herren sighed. It hadn't been his plan to end his career turning pages in the mantrap at the FBI, but he had chosen it and here he was. It was a far different environment than the camaraderie of the police department. Only three people in the entire PD knew where he was and why he was here. His buddies thought he was working on some kind of federal task force on a theft ring.

He was supposed to be part of a team, but his FBI partner was an older man he'd only met a few times, a senior agent assigned to the civil rights division. Bill Fleming was as icy as the mantrap. As a welcome, he'd brought Herren a file and left him to try to figure out what the Bureau's codes meant. Like the keys to the bathroom, that was something they couldn't, or wouldn't, give him.

Herren clenched his jaw. He wasn't going to give up just because the FBI rules made things difficult, or because he was sitting alone at a desk, or because his supposed partner hadn't said more than a handful of words to him. That wasn't in him. He'd come by his stubborn streak honestly. Fairfield Highlands, a small community just to the west of Birmingham, was a good place to grow up, but it had its challenges. As a kid, when the boys on his block got into fights—pretty much an everyday occurrence—his father let them put on boxing gloves and go at it. Herren was usually the smallest, and he didn't often win, but he didn't stop until he couldn't raise his arms from his sides. Besides, he didn't intend to stay at a desk forever, no matter how much paperwork they put on it. At some point, he would be out interviewing people.

His plan was simple. He would take in information with an open mind. At this point, for him, no one was guilty or innocent. It was the investigator's job to look at the evidence and uncover the truth. He would see where the facts led. Maybe he would find a hidden pearl—an overlooked clue, a witness no one had followed up on, something that might break the case open. That's how it worked—when it worked. Unfortunately, the majority of crimes didn't have enough evidence to start with and, despite best efforts, they ended up just as statistics. But every now and then, you got lucky. Sometimes you could make your own luck with diligence and a little smarts.

He took a deep breath, picked up a thick file from the 1963 investigation, and got his first surprise.

2 | BAPBOMB

IN 1963, THE FBI'S code name for the Sixteenth Street Baptist Church bombing was "Bapbomb," which referred to the "Baptist Church bombing." While the Birmingham Police Department normally would have had jurisdiction over the crime as a homicide, and had even assigned Lieutenant Maurice House to lead the local investigation, President John F. Kennedy tasked the FBI with solving the case.

The FBI's original jurisdiction rationale appeared to rely on a law enacted in 1960 that made it illegal to transport dynamite over state lines. An early internal FBI memo referenced a newspaper article where a "Federal man" told a reporter, "Slim chance anybody bothered to bring dynamite in from somewhere else. There's enough dynamite already in Alabama to blow Birmingham off the map." J. Edgar Hoover wrote on the bottom margin, "I hope no FBI man made any such statement." The director's comment prompted a flurry of internal investigation.

Herren had never really given much thought to the case. Many believed the original investigation had been shoved under the rug without much effort being put into it. On the face of it, that was a valid supposition, considering the feds worked the case for years without revealing their findings or bringing anyone to trial. But the first volume of files indicated a different story entirely.

By the evening of the day of the bombing, two bomb technicians from headquarters in Washington, DC, caught military flights and landed in Birmingham. Almost two dozen people—agents, attorneys, and support staff—arrived in a short period of time, and more followed, about thirty "specials" called in from across the country to work with the two squads in the Birmingham office, a total of about fifty agents initially dedicated to the case. One memorandum from Atlanta notified the team that a secretary for Squad Three was en route to Birmingham "with her type-writer" to help. The massive amount of paperwork associated with the case gave meaning to the phrase "speaking volumes."

Herren was quickly convinced that the Bureau considered this a major investigation from the get-go, a conclusion reinforced by the con-stant reminders from headquarters to the Birmingham field office that "this case and related bombing cases are to be given continuous and pre-ferred investigative attention." On one memo was a recommendation that the attorney general be briefed as to the extensive nature of the investiga-tion. Hoover handwrote a note, "No . . . We want results, not publicity."

Hoover had a standing policy of moving southern agents to other locations and importing agents from across the country to southern sta-tions. He did the same across the country. Although the agents in Bir-mingham would not be as familiar with the local culture as agents from the South, the relocations reduced the possibility of having southern extremist sympathizers in the Birmingham office. Nevertheless, rumors were rampant in the community that both Birmingham police and the FBI were in league with the Klansmen, and both law enforcement agen-cies suspected the same of each other.

The Bureau's policy forbade tape recording an interview, so the results were written on summary forms called 302s. Also included in the files were letters, memos, and the agents' logs, which listed the individu-als they talked to and the interview results. Everything was written in what Herren came to think of as Bureau-ese. The thick files had a two-post center punch at the top and went chronologically from the bottom up. All the reports were typed on a manual typewriter. Only one of the six copies made resided in the case file, and it was hit-and-miss whether it would be on bonded paper or one of the fine onionskin papers that needed to be held up to the light to be read.

Prior to the church bombing, the FBI had seeded hate groups with informants, and the investigation began on a national level with all FBI field divisions directed to access their sources for any pertinent information. Numerous leads flowed in from across the country, many based on rumor or supposition, but each was investigated. A large-scale inquiry focused on the Southeast, particularly on the known leaders and most militant members of hate groups. The effort included extensive surveillance operations.

In Birmingham, the Bureau targeted members of the Ku Klux Klan, the National States Rights Party, and the United Americans for a Conservative Government. Agents were instructed to start checking out Asa Carter, an anti-Semitic, segregationist speechwriter for Alabama governor George Wallace, and Wallace himself. Eleven locations were bugged on seven suspects. Eventually the surveillances alone yielded twelve hundred pages of logs, transcripts, and summaries.

Roy K. Moore, the SAC in Little Rock, Arkansas, was sent to Birmingham to lead the special squad investigating the bombing. Moore would later run the Jackson, Mississippi, office, where he was credited with tracking down the Ku Klux Klan murderers of three civil rights workers—James Chaney, Andrew Goodman, and Michael Schwerner.

Herren was starting from scratch on the matter of suspects, and he needed to understand the context in which the crime had occurred. Like many who had grown up in Birmingham, he knew generalities about the time period, but not the historical specifics. Clues could lurk there. Birmingham had earned the nickname "Bombingham" in recognition of the fifty bombings of the homes and houses of worship of black citizens that had occurred since 1947. Ironically, only a week before the Sixteenth Street Baptist Church bombing, Governor George Wallace complained about recent court rulings on school integration, telling the *New York Times*, "What this country needs is a few first-class funerals."

In 1963 the Sixteenth Street Baptist Church, located downtown across the street from a small park, was the church of the black middle class. It was the oldest black church in the city, founded in 1875, and the building itself had stood since 1911. The church was part of a consortium of sixty African American churches Reverend Fred Shuttlesworth had brought together to mobilize the black community. Shuttlesworth was a local leader of the civil rights movement in Birmingham who believed in active demonstrations to put pressure on the status quo. His small church in the northern section of Birmingham, the Bethel

Baptist Church, became the movement's blood, but the Sixteenth Street Baptist Church was its heart. It was used as a meeting place and as a site to launch the various protests and marches, in part because of its convenient location near downtown businesses and city hall. From this church, activists launched the Birmingham Children's Crusade in early May 1963. Televised video of police dogs and high-powered hoses turned on protestors and children on the church steps and in Kelly Park, just across the street, played across the world.

On May 10, 1963, there were two bombings: one at the home of King's brother, followed by one at the A. G. Gaston Hotel, a meeting place for civil rights leaders, including Martin Luther King, and the only hotel for blacks in the city. Angered by the bombings, an estimated fifteen hundred people rioted around the Gaston Hotel, requiring hundreds of state troopers and deputized citizens to restore calm.

Church sign on the front corner after the bombing.

Federal Bureau of Investigation

Kennedy threatened to federalize the national guard in Alabama and sent in representatives to help mediate, and city leaders—in exchange for an end to the demonstrations—announced an agreement for the desegregation of public facilities, release of jailed protestors, hiring of blacks in downtown department stores, and the creation of a biracial committee to oversee the implementation of desegregation.

Earlier that spring, the same progressive city leaders had orchestrated a change in the form of municipal government—from a three-person commission system to a mayor–city council system—and new elections were set for that spring. The three commissioners at that time were Public Safety Commissioner Eugene "Bull" Connor, Public Works Commissioner "Jabo" Waggoner Sr., and Mayor Art Hanes Sr. With the aid of a bloc of black votes, Albert Boutwell beat Connor for the position of mayor. Though Boutwell was a segregationist, his views were moderate compared to the radical positions of the incumbents, who claimed their terms had not expired and refused to step down.

Bull Connor was still controlling the fire and police departments in May 1963 while a court case deciding the implementation of the structural change in government worked its way to resolution. Thus Connor was in a position to order the police dogs and pressurized fire hoses turned on protestors and fulfill his vow to "fill that jail full if Negroes violate segregation laws." Afterward, when Boutwell was finally installed into office, the community leaders were unable to get him to enact the promised changes, or even to get all parties to agree on how to implement them.

Progressive coalitions in Alabama had worked to end Klan violence and bring about racial reform since the 1920s, when opposition arose to the state's rampant "convict leasing" practices. Reform efforts picked up again in the 1940s, when the Klan's actions against a black Girl Scout camp brought national attention to Birmingham. Despite these and other efforts, Birmingham's Jim Crow laws were among the harshest in the country. When the 1954 Supreme Court ruling on *Brown v. Board of Education* ended legal segregation in schools, Alabama schools remained segregated.

Almost a decade later, in 1963, court orders were issued enforcing desegregation in Birmingham, and the reaction was fierce. In his inaugural speech that year, Governor George Wallace shouted, "Segregation

National States Rights Party and the KKK at West End High School with anti-Semitic and integration protest signs, September 4, 1963.

Birmingham, Ala. Public Library Archives

now! Segregation tomorrow! Segregation forever!" White protests continued and black protests continued, as did the bombings.

The Sixteenth Street Baptist Church was not the first bombing of a church. Between 1947 and 1965 about nineteen bombings involved places of worship or ministers' homes. In 1958, a janitor at the Jewish synagogue, Beth-El, discovered a bag near the building wall with fifty-four sticks of dynamite in it. The fuses had died out only five feet from the blasting caps, possibly because of rain the night before. Bombs exploded at the Triumph Church and Kingdom of God and Christ, New Bethel Baptist Church, and Saint Luke's AME Zion Church. The Bethel Church, where Reverend Shuttlesworth preached, was bombed on three occasions. In 1965, while mass services were taking place, a bomb with a ticking alarm clock was discovered outside Our Lady, Queen of the Universe Catholic Church. Although parishioners evacuated the building, the priest refused to leave, continuing his liturgy. Only minutes before the bomb was set to explode, a bomb expert was able to deactivate it.

Nor was this terrorism limited to public figures and locations. Several bombs exploded in or near the homes of blacks who had moved into what were declared "white neighborhoods," a trend that began after World War II. Herren found it interesting how the pattern of segregation in the city differed from those of many of the surrounding mining towns. In those mining communities, whites clustered around the convenience of the company store, while the blacks lived farther out in an encircling ring. But in a city like Birmingham, there were white sections and black sections, some even designated by city zoning ordinances, and the Klan was determined to send a warning to anyone trying to cross those invisible lines. One such area in the Fountain Heights neighborhood on the northwestern side of downtown was still called Dynamite Hill.

In August and again in early September 1963, Arthur Shores's home in that area was bombed. Shores was a local African American attorney who represented blacks on several high-profile civil rights cases. In the mid 1950s he, along with future Supreme Court justice Thurgood Marshall and future senator and judge Constance Baker Motley, had represented Autherine Lucy, the first African American to attempt to enroll at the University of Alabama. In the spring of 1963, he worked to get the children arrested by Bull Connor released, and that summer, Shores had represented Viviane Malone and James Hood, who sought to enroll at the University of Alabama—Governor George Wallace famously blocked them entry by standing in the doorway. Shores was an obvious target for the Klan's attention.

A little over a week after the church bombing, a bomb exploded on Center Street, not far from Arthur Shores's house. After a short period of time, another, larger shrapnel bomb went off, timed to catch those who responded to help the wounded from the first bomb. The explosion left a crater in the street and damaged a utility pole.

Although there were injuries over the years, amazingly, no one had been killed prior to the bombing of the Sixteenth Street Baptist Church. But 1963 was a hot year. Tensions had built throughout the spring and summer: the confrontations in the Birmingham park; demonstration marches; the national March on Washington where Martin Luther King gave his "I Have a Dream" speech; Governor George Wallace's stance in the doorway at the University of Alabama; Birmingham leaders' agreement to desegregate public areas; and, especially, the federal court orders requiring the integration of public schools. All this sparked flames to the tinder of racial unrest.

As Ben Herren read the files, he could imagine the chaos after the bombing and the tension involved in working a crime scene where such overwhelming grief and rage seethed. Birmingham police and state law enforcement were charged with keeping the peace—or often, containing the violence. The FBI's responsibility was to determine what happened and who was accountable as quickly as possible.

Immediately after the Sixteenth Street Church bombing, agents interviewed church members and canvassed the neighborhood, interviewing people employed by businesses in the area or who lived nearby. Reports stated some people at first thought the explosion was a Soviet bomb and that the Cold War had finally erupted.

Orders from FBI headquarters instructed the agents to protect their informants by interviewing them "in the same manner as Klansmen and hate group members." Agents were also advised not to give a blow-by-blow account of the investigation to the Department of Justice attorneys, lest the details of their investigation appear on the pages of newspapers. Despite Hoover's declaration that he wanted results, not publicity, headquarters' administrators were apparently well aware that the eyes of the world were watching to see how their organization handled the volatile situation. Administrators instructed agents to observe church services and the funerals and record tag numbers, and so forth, but not to interview anyone near a church or funeral. Thousands of people attended the public funeral held for three of the girls. (Carole Robertson's family held a private funeral.)

Herren found references to pieces of evidence collected from the scene—material from the ladies' lounge and soil from the crater—which were forwarded to the FBI for analysis. Results came back negative for explosive residue or indications of what kind of timing device might have been used. Dynamite was "strongly suspected." One tantalizing reference described a fishing float, a bobber, found on the street. A document said it had been sent to the lab, but there was nothing in the files indicating it was received by the FBI lab or where it might be. Herren made a note to discuss it with Fleming, who was more familiar with the FBI forms and policies regarding evidence—assuming his partner ever decided to expand his contribution from slapping a file on Herren's desk to having a conversation.

During the 1960s investigation, experts determined the damage done to the church wall was consistent with a minimum of ten sticks of dynamite, or some "equivalent explosive," placed under an exterior concrete stairway in front of a basement window near the northeast (rear) corner of the church building. The stairway ran parallel along the building's wall. Someone walking up it would be facing the rear of the church. A clump of brush grew underneath. That stairway no longer existed. When the church was repaired, it was not replaced.

Police block off the street after the explosion.

Federal Bureau of Investigation

Within a couple of months after the explosion, information from sources led the FBI to believe the bombers were indeed among the approximately twenty-five members of the Eastview #13 Klavern in Birmingham and possibly belonged to a splinter faction of dissidents, formed in the early 1960s, called the Cahaba River Bridge Group. This group held their meetings just south of Birmingham in a wooded area under a stone bridge over the slow-moving Cahaba River. The Cahaba Boys met in that remote location because they (rightly) believed the FBI had bugged their homes, cars, and meeting places. They were constantly suspicious of each other being paid informants or "government pimps."

The Cahaba Boys felt the Eastview #13 Klavern did not take the threats to their way of life seriously enough. They employed what they called missionary missions—beatings and acts of intimidation—to discourage desegregation and integration. Although the Cahaba Boys were not recognized as a legitimate Klan organization, there was speculation Klan leadership might have welcomed the missionary operations as a way to have the dirty work done while distancing the official Klan from responsibility for the radical and violent acts.

Troy Ingram and Robert "Dynamite Bob" Chambliss were militant segregationists and the leaders of the Cahaba River Boys. They were both known for their skill at making bombs. Two days after the church bombing, a source reported that Chambliss had made the church bomb at Troy Ingram's house on Saturday, September 14, 1963, the night before the church bombing.

Another interesting bit about Ingram surfaced in the files: Three witnesses observed two white men hastening from the scene minutes before the bomb went off. One had a limp. In another document, Herren found Troy Ingram had a limp from an engine block falling on his foot. The witnesses identified Ingram from a book of photos as someone who looked like one of the men running from the scene, but the second person was never identified. All three witnesses took and passed polygraphs administered by the FBI. Ingram failed his.

Herren checked the suspect list. Ingram had died in 1973 from a heart attack while driving a fire engine for the Cahaba Heights Volunteer Fire Department. He was never prosecuted. Still, Herren tapped his finger on the pages over Ingram's name and scribbled a note. Connections were an important part of putting the puzzle together.

Robert "Dynamite Bob" Chambliss had worked as an employee in the city's Street and Sanitation Department until he was fired (despite his close relationship to the public safety commissioner, Bull Connor) for smashing the flashgun of a newspaperman's camera at a Klan rally. He was already on suspension for "conduct unbecoming a city employee" in connection with the threatened bombing of a house in North Smithfield—Dynamite Hill. W. Cooper Green, president of the county commission, told him to "either quit or be fired." According to Green, Chambliss sat outside his house for several days afterward, upsetting Green's wife.

Chambliss had a history of violence. In 1949, he was indicted by a Jefferson County grand jury investigating "a wave of lawlessness" that included the infamous Klan raid on Camp Fletcher, a Girl Scout camp suspected of allowing white women to mingle with the black troop. In 1957 he was arrested for bombing the parsonage of Reverend Fred Shuttlesworth. After intervention by Commissioner Connor, police released Chambliss without filing charges.

One informant, Gary Thomas Rowe, reported that Robert Chambliss bombed black homes in Birmingham and "generally operated with four others." At first, Herren was surprised to see Rowe's name spelled out in a case file. The FBI protected their informants and used code names in case files. Informant names, to which Herren was not privy, were kept in separate top-secret files. But Herren learned Rowe's cover was abandoned in 1965 when he had to testify in court.

Herren ran through the list of the original targeted Cahaba Boys suspects:

> Thomas Edwin Blanton
> Robert Chambliss (convicted in 1977)
> Bobby Frank Cherry
> Herman Frank Cash (deceased)
> John Hall (deceased)
> Troy Ingram (deceased)
> Billy Neil Tipton
> Levie S. Yarbrough
> Charles Arnie Cagle

These men were interrogated repeatedly during the 1960s investigation. They all denied any knowledge of the bombing, claiming the blacks had done it to gain sympathy for their cause or for insurance money. Besides, they said, it couldn't have been whites because they would too easily be noticed in that area.

The FBI's informants, however, claimed Imperial Wizard Robert Shelton, who was the national Klan leader, ordered the bombing. That order might have come down to the Grand Cyclops of the Eastview #13 Klavern, Robert Sidney Thomas. Shelton insisted he did not support violence and would have disapproved it had he known about it.

In addition to surveillance of the key suspects and nightly patrol of hot spots in the city, the FBI planted electronic devices in the homes of several Klansmen. At the time, the level of unrest was so intense that the situation was declared a threat to national security and Attorney General Robert Kennedy signed off on many of the wiretaps. Unfortunately, those files were also off-limits to Herren, at least until his background clearance came in.

Tired, Herren closed the file he was reading and rubbed his eyes. He stood, stiff from sitting. Better get used to that, he told himself. He was going to be sitting for a long time.

When he went down to his car, parked on the street—because he was not allowed in the FBI's garage—he found a ticket on the windshield.

3 | THE CHAMBLISS CASE

THE NEXT MORNING, HERREN stopped outside the Sixteenth Street Baptist Church, a mottled sandy-brown brick structure he'd never paid much attention to. The square turrets topped with conical roofs of red clay tiles made him think of a fortress. Along the east side, a row of arched stained-glass windows lined the wall. The bomb had blown out only Jesus's face in the center stained-glass window, leaving the rest of the image eerily intact. Now it was whole again. Along the darker stone blocks of the wall's bottom section stretched a line of plain, white-trimmed basement windows. No indication remained that a concrete stairwell had once stood at the northeast corner, concealing a package of dynamite. The area was quiet and serene; a new Civil Rights Institute stood across the street.

The black community in Birmingham had responded to segregation by building their own vibrant community. In the 1960s this was a dense business area with row houses and retail stores, such as the Silver Sands Café, the Jockey restaurant, and the Social Cleaners. None of that remained. It was as if time had reached down with a giant hand and plucked it all up.

Back at the FBI office, Herren continued his isolated study of the files. Eager for any information he could glean, he read the transcripts of the 1977 trial of "Dynamite Bob" Chambliss. The Alabama attorney general at that time, William J. "Bill" Baxley, had led the prosecution. In the trial, he had to establish several facts, one being that dynamite had caused the explosion. The defense fought tooth-and-nail against the word "bomb" being used, insisting it be called an "explosion."

Captain William E. Berry, the assistant Birmingham fire marshal, took the stand as a prosecution witness. Captain Berry testified the smell of dynamite was present and the sound of the explosion and damage caused by it were consistent with dynamite. The defense insinuated it could have been a natural gas explosion, but Captain Berry explained the greatest devastation in a natural gas explosion occurred at the perimeter, as the force went outward. It would not be unusual to find a loaf of bread intact and unharmed in the center of a natural gas blast. In the instance of the church explosion, the force at the center had been so great, piles of brick and twisted heavy gauge metal screen from the

The Sixteenth Street Church prior to the bombing; note the back stairs (bottom right) where the bomb was placed.

Birmingham, Ala. Public Library Archives

Church basement window of the Ladies Lounge.

Federal Bureau of Investigation

window were thrown all the way against the far inside wall, clearly pointing to a high-powered explosive detonated outside the building.

Berry also testified that a fuse burned at three feet a minute and would have required a significant length to provide enough time to safely retreat. This set the stage for the possibility the bombers used a delayed timing device.

Special Agent John McCormick, one of the dozens of agents assigned temporarily to Birmingham to help with the case in 1963, was extensively trained in explosives. McCormick said the smell of dynamite always gave him a headache, and when he had sniffed the crater at the scene, he instantly got such a headache.

In the preliminary search of the scene, a small fishing bobber with a wire attached to it was found in the street about twenty feet from the crater made by the bomb. The wire was about six to eight inches long. Agent McCormick explained lighter objects could fly through the air without resistance and remain undamaged, where denser objects would be demolished by a blast.

It was not brought out in the trial that fishing tackle had been found in one of the damaged vehicles nearby, a possible source for the bobber. The wire attached to it, however, was thicker than normal fishing wire. A final answer to the bobber's origins would forever remain a mystery, since it had been lost somewhere in transit to the lab.

Herren stopped and pulled out the black-and-white, eight-by-ten-inch file photos of the aftermath. A fireman, debris piled at his feet, stood in the basement beside a huge hole in the brick wall. Cars parked beside the church were pushed askew into the street, their windows

Cars parked beside the church on Sixteenth Street North.

Federal Bureau of Investigation

The room where the girls were killed.

Federal Bureau of Investigation

smashed, metal sides punctured and rippled from the heat and blast. The explosion created a crater in the ground five and a half feet wide by two and a quarter feet deep, punched through a thirty-inch stone-and-brick masonry wall, and was heard miles away on the far side of the Birmingham airport.

The last set of pictures was the autopsy photos. Those blackened figures hardly seemed to have once been young girls. According to the reports, their mothers had to identify their daughters based on the remains of the clothes they were wearing. Cynthia Wesley had to be identified by her shoes and the ring on her finger.

Police work requires a professional damping of emotional response, similar to a doctor encountering a traumatic injury. Otherwise, a person can't function, much less do his or her job, although the long-term effects might help account for law enforcement's high rates of divorce, alcoholism, and suicide. Herren looked at each photo as a small act of respect. There was nothing of evidentiary nature to be seen that wasn't obvious—the bodies were mutilated and burned into featureless char. He put the photos aside and again picked up the Chambliss trial transcript.

Reverend John Haywood Cross, the church pastor, was at the women's Bible class near the upstairs window when the bomb went off. "It sounded like the whole world was shaking," he said. When he made his way through the thick smoke and debris in the basement, he found Sarah Collins, age ten, trapped in the Ladies Lounge. The last she'd seen of her sister, Addie Mae was tying Denise McNair's sash. Sarah Collins survived, but lost her right eye.

Herren developed a system for taking notes. Using a blank supplemental form from the police department, he made headings and

Debris blown across the street.

Federal Bureau of Investigation

subheadings, each on a separate form. Bobby Frank Cherry and Thomas Blanton became categories, their family history subcategories. The bomb itself was another category. He gleaned information from the files about what materials might have been used, what the investigators knew about it, and what they thought about it. He took his notes home and typed them up at night.

Days in the mantrap began to pass by in a blur.

Herren made a research trip to the archives of the Birmingham Public Library. He didn't reveal his identify, just claimed an interest in viewing the historical records. The archivist insisted he wear plastic gloves and that he hand over all ink pens. He was allowed a pencil to take notes. He found interesting documents, including a site map of the area that helped him place the location described by the FBI's first important witness, Kirthus (Gertrude) L. Glenn, an African American seamstress from Detroit. She had come to Birmingham, her hometown, to visit a friend who lived across the street behind the church. Glenn and her friend's brother, Henry Smith, were returning from taking another friend home in West End at about 2:10 or 2:15 AM on the morning of the bombing.

As she searched for a parking space on Seventh Avenue North, Glenn saw a car parked there. The dome light was on, illuminating a white man in the rear passenger side. The man was twisted around in the back passenger seat, looking right into her high-beam lights. She saw his face clearly. The car went east and turned north on Sixteenth Street, headed away from the church. Nervous at the presence of white men in the neighborhood at that time of night, she parked three cars up and went straight to the house.

The day of the bombing, word reached Special Assistant in Charge Robert Jenson that a "Negro woman had observed the bombing and described the car." She gave a tag number, but the car's owner was quickly ruled out as a suspect. The source of this information was not given in the report, nor was the woman named.

It wasn't clear how the FBI obtained Glenn's name, but almost two weeks after the bombing, agents interviewed her at Harper Hospital where she worked in Detroit, Michigan. Glenn described the car she'd seen as "two-toned with a light top" and an extremely tall antenna mounted on the left rear fin. Later that day, after the bombing, she had

The church window where the head of Jesus was damaged.

Federal Bureau of Investigation

seen the same car two or three times in the area and confirmed the car's top half was white and the lower half turquoise. Henry Smith, the man who accompanied Glenn the night of the bombing, admitted to drinking heavily and was not able to recall the details of what they had observed. Glenn, however, was able to pick out the car from photos of different cars. Investigators knew Thomas Blanton drove a 1957 Chevrolet matching that description. In court, Special Agent Timothy Casey identified the photo Glenn had picked as a photograph he had personally taken on surveillance of Blanton's car in the 1960s.

On October 23, 1963, Glenn saw a photo of Chambliss in the October 17 issue of *Jet* magazine and telephoned the FBI to tell them he was the white man she had observed in the car. The article and photo in the magazine related the story of Chambliss's arrest for possession of dynamite shortly after the bombing. When agents brought Glenn a book of photos from the Birmingham office, she was able to pick out three photos of Chambliss.

Because of previous bombings, the police department had assigned Unit 14, a special patrol car, to keep an eye on the Sixteenth Street Baptist Church, Arthur Shores's house, and the A. G. Gaston Hotel, but at 1:35 AM the morning of the explosion, that unit responded to a bomb threat at the Holiday Inn Motel, blocks away. Who made the false alarm call was never determined, but there were some odd circumstances surrounding the incident.

There was no dispatch log on the call. A police report reflected that Sergeant Wilson located Unit 14 around the Gaston Hotel and told the officers in person that the woman who received the threat at the Holiday Inn said the caller was a black male. Perhaps Sergeant Wilson had been at the Holiday Inn when or just after the bomb threat came in, but even so, it was unusual for that information not to be shared with the dispatcher and other units. No evidence of a bomb was found. Regardless, the incident had the effect of keeping at least one patrol car away from the church around the time Glenn saw Chambliss.

When Baxley's team located Glenn in Detroit in the 1970s, his chief investigator, Jack Shows, flew up to talk to her. On his return, Shows reported to Baxley, "I have good news and bad news. The good news is she would be an excellent witness; the bad news is she is not returning to Birmingham to testify." Baxley was not one to give up easily; he sent Shows back to Detroit with a black attorney from his office. Once again, Glenn refused to come. She said she was never going to Birmingham under any circumstances.

"Do I have to do everything myself?" Baxley asked in exasperation and then flew to Detroit himself. Glenn received him warmly, fed him cookies, and firmly refused to go, in spite of all the attorney general's efforts. While he was in her home, Baxley's gaze fell upon a copy of *Jet* magazine on her coffee table, and he thumbed through it, running across a historical article about the Montgomery Bus Boycott and a photograph of attorney Fred Gray with Martin Luther King. Baxley and Gray were friends.

With sudden inspiration, Baxley showed the magazine to Glenn. "You see this picture?" he asked her. "This is Fred Gray. This is the man Martin Luther King turned to in the beginning. This is the attorney who represented King and Rosa Parks. If this man comes up here and asks you to testify, would you?"

"Well," she said slowly, "I'd think about it."

As soon as he got to his hotel, Baxley called Fred Gray and explained the situation. The next day, a state plane picked up Gray and took him to Detroit. Glenn held the magazine beside Gray's face and compared them for several long moments before she was satisfied the man standing before her was the same man as the one in the magazine. She listened to him and changed her mind, agreeing to go to Birmingham to tell what she had seen behind the Sixteenth Street Baptist Church on September 15, 1963. Her testimony was a critical part of the 1977 case—but Herren found her name, too, on the deceased list.

James Edward Lay, however, was alive. In 1963, he was a US Postal Service employee and captain of the Negro Civil Defense Workers in Birmingham, a respected man in the black community. On the day of the funeral for the slain girls, Lay was one of three men who stopped a spontaneous, angry demonstration outside the church. The others were Reverend Charles Billups, assistant pastor of New Pilgrim Baptist Church, and Charles Evers, brother of Medgar Evers, a civil rights activist assassinated only three months earlier in Mississippi by a member of the White Citizens' Council. Evers's murderer, Herren noted, was tried and convicted thirty years later based on new evidence. That was encouraging. But he was a long way from uncovering new evidence, and he went back to reading about Lay.

When the church explosion occurred, Lay was at Poole's Funeral Parlor, a couple of blocks away. Thinking an airplane had crashed nearby, he jumped into his car and arrived at the church within minutes. Members were still inside.

Newspaper articles were part of the FBI files, and Herren had read a *Los Angeles Times* article written the next day by William A. McGriff, who had been at the scene right after the bombing. McGriff reported that some people picked up stones and threw them at the police as they arrived, causing one officer to shout, "We didn't do it; we are here to protect you!"

Herren could imagine the chaos, grief, and anger that Edward Lay must have seen when he arrived at the church. Grabbing a bullhorn from his car, Lay tried to direct the gathering crowd back. An injured man hobbled out of the rear entrance of the church, and Lay rushed to help him. At the same time, a boy about fourteen years old grabbed Lay's arm and told him that he had seen "the two white men who threw the bomb." Lay decided helping the injured was a higher priority. Afterward, he looked for the boy but couldn't find him.

On the day of the bombing, Lay reported this to FBI agents and also told them about an incident a couple of weeks prior. As part of a volunteer group performing a nightly surveillance of attorney Arthur Shores's residence, Lay's job was to look for anything suspicious or out of the ordinary. Just after midnight on September 2, 1963—a weeknight about two weeks before the church bombing—Lay was driving north on Sixteenth Street. He noticed a black 1957 two-door Ford sedan with Alabama tags parked near the concrete steps on the northeast side of the church where the bomb was later placed. To see better, he flicked on his bright lights and stopped on the opposite side of the street.

The driver, a white man, was sitting inside the car. Another white man was standing on the sidewalk near the concrete steps with a black satchel in his hands. Seeing Lay, he hastened back into the vehicle, which proceeded north a block and then turned, switching off its lights as it sped away. According to Lay's report to the FBI, another man—"Tall" Paul White, who was a local black radio personality—observed the same thing, but wasn't in a position to see either of the men closely enough to identify them.

What was this? Herren wondered. Was it possible the two white men had been trying to plant a bomb at the church *prior* to September 15? What else would they have been doing? It was clear they did not want the eyes of witnesses on them.

Lay had immediately reported the incident to the police. The officers who responded to that call did not make a report, but police dispatch recordings confirmed such a call at 12:43 AM, given to Car 25. The precinct work list had Officer R. F. Reese and L. R. "Lying Louie" Cockrum assigned to that car. An FBI agent interviewed the officers, who remembered the call.

The FBI had shown Lay a large number of color photographs of people who'd been interviewed in connection with bombing investigations. He looked through them and pointed to a picture he said "closely resembled" the white man he saw on the sidewalk with the satchel. This was a photo of Thomas Blanton—whose car Gertrude Glenn had identified as being in the alley behind the church in the early morning the day of the bombing. Lay also picked another photo of a man he said closely resembled the driver of the black car he had seen two weeks prior to the bombing. That man was Robert "Dynamite Bob" Chambliss—whom Glenn had identified as being inside the car she saw the morning of the bombing.

Herren called for another file, and it seemed like Fleming took his sweet time bringing it. In disgust, Herren stood up, stretched, and got buzzed out into the waiting room to use the public bathroom, still irritated that they wouldn't let him into the "inner sanctum" to use the john. When he returned to the mantrap, Fleming was there.

"What are you doing?" Fleming asked, indicating the growing pile of handwritten supplemental reports.

Herren shrugged. "Taking notes." He smiled at the older agent, who presented a somewhat rumpled appearance and expression, not Herren's mental picture of an FBI agent. "I know," Herren said congenially, "I'm anal on my organization, though you'd never know it to look at my woodworking shop. Some things can just get a foot deep in dust, it don't matter, but some things I gotta have organized."

Fleming did not respond with the grin Herren hoped for. His mouth was a grim, downcast arc. Maybe he was angry about having an outsider working on his case, or angry about the case itself, or maybe he ate something sour for breakfast. Every day.

4 | AGENT BILL FLEMING

SPECIAL AGENT BILL FLEMING was seething. He was a senior agent—no, he was *the* senior agent in the Birmingham FBI field office. Why had they assigned him this unsolvable, thirty-three-year-old case? All the years of service he had given, and now he'd been thrown on the trash heap.

He'd never particularly wanted to be an FBI agent. After serving two years in the army as a lieutenant and having his fill of Korea, he'd flown home to Albany, Georgia. Somewhere up in the air it hit him: he needed a job. As a youth, he had hunted and trapped. He loved animals and the outdoors and always thought he would end up a forest ranger or an archeologist or a veterinarian. Law enforcement never entered his mind.

But it was 1969, and, for the first time in its history, the FBI was advertising for agents. They needed one thousand people. Although he had started management training for Kmart, the Bureau seemed like a better opportunity, and Fleming applied. The first time he was turned down. If not for the kindness of a secretary, he would never have made it on his second try. He had flunked the spelling test on the first go-around. So this time, possibly feeling sorry for him, the secretary stood up, stretched, and announced, "I've got to leave the room." On her way out, she slapped a sheet of paper with the spelling words onto his desk. His first thought was that this was part of a test to see if he would cheat, and he glanced nervously around, looking for hidden cameras.

That was almost twenty-seven years ago. If he hadn't been so angry, he would have smiled at the memory. He owed that lady. Her name, however, he had long ago forgotten. He forgot a lot of things nowadays, especially names. Was that why they had given him the '63 bombing case, this "bomb" of a case? Was he so old that he was no longer valuable? *We don't want to waste the time of a younger agent, but we can give it to Fleming.*

This was Fleming's state of mind when he encountered his boss, Special Agent in Charge Rob Langford, at a social event. Fleming took the opportunity to speak to him. Langford was an easy man to talk with, not like other SACs he had known. Maybe he would listen to reason. Fleming understood it was the SAC's job to keep his finger on the pulse of the community, and Langford was good at that. Langford had talked to the black community leaders and to Petric Smith. Langford thought enough of Fleming to give him Smith's book, *Long Time Coming*, to read, trusting him to report back on anything pertinent. It was an interesting book, a fascinating story. Who would have believed the niece of one of the Sixteenth Street Church bombing suspects, despite her fear for her life, would step forward and testify against him, and then have a sex-change surgery, altering her identity from Elizabeth Cobbs to Petric Smith? Next thing Fleming knew, Petric Smith came to the office for a meeting with a girlfriend. They met in the FBI conference room, and Smith gave a presentation about his story. Smith was a brave person, Fleming had to give him that.

But interesting was one thing; spending the kind of time it would take just to look through the files on this was ridiculous, a waste of his time and experience. Fleming knew he was the logical person to consult, since he was assigned the civil rights cases, but no one seemed to listen to him on this. He was just the guy they had designated to be the sacrificial lamb, so they could say they put somebody on it.

"About the case, sir, the bombing case," he said when he managed a moment alone with the SAC.

"Yes?"

"Mr. Langford, this case has been thoroughly investigated two times, and there's no evidence; nobody has come forward. We are wasting our time. I know you think it's the right thing to do, but we've got to stop now."

Langford looked him in the eye and replied in his characteristic calm, level manner. "Bill, you gotta keep on going with it. The people of Alabama deserve another look at this." Then he added with a grin, "Besides, I'm the boss."

Fleming said nothing to the younger Birmingham officer in the mantrap; he just laid another requested file on his desk. He had nothing personal against Herren. The sergeant seemed very competent and thorough. And the FBI had to partner with the Birmingham Police Department on this case because there was no federal nexus; the federal government technically had no jurisdiction to prosecute if it ever came to trial—not that there was a chance in the world of that happening. All that had been hashed out in the early meetings, and the district attorney had agreed to prosecute it as a state murder case if the FBI found enough evidence.

Back in 1963, prior to the 1964 Civil Rights Act, there had been slim legal grounds for allowing the FBI to investigate the case. Murder wasn't a federal crime unless the victim was a federal employee or federal judge. When they started this current investigation, they thought they might have jurisdictional grounds because a death resulting from interstate transportation of dynamite was a federal crime and carried no statute of limitations. Herren and Fleming eventually chased leads about dynamite shipments from Atlanta to Kentucky, but there was no evidence the dynamite was purchased across state lines. In the 1960s, there were four dynamite manufacturing plants in Alabama. Dynamite was used for coal mining, of course, and Birmingham was a center for mining. All the ingredients for making steel—iron ore, coke, and limestone—existed together in this city. It was built around mining and the railroad. Dynamite was a readily obtained commodity outside the city limits, and the dynamite houses that contained the explosives used in the mines were often burglarized.

In fact, later in September 1963, state troopers arrested Chambliss and two other members of the Eastview #13 Klavern for possession of dynamite. When investigators interviewed Chambliss, he claimed the Exalted Cyclops of Eastview #13 Klavern had ordered him to purchase the dynamite to blow up stumps on klavern property in preparation for construction of a lodge.

Fleming considered Sergeant Herren. The Birmingham detective was younger by maybe ten or twelve years. Fleming had been eighteen years old and living in Georgia at the time of the church bombing. He remembered hearing about it, but it was a casual comment from his neighbor a year later that hit closer to home and made a deeper impression on him. Only days after the passage of the Civil Rights Act in 1964, Lemuel Penn, a young army reserve officer and decorated World War II veteran, was driving with two other black officers from Fort Benning, Georgia, to Washington, DC. Two Klansmen spotted the DC tags. "That must be one of Johnson's boys," one of the men said, referring to President Lyndon Johnson, who was a supporter of the Civil Rights Act. "I'm going to shoot me a nigger," the other declared. They pulled up beside the car on a bridge in Madison County, Georgia, and fired their shotguns, hitting Penn in the neck and jaw and killing him.

Fleming's neighbor was a big man and very active in the church, a Christian role model in the community and particularly for Fleming, who thought he was as close to perfect as a man could be. One day after the death of Lemuel Penn, Fleming remarked to his neighbor, "Wasn't that bad about Mr. Penn?"

Without hesitation, his neighbor replied, "Well, he shouldn't have been down here flaunting himself."

Fleming could still feel that shock to his young self at those words, as his idol toppled from the pedestal he had stood upon for so long. The words ignited a flame of anger that such a man could tarnish the religion Fleming had been brought up to believe was founded on loving one's neighbor. His role model, it turned out, was a member of the National States Rights Party, which Fleming considered about the same as the Ku Klux Klan.

Fleming shook himself from his reveries. It wasn't that he didn't want to work on a civil rights case, for heaven's sake; his assignment was the Civil Rights Division. It was just an insult to give him a thirty-four-year-old case that didn't have a prayer of ever being solved. He sat down at his desk and wrote his resignation.

After the steno typed it, he put it in a drawer, feeling a little better at having written it but not quite ready to hand it in. Then he remembered Sergeant Herren was waiting on him to bring another file.

"Can you tell me who this code refers to?" Herren asked, pointing to a series of letters and numbers he had encountered several times.

Fleming shook his head. "That's classified."

Herren sighed.

"You need anything else?" Fleming snapped.

"No, I'm fine." Herren was already flipping pages.

Fleming went back to his office, still nursing his irritation. If he couldn't convince the SAC they were wasting time, he would just have to pull that resignation out of the desk drawer. He loved the FBI; it was his life, but he wasn't going to end his career on a boondoggle.

5 | OLD FILES AND RABBIT TRAILS

BEN HERREN HAD ALWAYS advised his young detectives that an investigation leads you; you don't lead the investigation. A detective should follow the best information available, not someone else's thoughts or hypotheses. He would take his own advice and pursue the facts until he could make a decision whether he was on the right trail or not.

Because of that determination, reviewing the FBI files from the 1963 investigation was a roller-coaster ride. In the early days, when the net was spread wide—across the nation—rumors flew, and there was no way to know which of the snagged flotsam had value and which didn't. It was all sent to the Birmingham FBI field office.

Herren would catch a new name dropped in an interview and scribble a furious note, thinking he'd uncovered a lead that had been missed in the 1960s, only to discover the investigators had already looked under that rock. He came to call those paths-to-nowhere rabbit trails. One such came from a man named Buggywhip who had just gotten out of jail and claimed to know about the bombing. Herren read on, only to find—thirty pages later—that the man was mentally unstable.

Another rabbit trail involved a tape recording by an undercover Miami police officer in which a man named Brown, a member of a "Constitutional Party," said he wanted to target Martin Luther King. The conversation included a discussion of how easy it would be to kill President John F. Kennedy by picking him off with a high-powered rifle from another building. The FBI identified Brown as Jack William Brown, a member of the Ku Klux Klan in Chattanooga, Tennessee. Herren also discovered Brown had been an early suspect in the 1960s, but pages later he learned agents had confirmed Brown was in Chattanooga at the time of the Birmingham church bombing.

Herren struggled to get a clear picture of the 1960s investigation, challenged by the fact that all the informant names were replaced by encryptions. He didn't have the clearance required to be privy to the files on the informants' identity, but eventually, by cross-referencing the codes, he began to pick apart who they were.

As a police sergeant in the 1980s, Herren had been part of an Organized Crime Drug Enforcement Task Force (OCDETF) case, a joint investigation of federal and local agencies. It covered a span of years before bringing down the ringleaders of a drug cartel that had held Birmingham hostage, and Herren had learned where the phrase "making a federal case of it" came from. The feds were notorious for stretching a case out for years, but he had to give them credit—they were thorough, at least as far as the 1963 bombing case.

Whittling away at a ton of paper was not his idea of a dream job, but at least he didn't have a dozen rookie detectives to supervise. There were other advantages: He had his own car, and he came and went as he pleased, if you didn't count the FBI's bathroom. Retirement was just over the horizon for him, and being stuck here in the mantrap would keep him out of trouble until then. He would ride this gravy train with biscuit wheels as far as it would go . . . and do his best while he was on it.

He plowed on.

The Klan was paranoid and had reason to be. One little klavern north of Birmingham had only three members; two of them were undercover informants and neither knew about the other.

In the early days when J. Edgar Hoover reigned over the Bureau, all agents were required to wear white, long-sleeved shirts and regulation haircuts. Unless they were working deep undercover, they were only allowed to disguise their presence by removing their signature fedora hats . . . not particularly effective. Klansmen could spot them a mile away. It reminded Herren of the days when the police department's idea of fashioning an undercover car was to remove the municipal tag and paint over the insignias on a standard police-issue Ford LTD. Every criminal in town could spot an undercover cop car. That didn't change until the police started confiscating cars in drug arrests.

Hoover directed the FBI to build intelligence files on the white supremacist groups, suspected communists, Martin Luther King, and even top government officials. Agents staked out the Klan's social haunts and drove by their houses day and night, sometimes giving the wheels a little squeal to let their presence be known. Klansmen referred to the FBI agents as Kennedy's boys, and, among themselves, the agents called Klan members Klackers.

One night, Thomas Blanton climbed a tree in the alley behind his house to get the tag numbers on the FBI cars watching his house. Bored from endless hours of surveillance, an agent rolled into the alley and threw a cherry bomb up into the tree, and was shocked when the *bang* knocked Blanton out of it. From then on, the feds would shine a light into the tree as they rolled by. Blanton returned the cherry bomb exchange, tossing one into the FBI parking garage from the alley behind the local office.

Herren found the interaction between the Klan and the FBI to be a kind of game. It had its own rules and sense of humor, such as the time when Mississippi agents sent a card to every member of a particular Klan, inviting them to a big fried chicken Christmas dinner at the Grand Titan's house. An RSVP was not necessary, the card declared; just drop in. The Grand Titan had quite a surprise as guests from across the state showed up for dinner.

When the FBI began investigating the church bombing, the game escalated. Agents were harassed: At one agent's home, a hearse arrived to "pick up a body." Another agent received a phony phone call stating his wife and children were hurt and in the hospital. Some agents had their homes picketed or mustard gas put in their cars, and some were actually arrested by local police on trumped-up assault charges. Tensions were high.

At one point, Thomas Blanton and his father, "Pop" Blanton (sometimes "Pops"), were handing out leaflets in Agent Neil Shanahan's neighborhood. Pop Blanton was known as a blatant racist, but he apparently didn't see himself that way. He once told an agent, "I got nothing against niggers; it is the white people backing them that are causing the trouble—the communists." The leaflets made outrageous claims about the FBI. When Thomas and Pop Blanton came onto Shanahan's property, the agent stormed out of his house, picked up Pop Blanton—a small, skinny man—and stuffed him through his car window.

On another occasion, Thomas Blanton was arrested for taking a swing at Agent Bernard Cashdollar and putting his hand on a knife in his pocket. The grand jury refused to indict him for assaulting a federal officer.

In a memo dated April 10, 1964, the Birmingham FBI office reported:

> In our investigation of the church bombing and related incidents in the Birmingham area, we have practically torn Birmingham apart and have interviewed thousands of persons. We have seriously disrupted Klan activities by our pressure and interviews so that these organizations have lost members and support. We have harassed the principal suspects in this case by every possible means in an attempt to bring about a solution. We have made extensive use of the polygraph, surveillances, microphone surveillance, and technical surveillances.
>
> Our Agent personnel have used imagination and ingenuity to seriously hamper the activities of the suspects in this case to such a point that the suspects have at times attempted to have our Agents arrested.
>
> This is the type of case that until a confession or witnesses from within come forth the evidence is not obtainable upon which to base a prosecution. The very nature of the crime destroyed all physical evidence and the brutishness of the way it was perpetrated leaves the criminal the opportunity to be far removed from the scene when the actual explosion took place.

From photos and reports, Herren began to put together a profile of the FBI's suspects. Bobby Frank Cherry, a tall, muscular man with lots of wavy hair, a reddish complexion, and a bulbous nose, was a braggart and womanizer. Thirty-three years old with an eighth-grade education,

Cherry did not like being alone, evidenced in a succession of five wives with whom he fathered fifteen children. More than one wife claimed he abused her and sexually abused their children or grandchild. The US Marines had provided Cherry training in demolitions—he served from 1957 to 1959. Cherry worked as a welder, a carpet cleaner, and a truck driver, and was a member of the Teamsters Union, the Eastview #13 Klavern, and the Cahaba Bridge Boys.

His violent nature extended beyond family matters. On April 6, 1961, he was involved in a shooting—one of the Klan's missionary missions—at the residence of a white family who was trying to raise a black child. He was never charged.

FBI investigators questioned him repeatedly. One report stated that he "admitted to firing his rifle at Negroes outside his house within the past two months." On August 20, 1963, a month before the church bombing, the residence of civil rights attorney Arthur Shores was bombed. The front door, windows, and part of the roof were blown away, and one of the family dogs was killed. When agents asked Cherry about it, he responded that he hadn't done it, but when he heard about it, his thought had been, "'I hope it killed him.'"

In front of an FBI source, Robert Chambliss said, "I hope to God Cherry won't talk, because he knows too much and was guilty as hell." Chambliss also said, "They're going to get me, Blanton, Cash, and Cherry."

Cherry himself was heard to say, "They are going to get me before it's over." And, "It'll be mighty hard on me if they get old Chambliss."

To the FBI directly, Cherry said he was not and had never been a member of the Ku Klux Klan, the National States Rights Party, or any similar organization. He said he didn't know Thomas Blanton or Robert Chambliss. At one point, Cherry was examined by polygraph, which indicated he was not being truthful in his denial of knowledge of the bombing. Polygraph evidence would not be admissible in a trial unless both the prosecution and the defense agreed to it—a highly unlikely scenario—even if the polygraph examiner were still alive.

Since Herren wasn't allowed to park inside the FBI garage, he had to struggle to find a parking place every morning. Finally, irritated at the hassle, he started leaving his unmarked police car in a "No Parking" zone near the building. Each evening he found a ticket on his dash. He routinely took them to his lieutenant to be voided, until he decided enough was enough and removed the tag from his car. The parking enforcement officers were too lazy to go read the vehicle identification number on the dash. No more tickets.

Gradually, he and Fleming developed a working relationship. Fleming was "Old Bureau." He had come into the agency in the days of J. Edgar Hoover, when things were done by the book—Hoover's book. Hoover, alone, used a blue pen; agents used only black pens. And by Old Bureau standards, Herren was an outsider. Still, despite Fleming's anger—and perhaps embarrassment—at being assigned such an impossible case, Herren could tell Fleming was trying to answer his questions indirectly.

It took more than six months for Herren to receive his interim clearance. Pending a complete background investigation for his top-secret clearance, the Bureau now had enough background to allow him to come inside the hallowed inner ground of the FBI headquarters. More importantly, he had access to the twenty-five to thirty pertinent informant files.

He moved downstairs to the seventh floor, where Fleming was the civil rights investigator for the squad in a much bigger space than the mantrap. It was a long room with two six-foot tables, a few chairs, and a window that looked out over the county courthouse across the street. He began accumulating office equipment through the "BBA" skills he had learned in the police department—begging, borrowing, and appropriating when someone left an office. He used his carpentry skills to build an expandable wooden rack to hold the growing number of notebooks they had read.

Both Herren and Fleming pored over the files together now.

Tina Mauldin came on board to assist them. She was an IRS—intelligence research specialist—and a jewel. Her first task was to draw out family trees so they could see the relationships, which was especially important with Bobby Frank Cherry, who had so many wives and children. Mauldin had a knack for tracking down people and addresses.

She, along with Charlotte Kessler, who had done the early workups on possible suspects and witnesses, were invaluable.

Herren made notes on everything. Occasionally, he'd get excited. "Bill, I think I got something here they missed."

Unperturbed, Fleming would reply, "Wait till you get to the next volume." Each time, the next volume would resolve the question in Herren's mind, and Herren would mark the lead as another rabbit trail.

They compiled a list of hundreds of people to contact, including Klansmen and their relatives, FBI agents, and church members. The clerks had already established that 160 of them were dead. That still left a long list.

Now that they were working in close proximity, they began to go out to lunch together. That was when the ice began to thaw. They were both southern boys raised with strong fathers and shared the same solid values and dedication to their work. Both agreed this investigation was a wild-goose chase, but they were professionals. They didn't get mushy about the case; but both knew a great wrong had been committed, and they were going to do everything in their power to right it. For a law enforcement officer that meant one thing: find the bad guys.

6 | THE CHAMBLISS CASE: BEGINNINGS

AS HERREN AND FLEMING dug through the files, going over each one at least three times, they came to respect what Bob Eddy, the investigator in the 1977 trial of Chambliss, had been faced with and what he had accomplished. When Alabama attorney general Bill Baxley reopened the case of the 1963 Sixteenth Street Baptist Church bombing in 1971, he hired three investigators experienced in both bombing and Klan cases: Jack Shows, Tom Ward, and Joe East.

It became apparent that the 1960s files were critical to making any substantial headway, but Baxley's efforts at obtaining the case files were stymied by the FBI for five years, despite several visits to both the Birmingham and Washington offices. Baxley did not know until 1978, when Bob Eddy was going through files in Washington, DC, that Director J. Edgar Hoover had ordered the FBI to withhold the files from him. According to Eddy, Hoover's given reason was that he felt Baxley only wanted to further his political career, although documents also reflect a concern that one of the part-time consultants Baxley had hired worked for the local newspaper. The FBI considered the case open until 1973 and did not want information leaked to the media.

Even after Hoover's death in 1972, his successor Clarence M. Kelley (who had been the SAC in the Birmingham field office from 1957 to 1960) refused to release any files to Baxley until 1976. Baxley had requested that the FBI "participate in a joint investigation," but, perhaps because Baxley stipulated he wanted his office to have investigative control, he was told "this could not be done." By 1976, internal memos at the Bureau reported that the reason no action had been taken on Baxley's requests was that the FBI had handed Baxley's request over to the Civil Rights Division for permission and had never heard back from them.

Baxley finally obtained some of the FBI files by laying the situation before the Washington bureau chief for the *Los Angeles Times*, Jack Nelson, who was originally from Alabama. Nelson was a prominent reporter, well known in Washington, DC. He contacted the US attorney general, Edward Levi, and let it be known he was considering writing a story about how the FBI refused to give the Alabama attorney general the files he needed to prosecute the most heinous civil rights crime of the century. Some files were then released to Baxley.

In 1976, Baxley hired Lieutenant Colonel Bob Eddy, a trim, medium-sized man with a nose for investigation, from the Alabama State Department of Public Safety. Eddy was hired to work on organized crime, but in 1977 Baxley gave him the box of files he had received from the FBI on the church bombing case and told him to read them.

Eddy had a good reputation with federal agents in Huntsville and across northern Alabama where he had worked in the Madison County sheriff's department, and he was a graduate of the FBI National Academy, a program offered to select law enforcement officers. Being an academy graduate meant his background had been thoroughly vetted and made him more likely to be allowed access to the rest of the files in the Birmingham office. Baxley sent Bob Eddy to Birmingham with a mandate to take three months and focus on digging through the files the FBI would not let out of the office. "Don't let anybody from this [Attorney General's] office distract you with other things," Baxley admonished him. "If they try to, you send them to me."

Baxley needed to move quickly if he was going to resolve the case. His time as attorney general was running out, and he planned on a bid for the governor's seat. Obsessed by the 1963 church bombing since his law school days, Baxley still carried in his pocket a worn card on which he had written the names of the four little girls. When a Klansman wrote a threatening letter comparing him to JFK and calling him an "honorary nigger," Baxley wrote back on state letterhead, "My response to your letter of February 19, 1976 is—Kiss my ass."

When Bob Eddy arrived at the Birmingham FBI office in 1977, they told him up front what the ground rules were: They would give him a specific person's file if he asked for it. If they could find it, it would be put on his desk. Eddy was to give the FBI copies of any reports he sent to Baxley. In return, they gave him a small room and brought him the files he asked for. Timothy Casey, the agent assigned to help him, had worked civil rights cases in Tuscaloosa, Alabama, but he had never worked the Sixteenth Street Baptist Church bombing case. The attitude Eddy encountered in the beginning was: the FBI has already investigated this case—what makes you think you are going to do better?

It sounded remarkably like Herren's days in the mantrap, but the key difference was that in 1996 the state and federal government were collaborating. In Eddy's day, two decades earlier, the attitude was more a tenuous, grudging tolerance.

Eddy had some names Baxley's team had developed over the years and that he had gleaned from the FBI files Baxley finally had been given. Eddy read, made notes, and requested files, some of which he received and some he didn't.

Herren sympathized with what Eddy must have gone through. The Bureau was traditionally very close-knit and exclusive. From the outside, it was often seen as snooty or even arrogant. But Herren did understand their reluctance to share informant files. He had worked in Vice and Narcotics and knew the whole house of cards was built on the confidence of secrecy between detective and informants. Informants risked a lot, often their lives, to give information, and information was the lifeblood of the FBI. Hundreds of interviews had taken place in the 1960s on this case, but most useful information came from informants.

Through a contract with the Department of Public Safety, Eddy now provided consultation to Herren and Fleming when called upon. Herren and Fleming both had a tremendous respect for Eddy's knowledge and what he had accomplished, and Herren talked with Bob Eddy whenever he could, wanting to learn from the story of that previous investigation. Eddy had developed the key witness in the Chambliss trial—his niece Elizabeth "Libby" (Cobbs) Hood. To a large degree, the eventual indictment and conviction of Robert "Dynamite Bob" Chambliss resulted from the bravery of this woman who lived in the shadow of the Klan's "kiss of death" to anyone who challenged or betrayed them. She told Bob Eddy that a few days before the bombing, she stopped by her uncle's house and sat at the table with him. They talked about a young black man who had cut a white girl with a knife as the girl leaned out the window of a bus. The girl was the sister of a schoolmate of Elizabeth's.

Chambliss complained to Elizabeth that if any of his fellow Klansmen would have backed him up, "we would have had the God damned niggers in their places by now. I've been fighting a one-man war since World War II. If the boys had backed me up, we wouldn't have the nigger problems on our hands." When he added, "I've got the address of that nigger girl that was going to integrate the school," Elizabeth cautioned him not to do anything foolish. "Don't worry," he replied, "if I do anything . . . [I] would be in something that I could get away in."

He bragged he had enough stuff put away to "flatten half of Birmingham." At that point, he put his hands on the newspaper and looked her in the eye, "You just wait until after Sunday morning; they will beg us to let them segregate." Frightened, Elizabeth asked, "What do you mean?" All he would say was, "Just wait. You will see."

A week later on Saturday, September 21, 1963, she was sitting on a chair in her aunt's living room when Chambliss came into the room and sat on the sofa to watch the news. The announcer said there was a possibility of murder charges arising from the Sixteenth Street Baptist Church bombing. Leaning toward the television and speaking as if to himself, Chambliss said, "It wasn't meant to hurt anybody. It didn't go off when it was supposed to."

Eddy also uncovered the name of Yvonne Young, a white woman who was at Chambliss's house two weeks prior to the bombing. Looking for the restroom, she opened a door and saw bundles of packaged dynamite on the floor. At the trial, the defense attorney asked her if she had been promised any reward money. "That's blood money," she said, "and I want no part of it."

Cobbs had testified despite her fear of retaliation from the Klan, and especially from her Uncle Robert, should Chambliss not be convicted. As he had promised, Eddy stayed beside her, holding tight to her hand and escorting her into the courtroom through a cordon of deputies. But after the trial, she received continuous harassing calls and death threats, and

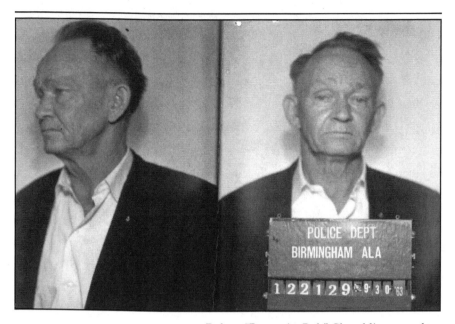

Robert "Dynamite Bob" Chambliss, mug shot.

Birmingham, Ala. Public Library Archives

she left Birmingham in 1979 under an assumed name. Eventually, she had gender reassignment surgery and became Petric Smith. He returned to Birmingham in 1985.

Chambliss, who was seventy-three, went to prison for the murder of Denise McNair, one of the little girls in the church basement. Since Chambliss had a life sentence, the other charges were never pursued. Baxley said he only tried Chambliss on one count of murder to preserve future prosecutions should he not get a conviction. Chambliss died in prison in 1985.

Right after Chambliss's trial, Governor Wallace appointed Bob Eddy sheriff of Madison County in north Alabama. The previous sheriff there, Eddy's former boss, had been sent to prison on corruption charges. Eddy later lost a bid for election as sheriff, and Baxley asked him to return to the attorney general's office, which he did.

Baxley felt there was more work to be done on the Sixteenth Street case and wanted to keep the files out of the press's hands. Concerned

Lt. Col. Bob Eddy, investigator for Attorney General
Bill Baxley on the Chambliss and Stoner case.

Kay Eddy Schuffert

that a national network, CBS, had filed a Freedom of Information Act
request on all the material in the bombing case, Baxley asked Eddy to go
to Washington, DC, to review the files about the Sixteenth Street bombing case in that office. It was somewhat of an irony that Baxley had originally used the threat of the press to get information from the FBI, but
now he was trying to keep it out of the press's hands. But Baxley's goal
was to be able to make a solid case, and he feared that having the information public before a trial might hinder that. While Eddy was in the DC
office on this mission, he saw the original memo from Hoover directing
the FBI to withhold the files from Baxley.

Baxley was never able to prosecute the other prime suspects, and he
failed in two subsequent bids for governor of Alabama. It was another
irony that the case he was accused of using for political advance may
have cost him the governorship. The attorney general who succeeded
Baxley, Charles Graddick, did not pursue the bombing case.

Working under Graddick, Eddy was investigating a widespread public corruption case in Huntsville and had witnesses lined up when he

received a sudden and unexplained order from Graddick to drop the case. On his return to Montgomery, he was informed he was being fired, prompting Assistant Attorney General John Yung, who had been part of Baxley's prosecutorial team on the Chambliss case, to resign in protest. Eddy was asked by Mobile County's district attorney to fill the position of chief investigator.

In 1988 Don Siegelman (who later became governor of Alabama and was subsequently convicted on bribery charges) was elected Alabama attorney general. Siegelman asked Bob Eddy to meet with him and his staff at the attorney general's office in Montgomery. Several lawyers were present, including the attorney general's chief investigator, Jesse Seroyer. They spent a couple of hours asking questions about where they should start and what witnesses Eddy thought were important. "The best thing you can do is pull the files," Eddy told them. "All of my memos should be in the AG's office."

Afterward, Seroyer asked Eddy to join him for a cup of coffee. When they were alone, Seroyer told him, "You and Baxley convicted the wrong man in Chambliss." He let Eddy know he thought Baxley sent an old man to jail to further his political career. Eddy asked, "Do you have some information that would lead to anyone else?" Seroyer didn't, so Eddy just listened to him and then left, thinking Siegelman was doing exactly what Seroyer accused Baxley of doing—making decisions for political reasons. J. Edgar Hoover also had accused Baxley of wanting to open the case for political reasons. Eddy had heard the same theory from other people. From a law enforcement perspective, it seemed a particularly flimsy reason to disagree with years of research, investigation, and a jury's verdict, but it was certainly a dismissal.

In 1988 Siegelman did ask Eddy to write a summary of what he thought should be done in the case and how to go about it, who to interview first, and what each one might be able to tell them. Siegelman said he would have someone pick up the summary. Eddy returned to Mobile and wrote the requested document . . . which was never picked up or requested.

Eddy never heard from anyone about the case again until FBI SAC Rob Langford contacted him in 1995 and asked for his help.

7 | THE TRUNK TAPES

THOMAS BLANTON WAS A prime suspect in the 1960s. His house had been searched as early as October 1963. He had a particular hatred for Catholics, though his mother was Catholic. Blanton was five foot ten and weighed 174 pounds. He had black hair, blue eyes, and, at that time, a tenth-grade education, although he later earned a law degree from the Birmingham School of Law.

Bobby Frank Cherry told investigators Blanton was known to carry "a big old knife," which he "was always flipping." The FBI questioned Blanton multiple times, but their primary source of information about him wasn't developed until 1965 and came from a paid informant, Mitch Burns. Mitch Burns's membership in the Warrior Klavern (north of Birmingham) was primarily a family tradition and "something you just did." He did not hold their ideological views deeply, but he did attend meetings.

FBI agents were tracking Tommy Blanton, who lived with his father, Pop Blanton. A young woman named Marie Aldridge rented a room from Pop, and agents soon realized Klansman Mitch Burns was eating every day at the restaurant where Aldridge worked as a waitress. The restaurant was only a block from his workplace in north Birmingham. Burns appeared sweet on the waitress.

One of the Bureau's best agents was Brook Blake. Blake began "courting" Mitch Burns after he ate lunch, inviting him to ride around with him to talk. Agent Blake would stop by and pick Burns up maybe once or twice a month, and they would ride together for a short distance until Burns would say, "Take me back and let my butt outta here. You can go to hell. I don't want to talk to you."

Reading the case file, Herren couldn't quite figure out why Burns, who was a Klansman and a tough-looking ex-Marine, even got into the car with an FBI agent. Maybe he thought his waitress wanted him to, or Agent Blake found something to hold over his head, or Blake was just persistent. Fellow agent Neil Shanahan referred to Brook Blake as "a good agent; a 'ballsy' agent. If we got a call out at two AM in the morning, you couldn't beat Blake to the front door."

In any case, the record was silent on possible motivations to ride in the car, but it was no mystery why Burns would hesitate to talk. Helping the feds was risky business—his wife was dead and he had the total responsibility for two children. Regardless, the fact was they rode together several times, Mitch Burns listening to what Agent Blake had to say but always rejecting the idea of helping the FBI, until one night, after the church bombing. Agent Blake offered Burns a ride home and stopped the car, pulling out a folder. "I've got something I want you to look at," he said.

Burns's face paled in the overhead car light. In silence, he stared at the enlarged black-and-white autopsy photos of the dead little girls, one of whom had been decapitated. Burns, an orphan, had joined the marines when he was sixteen, falsifying his birth certificate to get in. In World War II, he never made it out of the states because of a medical condition. Perhaps looking at those burned, savaged bodies made him think about his friends who died on Iwo Jima, or perhaps he thought of his own two daughters.

Burns was quiet. He took several deep breaths and swallowed, then said, "I'll do whatever you want me to do."

The waitress Marie Aldridge told Tommy Blanton about Mitch being beleaguered by the FBI, and Blanton contacted Mitch Burns to commiserate with him. He asked Burns if he could help get the FBI off Blanton's back. Those efforts involved picketing and giving an interview to a magazine about FBI harassment. Blanton had no idea he was asking for help from an FBI informant. He and Burns became "friends," riding around together every Friday night and sometimes more often.

Although Blanton always drove, he insisted on using Burns's car because he feared the FBI had bugged his car. Ironically, it was Mitch Burns's car that was bugged. A microphone was installed under the dash in the disabled radio. Cumbersome, seven-inch reel-to-reel recording equipment was hidden behind the spare tire in the trunk. Some of the conversations took place outside of the car, and Burns wrote those down as soon as he returned home, giving them to Agent Blake weekly. Throughout 1965, Burns rode with Blanton.

On March 1, 1965, almost two years after the bombing, Burns reported that Blanton, who had been drinking heavily, made a wrong turn into an alley near Cherry's house. Blanton said he drove up "this same alley the night we made the bomb at Cherry's house, [the bomb] we used to blow up the Sixteenth Street Baptist Church." Then he laughed.

Burns said, "So, this is the place you made it at."

Blanton only laughed again.

Later in the evening, when they were inside Cherry's house, Blanton mentioned to Cherry the conversation he'd just had with Burns in the car. Cherry laughed and said, "The FBI thought it was made at someone else's house."

On another occasion, Blanton said, "I'm gonna stick to bombing churches. . . . They ain't gonna catch me when I bomb my next church." Burns and Blanton discussed how much they hated the church (possibly meaning the Catholic Church), and perhaps they should start their own church and use their urine as holy water.

Fleming had found some transcripts of the car conversations between Blanton and Burns in the technical files. Many of them were dotted throughout with "UNI," for "unintelligible," but there was one transcript of a conversation between Blanton and his wife that referred to a meeting under the bridge, another meeting at the sign shop, and a bomb. Fleming knew the tapes had been inadmissible as evidence in the 1960s because they had only been permitted for national security purposes, not for criminal evidence, but he couldn't help think if they could just listen for themselves, they might find a pearl or two that had never come to light. Even if the tapes themselves weren't useable, it might give them some additional insight or take them down a path where they might develop something useable. It was a long shot, but he asked the ELSUR (electronic surveillance) clerk to look for the tapes.

On June 12, 1997, she found three of the large reel-to-reels in a cabinet. Fearing the act of playing them might damage the tapes, Fleming sent them off to the FBI lab with a request to duplicate and enhance them, if possible. It was apparent from the information in the files that many more tapes had existed, but they, like the fishing bobber, had disappeared.

8 | DALLAS BOUND

THIS WAS DO-OR-DIE DAY. Herren and Fleming had spent fifteen months researching the files and making lists of possible interviewees. The two prime suspects who still were alive were Thomas Blanton and Bobby Frank Cherry. Tomorrow would start the active phase of the investigation, yet they had next to nothing substantive to pursue. Rob Langford, the SAC who had begun the investigation, had retired in November 1996. The new special agent in charge, Joe Lewis, called Fleming and Herren in for a meeting.

A large African American man, Lewis loomed over them both. He asked for an update, and Fleming told him that over a hundred of the potential witnesses mentioned in the files had died. Eighty-eight of them would have had significant potential value as witnesses. There were forty-two left—agents, church members, and Klansmen—but no reason to believe any would have relevant information or even give them the time of day.

"Sir, I feel it is my duty to say this," Fleming said. "I think spending more time on this case is not in the interest of the Bureau. We could spend a very long time on this and never get to a prosecutable case. Ben and I have been through all the files at least twice or more and based on our analysis and what we have seen and read, and on the list of witnesses, these people aren't going to tell us anything different." He took a breath, "There's nothing here; we're gonna embarrass ourselves again with a big effort."

He didn't need to explain to Lewis that he was referring to Trans World Airlines Flight 800, a Boeing 747 that exploded in midair and crashed into the Atlantic Ocean on July 17, 1996. A drawn-out investigation involving eighty agents and several contentious stands with the National Transportation Safety Board looked as if it would end with a whimper.

"This is where we are," Fleming said. "We are going to interview Bobby Frank Cherry—but if he doesn't confess, we'll be standing in the wind. I don't see it going any further."

Herren agreed but kept quiet. Although he had background clearance and he and Fleming had developed some trust between them, Herren was still an outsider.

"There's nothing new here," Fleming repeated. "We have been through everything."

Lewis nodded. "I understand, Bill." But Lewis felt strongly that this was a significant and historic crime, and this was the last chance for closure.

Herren spoke up then, "Well, if we're going to do it, we need a pin resister on Cherry's phone to see who he calls after the interview. It would be interesting if he tries to contact Blanton or any of the old gang. When Bob Eddy interviewed Cherry in 1977 in Texas, Cherry made a call back to Birmingham, and we think he got word to Chambliss through a friend."

"Do it," Lewis said.

As they left the SAC's office, Herren said, "Well, looks like we're in this thing, whether we want to be or not."

"That it does," Fleming echoed.

Their next move was to fly to Texas where Cherry now lived and see what they could get out of him. "I guess all we can do is the best we can do. This is the last shot anybody's ever gonna have at this."

Fleming grunted.

"Well, let's look on the bright side."

"What's that?"

"Maybe Cherry will have a heart attack when he sees Bob Eddy and that will be the end of it all."

Herren wasn't an experienced traveler. His first airplane ride in 1986 had been in a small Bureau plane, a Cessna 182, following bank robbers—not exactly a sedate ride. So now, to distract himself, he went over his notes with Bob Eddy, who sat beside him.

When Eddy interviewed Cherry during the investigation in the 1970s, he felt he had been close to a confession until he told Cherry, "Now don't

FBI Special Agent Bill Fleming (left) and Birmingham
Sergeant/FBI Analyst Ben Herren (right).

Larry Harris

lie to me. I know about the trip down the alley when you went and placed the bomb."

Cherry's response was, "They're gonna hang this on me now?"

"Looks like it," Eddy said.

"I'll come back tomorrow and tell you more," Cherry replied, cutting off the interview.

About six that night Cherry called Robert Gafford, and Gafford was seen talking to Chambliss, who lived close by. Gafford had an auto parts business in north Birmingham, and in 1977 was elected to the Alabama senate. He was also the treasurer of the United Americans for Conservative Government, an organization Chambliss also belonged to.

About midnight, Cherry called Bob Eddy at his hotel to confront him. "Chambliss says he didn't talk to you. You're lying."

"I didn't say I talked to Chambliss," Eddy said, but Cherry refused to talk further.

Herren mulled over how he had come to be sitting in this plane headed to Texas with Fleming, Eddy, and two Justice Department attorneys. After endless conversations over strategy, all involved parties had decided the first interview should be with Bobby Frank Cherry. Blanton's nature was reticent, while Cherry had always been talkative. They also decided the shock value of confronting Cherry with Eddy's presence could be an important tool.

Deputy District Attorney Jeff Wallace would stand by the phones while the investigators were in Texas, in case Cherry indicated he wanted to make a deal in exchange for a confession. Wallace had been chosen a few months earlier to represent the state on the prosecutorial team. John Ott, an assistant US attorney, had called Wallace and said, "I have something to give you; can I meet you somewhere?"

Wallace knew Ott had to be referring to a criminal case, but the question sounded so clandestine that he couldn't resist replying, "Yeah, meet me by the fountain [in Linn Park]. I'll be the one wearing a trench coat." They did meet there, a logical place between the US attorney's office and the FBI headquarters, and Ott gave him an envelope with information on the investigation. That was Wallace's first clue that he was the assistant district attorney assigned to the case. It took a while before it hit him— "This is the Sixteenth Street Church bombing case; this is history."

The two Department of Justice lawyers were accompanying Herren, Fleming, and Eddy to Texas in an advisory capacity, but only Herren and Eddy would be conducting the actual interview. Fleming was also coming with them but would not be present at the interview. He had been stubborn on that point. "Two is enough. Any more would be too many."

That was one of the many things Herren was coming to admire about Fleming. He chose to do the best thing for the case. He wasn't after glory. Herren sincerely hoped he was right, because it put the responsibility squarely on him. But that was something you did as partners—you talked it out, and then you trusted each other.

Ben's longtime patrol partner in the Birmingham Police Department was also that kind of partner. The 11 PM to 7 AM shift—dubbed the morning shift for the wee hours before dawn it covered—was home to several characters nicknamed after the children's show *Sesame Street*, including Big Bird, Bert and Ernie, and Cookie Monster. Herren had the fortune of pairing up with Mike Crawford, a.k.a. Cookie Monster. He considered Cookie "one of the best police officers to ever put on a pair of pants." They were like brothers. When a tense situation arose, they didn't have to communicate; each knew what the other was going to do without having to think about it. It was a good feeling to know your partner had your back.

Cookie Monster was at least six foot three, claiming 360 pounds but probably closer to 400, a big guy, while Herren was short and underweight. One thing Herren could never figure out was that every time someone tried to fight or, in police lingo, bowed up on them, they took on Cookie first. Why tackle the big guy first? People were strange. They didn't always react like you thought they would.

That was the thing worrying him, far more than being thousands of feet above the ground. He'd spent over a year and a half reading and studying the files on this case, making notes and then going home and typing up the notes. Even as late as last night, he and Fleming had gone over everything again, posing questions, trying to guess what Cherry might say, what strategies would have the best chance of working with him. The worst thing in an interview was to have to stop to look something up. He'd had good success with interviews as a burglary detective, and he knew it was important to keep it flowing, to pop questions as fast as your subject could answer them, keeping him off balance so he wouldn't be able to think of lies. If the suspect wasn't prepared, the truth might come out. For that very reason, they were bringing Bob Eddy to the interview—to make Cherry see a ghost.

Police work had taught him, however, that all the preparation in the world couldn't predict what would happen when you stepped out of the patrol car or sat down to interview a suspect. Cookie being a big guy didn't guarantee someone wouldn't tackle him. The unpredictable element was the main reason Herren was nervous. That—and the fact he had slipped his gun into a camera case inside his luggage and not declared it at the airport. The FBI was strict about their rules, but Herren wasn't about to be anywhere without his gun.

He had grown up with guns around him. His father bought him his first BB gun when he was six years old, a Daisy Red Rider. Later, when his brother was old enough, they'd gotten a set of Target air guns. He smiled at the memory. They didn't have a clothes dryer back then, and it was his job to hang out the clothes on a line and to bring them back in when they were dry or if it looked like rain. When there weren't any clothes hanging up, he'd stick clothespins on the line and shoot them with the BB gun. A good hit would make the pin spin. The satisfaction was worth his mother's ire, perhaps even the whipping he got for breaking all her clothespins.

But his introduction to serious guns came courtesy of J. O. Duke, a Jefferson County sheriff's deputy and a friend of his father's. His dad was skilled in woodworking, a passion he passed on to his son, and his father made Deputy Duke nameplates for gifts to his supervisors. Duke had a huge gun collection and gave Herren his first real gun. The age limit for a gun permit was twenty-one, but Duke wrangled Herren a permit when he was eighteen, perhaps because he had proved himself a responsible kid, earning his Eagle Scout rank and staying out of trouble. In the neighborhood Herren grew up in, you either joined the scouting program or you joined the hoodlums.

Duke also got him into the county's Explorer Program, a youth training program focused on learning about law enforcement as a career. No doubt Duke had been responsible for stirring Herren's interest in police work. If Duke and his father had not met and become friends, where would he be now? On such a small thing, a life could turn.

9 | BOBBY FRANK CHERRY

THE ENTIRE LENGTH OF the Dallas airport, Herren expected a hand on his shoulder and a quiet, authoritative voice in his ear saying, "Ben Herren? We need to speak to you." It was a great relief neither the hand nor the voice arrived, and, first thing in the hotel, he fished his Sig Sauer .45 out of the camera case.

They checked in with the Dallas division SAC. It was FBI protocol to send an electronic communication to let the local division know they would be on their turf doing interviews. The Dallas SAC assigned an agent to be their guide and, Herren suspected, to keep his finger on what was happening.

That night, there were more of the endless discussions about the upcoming interview. Herren was impressed with the Justice Department lawyers, who seemed as informed on the case as he and Fleming were.

Everything they could think of to be prepared had been done. They had even consulted a behavioral scientist, as well as a repentant "free-lance bomber" for insights on how to deal with Cherry. By the time Herren's head hit the pillow, it was buzzing with everything he knew about Bobby Frank Cherry.

Athens, Texas, was a seventy-mile drive southeast of Dallas. It was July 9, 1997, and hot, but both Herren and Fleming were southern boys. They knew hot, and this heat was drier and easier to bear than a humid Alabama summer. Their route to Athens took them through Mabank, the town where Bobby Frank Cherry now lived. A small city, Mabank's major attraction was a lake resort. Some of the folks from Dallas built nice houses lakeside, but at heart, the town was rural.

Herren was as prepared as he could make himself, but that didn't help the fact he was shouldering the responsibility of getting Cherry to talk. He was accustomed to tape recording important interviews, but FBI rules still forbade recording interviews, a holdover from the days of J. Edgar Hoover. He and Fleming had even tried getting approval, under an officer safety rule, for Herren to wear a wire, but that was also denied. On several levels, he was glad Bob Eddy was with him, but Eddy wasn't saddled with note-taking duty, so Herren was going to have to write fast and think faster.

It was not considered a good technique to do an interview on a suspect's turf, so Stan Strauss, the Dallas agent who had done a lot of footwork for them, set up the meeting with Cherry at the Henderson County sheriff's office in Athens. Deputy Wayne Carroll was bringing Cherry in. Carroll had been asked to tell Cherry only that some people wanted to talk to him. Cherry had several children who had gotten into trouble with the law. They hoped he would assume his children's behavior to be the purpose of the sheriff's call. This meeting was top secret, but Cherry must have had his own sources or smelled a rat in the woodpile, because on the way to the sheriff's office he announced to Deputy Carroll, "If them boys are from Birmingham, I ain't talking to 'em."

Cherry's instincts or information proved correct, but contrary to his pronouncement, when Herren and Bob Eddy stepped into the room, his reaction was neither what he predicted nor what they had planned for. Instead of shock, Cherry greeted Bob Eddy like an old friend, "Boy, I thought you retired and was raisin' cattle somewhere in Alabama."

"I am," Eddy said.

"How long has it been?"

"Over twenty years."

"What you doing here?" Cherry asked.

Eddy's mouth was grim. "Things like this never go away."

Herren took a breath to recover from his surprise at Cherry's reaction. This was not what they had hoped for. Seeing Bob Eddy should have been like seeing a phantom from his past, but Cherry was calm and cool. This did not bode well for the interview. Herren held out his hand and introduced himself as a Birmingham police sergeant.

In a pleasant good-old-boy fashion, Cherry started naming people in Birmingham and asking Ben if he knew so-and-so. "Hey," he added, "I got to take my wife to the doctor at one thirty, now."

"No problem," Herren said, glancing at his watch, "We'll try to see if we can be finished by then."

Cherry began talking about his last meeting with Eddy and Attorney General Bill Baxley in 1977. "I remember I slapped that Baxley," he said, giving a self-pleased chuckle.

Herren recalled Eddy telling them about that interview—Cherry would periodically flare up in anger and then "sull up" in silence during the five hours with him and Baxley.

"That's not true," Eddy said at once. "I was there. If you had done that, we'd have put you in jail."

As they had planned, Herren let Bob Eddy lead on the interview. The idea was for Eddy to ask the softball questions, because they knew each other and had a rapport, and Herren would follow up with more confrontational questions. While Eddy was warming Cherry up, Herren did a quick study of the man. Cherry had aged; he didn't look anything like the pictures taken of him three decades ago, though he still had the thick wavy hair, ruddy complexion, bulbous nose, and straw cowboy hat.

Deputy Carroll, who had simply walked into the interview room with them, sat quietly in the corner. That wasn't planned, but Herren didn't feel like asking him to leave while they were guests at his agency.

Even though Eddy was handling the opening questions, Herren had to write fast because Cherry was like a spigot, and there was no way to distinguish bull from something that would turn out to be important later on. But he was not complaining. The most difficult suspects were those who lawyered up. They made it hard, if not impossible, to make a case. But if they kept talking, there was a chance for a confession. And if you couldn't get them to tell you the truth, the next best thing was to get them to lie, because you could bust them on lies.

Hours later, Cherry left the room and made a phone call, getting one of his children to take his wife to the doctor. Herren was afraid it would be a repeat of his break in the previous interview with Eddy, and that Cherry would return and refuse to say anything more. Instead, he came back and talked on.

When he did return, Herren jumped in. "Well, you know, like Colonel Eddy said, this thing's never goin' to go away until the truth is known; that's the reason we're out here. The truth has been with you, but it's been weighing on the public all these years. We're just out here to talk to you, find out what the truth really is. You hold the key to the whole story."

Herren, realizing confrontation was not going to get them anywhere, tried a different tactic from what they had planned. "Who do you think planted the bomb?" he asked.

"Other folks in the Klan," Cherry responded with a shrug. "There are two organizations I regret joining. One was the US Marines and the other was the Klan."

"Why would they have done it?" Herren asked.

"Don't know," Cherry responded, shaking his head. "I guess because they just wanted to kill somebody. They're all trying to frame me."

"Now why would they want to do that?" Herren asked again, keeping the tone conversational. "You're just a good old boy; why would they do that?"

Cherry gave a snort. "They were just laughing and sitting back in their Cadillacs."

Herren knew the southern phrase from his childhood. It meant somebody had left you hanging and was driving off unencumbered.

Herren asked him if it were true Cherry was kicked out of the Klan. Cherry denied it vehemently. "I could go back to the Klan today if I wanted to. I could march right in there and be a member."

Herren asked him about his children. There were several ex-wives and descendants he wanted to interview, and he was hoping for enough information to locate them. He asked where they lived and whom they had married, working his way down the family tree he had laid out thanks to the files and the background work done by FBI staff. When he got to one son, Cherry said, "Oh, he's dead."

"Oh man, I'm sorry. How'd that happen?"

"Police killed him in Arlington, Texas."

Herren swallowed, afraid all the rapport he'd carefully built had just flushed down the toilet. How was he going to recover from this?

With only a brief pause, Cherry added, "But he deserved it; he had a gun," and kept right on talking.

When Herren asked about his whereabouts since 1963, Cherry said he had worked at Wyatt Industries from 1977 to 1981 and then started a carpet business and a small trucking company. Herren worked the conversation back to 1963. Cherry insisted he had quit the Klan a year or so before the bombing because "his old lady was sick with cancer" and he had to take care of her. He said that while he was a Klan member, Robert Sidney Thomas was the Exalted Cyclops of the Klavern. Thomas, Cherry declared, was a "government pimp" and had a "nigger maid he refused to fire." To add insult to injury, some of the other leaders were sending their children to Catholic schools, and this was "delivering a bad message."

"Did you ever attend the Cahaba Bridge meetings?"

"Once, but I didn't ever go back because they looked like a mean bunch of fellows."

At first Cherry said he did not know Chambliss very well and only saw him "at meetings and such." Later, he said he knew Chambliss about "as well as anyone did" and described him as a good friend who worked for the City of Birmingham.

Herren wrote furiously. "Did you know a Mr. Fields?"

"Yeah, he wrote something about me in a paper, the *Thunderbolt*, but it was about ninety-nine percent fiction just to upset people to sell papers. I did help Mr. Fields put up a sign one time, because everyone else was afraid to do it."

"What about Robert Shelton [the Klan Imperial Wizard]?"

"I was Bobby Shelton's bodyguard," Cherry bragged.

Herren tried to write quickly, wishing yet again for a tape recorder.

"I still believe in segregation," Cherry volunteered. "I do not want my kids to be forced to associate with niggers. And I don't like the government telling me what to do. I don't mind niggers; in fact, I grew up with some niggers. I did not just hate niggers, I would have hated white people too if they were going to jump on me." He launched into a story about going with other Klansmen to talk to a white preacher who was raising a "nigger kid."

"What happened?"

"The man's wife came out with a gun and started shooting, and we all high-tailed it for the cars!"

"Would something like that be considered a missionary operation?" Herren asked.

"The Klan was set up to help people," Cherry said evasively.

Hours ticked by; the deputy sheriff sat still in the corner, saying nothing, giving no clue to his thoughts. Herren felt they were not hitting the right emotional buttons to make Cherry want to tell the truth and get it off his chest. Or maybe Cherry just didn't have the same kind of buttons a normal person had. His mindset was different.

Herren knew he needed to think outside the box. Realizing Cherry's weakness was his ego, Herren offered him avenues to save face. "What the white population wanted back then was segregation, not integration," Herren remarked, in the hope Cherry's tendency to brag would spill over into the church bombing. "The Klan and your group were doing what others didn't have the guts to do."

"Well, you know," Cherry responded, "I did bop old Reverend Shuttlesworth right between the eyes with a pair of brass knuckles. Then I hit the car window with my fist and almost cut my fingers off."

"When was that?"

"It was during a high school demonstration in 1957."

"Really?" Herren said. "So you do believe violence is sometimes called for?"

"I don't like it, but it can be necessary if you're protecting yourself or what belongs to you."

"Like that incident at the Krystal Kitchen?"

"I had to split open a nigger's head with a pistol once at the Krystal Kitchen," Cherry concurred.

"How come?"

Cherry shrugged. "He called me an SOB."

Herren nodded, as if that were perfectly understandable.

Cherry shifted in his chair. "Statute of limitations has run out on that one."

When Herren asked him again about his possible role in the church bombing, Cherry said his back was broken during that time and he could not have carried a big bomb.

"How do you know it was big?" Herren asked.

"Well, I just thought it would have been big."

"Could you have carried ten to twelve sticks of dynamite?"

"No."

"What about a lunch box?"

"I couldn't have carried anything."

"Why did you join the Klan in the first place?" Herren asked, switching the topic.

"Well, back in 1955, or maybe it was 1957, it was a political group out to help get good people elected to office. And I also joined," he added with a chuckle, "so I could chase women when I went out of town to the rallies."

"Where were you on Saturday, September 14, 1963, the Saturday before the church bombing?" Eddy asked.

"I was at the Modern Sign shop running a silk screen."

"How were you able to run a silk screen with a broke back?"

"Actually, it was good exercise for my back."

"Was anyone with you?"

"Yeah, Tommy Blanton and Bob Chambliss."

Herren wrote quickly. "Let my crayon catch up with us. Are you sure that was Saturday night?"

Cherry explained he was certain because there were relatives visiting (now dead) from out of town and his wife had cancer, and he had gone home later to watching "wrasslin'" on TV with her.

A few minutes later, he added, "The Klan is a Christian organization and would never blow up a church, because the church is a Christian place. I sang in the Klan choir at churches and funerals."

"Well, you know, that church was where all the rallies were taking place," Herren said. "We know that bomb wasn't meant to kill those innocent little girls. It was just an act against the church."

"I thought it was a gas explosion," Cherry said.

Herren showed him the autopsy pictures, his last hope of breaking through Cherry's shell.

In that moment, Cherry became very still, taking a deep breath, his head dropping a bit. All the braggadocio vanished from his voice. "Goddamn. Good God Almighty." He took another breath. "Well, you know, Mr. Herren, it's like pulling the trigger on the gun. After you do that, it's too late. . . . I would never bomb a church."

As he was walking out the door, Cherry looked back over his shoulder. "Birmingham is a little Africa now, more niggers than whites."

After four hours of interviewing Bobby Frank Cherry, Herren left the sheriff's office without a confession, but with a certainty in his heart the man was guilty of helping to plant that bomb. Some part of Cherry, Herren believed, really wanted to confess.

Herren and Bob Eddy interviewed other people who had known Cherry in the towns of Mabank and Gunbarrel and then met Fleming back in Dallas. "Well, he didn't confess," Herren told his partner, "but he did talk for four hours."

"Oh, that's good," Fleming said. "That's very good you kept him talking that long."

They went out for a steak and a beer in Old Towne. Despite Fleming's encouragement, Herren knew it was the beginning of the end of the investigation. He felt like he had run a marathon and lost. Except for a few loose ends interviewing old Klansmen and family members who weren't likely to give them much, the fuse had fizzled.

He was unaware Cherry himself would ignite it again.

10 | TIPPING POINT

WHILE HERREN WAS INTERVIEWING Bobby Frank Cherry, Fleming was talking to other people they had identified as related to or knowing Cherry. He found Tommy Frank Cherry Jr., a grandson of Bobby's, in a Henderson County jail. Tommy said he had never heard his grandfather discussing anything remotely related to the incident.

Robert L. High, a part-time preacher who knew Cherry from working at Wyatt Industries in Dallas, painted a glowing picture of Cherry, claiming he got along with both white and black employees with no indication of prejudice. Cherry and his wife were the godparents of High's children.

When Herren and Fleming returned to Birmingham, they attempted to interview Thomas Blanton, but he refused to talk to them, so they went back to the list of Klansmen, their relatives and associates, and other possible witnesses compiled during the months of studying the files. Their plan was to prioritize the list and interview everyone they could find. Making the list had been a huge undertaking itself, but staff's help with the tedious task of obtaining contact information was invaluable.

Herren wrote twenty pages for the Bureau 302 summary file on the interview with Cherry, and they began to look into the information Cherry had given them. They checked newspapers for September 15, 1963, and television schedules and found Cherry had lied when he claimed he was home watching wrestling with his sick wife. No wrestling had been playing.

Hospital records revealed Cherry's wife, Virginia Cherry, did not have symptoms of cancer until 1965, two years later. Another lie, but they did not have nearly enough for an indictment. An indictment required probable cause, a subjective standard beyond suspicion. Probable cause was a standard based on what a reasonable person would believe when confronted with the evidence. It was subjective, but, after a while, a law enforcement officer pretty much knew when he had it or not.

Disappointingly, the pin register they had put on Cherry's phone to identify the person(s) Cherry called after the interview did not provide any useful names or connections.

Now what? Herren and Fleming decided they would continue interviewing the people on their list—stir the ant bed and see if anything came out.

The case was announced publicly July 10, 1997, the day after Cherry's interview. Herren, who had two large scrapbook volumes of mementoes and newspaper clippings from his police days, began to collect articles. In an article in the *Birmingham News*, Carol Robinson wrote:

"It's a crime that has gone unsolved except for one local conviction, and it remains a sore part of American history that we would like to heal," said Joseph Lewis, FBI SAC of the Birmingham field office. "We feel we have an opportunity to do so this time, and we want to take one last shot at it. This is the last grand hurrah we'll have."

There was a scramble of speculation that Spike Lee's newest film, *Four Little Girls*, was the catalyst for reopening the bombing case, but that was just coincidence.

No one was more surprised than Agent Fleming when Henderson County's Deputy Carroll—the deputy who had sat quietly in the corner throughout the interview with Bobby Frank Cherry—called to let them know what Cherry had been up to. Cherry had hired a lawyer and called a news conference in Athens, Texas, on July 14, 1997, to complain about the FBI reopening the bombing case and harassing him. Deputy Carroll was in the crowd, videoed the conference with a hand recorder, and sent it to Birmingham.

Fleming and Herren watched the video in the office. Less than a dozen people had gathered as Cherry stood on the courthouse steps in his big Western straw hat, his son Tommy Cherry at his side. "Them feds won't leave me alone!" he railed. "They've been harassing me for thirty years. I'm innocent! I ain't done nothin'."

Shortly thereafter, the phones at the Birmingham FBI office began to light up. Just a few days after Cherry's interview, the switchboard operator forwarded a call to Fleming.

"This is Agent Fleming," he said.

"Thank God somebody's doing the case. I've heard about this all my life." Those were the first words out of Teresa Stacy's mouth. Stacy was one of Bobby Frank Cherry's granddaughters. When she was younger, she'd overheard her grandfather bragging at a family reunion: "We took care of 'em up there in Birmingham. We blowed that church up." When they moved to Texas, Cherry told his family he'd been indicted in Birmingham and that if he ever moved back, he'd be put in jail.

That same day Fleming was on a plane to Texas to interview her in person, excited at their first real break, but his high deflated quickly. Teresa Stacy could have been a movie star or a model; she was a knockout, not to mention, he thought, about the only person in her family with all her teeth. Her childhood desire was to be a veterinarian, but Bobby Frank Cherry, her grandfather, had sexually molested her at age twelve. Her father, Tommy Cherry, beat her mother, and, at sixteen, Teresa ran away and became an exotic dancer—with a cocaine habit.

What she had to offer the case was similar to what Elizabeth Cobbs contributed in the 1977 trial of Robert Chambliss, which sent him to prison. But Elizabeth Cobbs had testified when she was a Methodist minister—nobody knew how it would have affected the credibility of the witness if Petric Smith had testified. Teresa Stacy would have to take the stand as a former exotic dancer and drug addict. The defense, Fleming worried, would eat her for lunch.

11 | MITCH BURNS

BILL FLEMING WAS IN Dallas the day Herren had arranged to interview Mitch Burns. Burns, now elderly, had been the informant who was moved to help the FBI after he saw the autopsy photos of the four girls.

The backcountry of northern Jefferson County was beautiful, winding between patches of green forest and rolling pastures. Burns, now over seventy years old, lived way off the main road in Warrior, Alabama. An American flag flew at the driveway entrance, and when Herren finally arrived, he saw a well-kept house and land neatly divided by a creosote fence. In fact, Burns was painting the thick black mixture onto the fence when Herren found him. He was a spry man with silvered hair and a face browned by the sun.

Herren introduced himself, his eyes watering at the bitter stench of the inky black mixture of turpentine, kerosene, and roofing tar. Nasty stuff to work with.

"I make it myself," Burns told him.

He invited Herren into his house. The smell of coffee was a welcome alternative to the creosote. Herren accepted a cup, not bothered by the statuette of a hooded Klansman or the revolver—a chrome-plated .38 with imitation ivory handles—that lay in plain sight on the Formica kitchen table. He had read enough about Burns to know what kind of man he was. Cooperating with the FBI all those years ago had put Burns at a terrible risk. He would never know if or when the Klan might come for him or his family. That gun had most probably been at hand for the past thirty years. The statuette of a hooded Klansman was evidence of how deeply Burns played his role, even now.

"You sure do keep your place looking good," Herren said.

"I try to stay active. Got a girlfriend that lives in Mount Olive, and we go dancing regularly."

Herren grinned. "I hope I am still going that strong when I'm your age."

"Where's the FBI man that was coming?" Burns asked.

"He's in Texas and wasn't able to be here. We wanted to talk to you about the Sixteenth Street Church bombing. You're not under investigation; we've reopened the case and discovered you had been an acquaintance of Thomas Blanton and possibly Bobby Frank Cherry, two of the suspects we are looking at."

"Can I see your identification again?" Burns asked.

"Sure." Herren took out his police badge and handed it to Burns, who studied it carefully. He handed it back and with a steady hand lit an unfiltered cigarette, offering one to Herren.

"No, thanks. I don't smoke."

Burns took a sip of his coffee. "I met Tommy Blanton through a waitress by the name of Marie. She worked at a café where I had lunch a lot. One day two FBI agents came to the café to talk to me there. They were talking to everyone who had ever been connected to the Klan."

"Were you a member?"

"In those days, it was just the thing to do. I never done anything as a Klan member except burn a cross once, and I'm ashamed of that. But getting back to how I knew Tommy Blanton, Marie saw the FBI talking to me, and she told Blanton about it. She knew him because she rented an apartment from his father, Pop Blanton."

"Did you know Pop Blanton?"

Burns made a dismissive sound. "Pop was a strange one." He took a drag on the cigarette. "His car had Wallace stickers all over it; you could barely tell what the color was."

"So, what about Tommy Blanton?"

"Tommy was running around with a lawyer named J. B. Stoner at the time. Blanton asked me to give a statement to Stoner for a paper called the *Thunderbolt*."

"Did you?"

"I did."

Burns breathed out smoke. "When the FBI found out I knew Blanton, they came back and showed me the pictures of the little girls from the church bombing, and I told them I would work with them to get the people responsible for killing them."

Herren played ignorant that he knew Burns had been an FBI source. He didn't want Burns to think the FBI would divulge he had worked for them. "Oh, so you worked for the FBI?"

Burns eyed him and stubbed out his cigarette. "No offense to you, but I would be more comfortable talking to an agent, because I just don't know how much them fellas want me to tell you."

Herren was not offended. He respected Burns's keeping the FBI's trust, even now.

"I understand. Can I come back with an agent?"

"Sure."

And he did return with Fleming, on several occasions. They met Burns's two daughters, admired his belt buckle collection, and talked with him about the straw cowboy hats he painted and sold. Burns would not, however, agree to take the stand—and that was critical to their case.

The prosecution needed a witness—assuming they got far enough to prosecute anyone—who could vouch for the authenticity of the transcripts of conversations between Burns and Tommy Blanton. The problem seemed to lie in Burns's feeling that Bill Baxley had tried to bully him into testifying in the 1977 case. Also, one of Burns's daughters was a special-needs child, and Herren wondered if that entered into his stubbornness about not testifying. Herren could understand a father's protectiveness toward his vulnerable child, but they needed Burns's testimony.

12 | BOBBY BIRDWELL

SINCE CHERRY'S TELEVISED PROTEST, the media attention Herren and Fleming had avoided for almost a year and a half was now recognized as an important tool, but they couldn't comment about the case, so the media was often referred to Bob Eddy. This kept articles and stories going and calls coming in. Some were from outrageous liars only after the offered reward money; others were well meaning but had little to contribute.

One important call came in during the night, but the night duty operator didn't try to contact Fleming, he just left the information. The call was from a Vietnam veteran named Bobby Birdwell who said he had been a school friend of Tommy Cherry, Bobby Frank Cherry's son. They both had attended Bush Elementary School in Birmingham.

Bobby Birdwell came to headquarters for an interview. He was working in Utah and never knew about the 1977 investigation, but he saw a recent newspaper article about the reopening of the case in which Cherry claimed he was not part of the Klan. Birdwell said he remembered being at Tommy's house one Friday when he was an adolescent. Tommy was bragging about his father being a member of the Ku Klux Klan and showed him—spread in all its glory across the couch—his daddy's white satin robe, emblazoned across the heart with the MIOAK patch that looked like a tilted, blood-drop cross.

In the kitchen, several men were sitting around a table talking. They ignored the boys, who were on their way out, and Birdwell heard, "The

81

dynamite is there," and the words, "bomb" and "Sixteenth Street." Bird-well didn't know the other men at the kitchen table, but he knew his friend's father, Bobby Frank Cherry. He didn't think much of it until a few days later—Sunday, September 15, 1963—when the bomb ripped through the basement wall of the Sixteenth Street Baptist Church.

He didn't call the police; he was a young boy and was afraid. His parents also had strong segregationist feelings at that time. But now, when he heard about the investigation being reopened, he came forward. He didn't want any of the reward money. He just wanted to tell what he knew.

13 | MICHAEL WAYNE GOWINS

FLEMING WAS AS CONVINCED as Herren about Bobby Frank Cherry's part in the bombing, but as far as evidence, they had very little—only Teresa Stacy's statement. Which was good, very good—he'd gone to "the top of the moon" about it at first—but she would be so vulnerable on the stand. They had to have much more before the US attorney would even consider taking it to court. He'd gotten over his initial anger at having been given the case. Now, he just wanted to solve it.

Only two days after the interview with Cherry, Herren picked up the phone. "Yes, sir, this is Sergeant Herren."

"I've heard Bobby Frank Cherry talk about the bombing," the raspy male voice on the phone said.

Herren wouldn't let himself get excited. They were getting lots of calls from people who couldn't offer anything of substance. "In what context did you hear him say it?" Herren asked.

"Well, my mother ran some apartments out in Texas. Bobby Frank Cherry had a carpet cleaning business. When people moved out of an apartment, we'd have to go in and paint the walls, clean the carpets, clean it up before we could rent it out again. And he said things during the time I was in there painting and him cleaning carpets."

Herren felt his pulse quicken. In the interview, Cherry mentioned he'd had a carpet cleaning business. There could be something to this. When he hung up from the call, he turned to Fleming. "We gotta go talk to this guy."

———————

Herren and Fleming drove for hours through the flat countryside of rural southern Alabama, looking for Mike Gowins's trailer. It was a hot August day in 1997.

Finally, they gave up and stopped at a post office in a small town to ask for directions. Fleming approached the woman behind the counter. She was in her sixties, Herren guessed, maybe a little older than Fleming.

Herren had never met anyone more of a proper southern gentleman than his partner. He'd never heard an exclamation from Fleming stronger than "Golly Moses!" or "Good Lord!" or an occasional "Oh my goodness!" Fleming seemed a man from a different time.

The woman had her back to them, busy with something.

"Excuse me, ma'am," Fleming asked. "Are you the postmistress here?"

She turned around and eyed him. "Sonny, the government don't pay me enough to be a mistress."

At the stricken expression on his partner's crimson face, Herren burst into laughter. When Fleming recovered enough to get the directions they needed, they headed out, following the postmistress's instructions.

———————

Gowins's home was filled with tiny, intricate model cars encased in glass cubes. A thin man with brown hair and eyes, Gowins was in a wheelchair when they arrived and not in good shape. Clear twin tubes fed from a tank of oxygen to his nose. He looked like a man living in death's shadow.

"I'm dying of asbestos poison," he wheezed in answer to their unspoken question. "Worked with tile embedded with it." He had to pause to catch his breath every few words, but he was earnest and wanted to talk. Herren and Fleming wanted to listen.

"Tell us how you came into contact with Bobby Frank Cherry."

"Well, it was 1982. My mother managed the Munger Apartments on Munger Avenue in eastern Dallas. I was visiting her with my girlfriend for about a month and a half. Like I said on the phone, I would help out sometimes when apartments became vacant, help her clean up and repair any damages. That was a second job for me. I was also a security guard."

Herren looked at the wasted man before him who struggled for breath, trying to imagine him as he had been.

"Bobby Cherry had a carpet cleaning company, a van with hoses, but I don't remember the name of it. I saw him four or five times."

"Do you remember anything about what Cherry said when he came to clean carpets for your mother?" Fleming asked.

"Sure I do. That's why I called," he wheezed. "I saw it on television, and then I saw a picture of Cherry in the newspaper, and that brought it all back. He was different, older, but I knew it was him. Back then his hair had a reddish tinge, and he wore it combed straight back. I remember exactly what I was doing—I was in the kitchen in an upstairs apartment, and my girlfriend was there in the apartment. I didn't call anybody about it. I didn't know who to call."

They paused to let him catch his breath.

"What he said just seared into my mind," Gowins continued when he could. "It shocked me. I'll never forget it. Cherry was talking about the Mexican problem. He says, 'What are you guys gonna do about all these Mexicans down here?' Then he says, 'Y'all need to handle these dad-gum wetbacks like we handled the blacks up in Birmingham and kill a few of 'em, and then they'll quit messing with you."

Once again, Gowins had to stop to catch his breath, though he obviously didn't want to. When he could, he added one more thing. "Cherry said, 'I had to leave Birmingham. I had bombed the Sixteenth Street Baptist Church.'"

Fleming and Herren left Mike Gowins with a mixture of elation and dread. They were getting somewhere. This was important new testimony and something that had happened in 1982, long after both the initial investigation and after the 1970s investigation. "What do you think?" Herren asked.

"He's a good man," Fleming said. "He really wants to help. He's poor as dirt, and he didn't ask us for a thing. But I don't know if he could make it to Birmingham for a trial."

Herren sighed. "I don't know that he's going to stay *alive* long enough for a trial."

———

Later, they interviewed Mike Gowins's mother, who Gowins said might have been in the room when Bobby Cherry made those remarks. She was curled up on her bed, very sick with cancer, when they found her. They thought she might want to talk with them, but she denied having heard Cherry's statements.

One of Gowins's ex-wives told them, "He [Gowins] was not a nice man. He was rough, physically and verbally. I didn't love him; I hated him, but he would not lie to you."

14 | DON LUNA, "CON OF CONS"

BILL FLEMING HAD PUT away his resignation letter after they had spoken to Burns, but he found the interviews to be difficult. Often it felt as if he and Herren were talking to their own grandparents. He felt badly going to sons and daughters who had never committed any kind of crime and asking them if they'd heard about the terrible things their fathers had done. Though some of the people they spoke with were what he called lowlifes, some were upstanding citizens.

They interviewed everyone they could find. A few of the original church members were contacted, although Herren and Fleming didn't devote much time to that, assuming they would not know about the conspiracy, only about what happened on that day.

———

As an assistant US attorney, Caryl P. Privett had watched the 1977 trial of Robert "Dynamite Bob" Chambliss from the balcony of the county courthouse. When Langford began the new investigation, she was the US attorney for the Northern District, which included Birmingham. Initially she had qualms about reopening the case. What if they decided not to prosecute? Or even if they did, what if they weren't able to get convictions? But FBI SAC Rob Langford had been persuasive in his presentation. His commitment to the investigation, even in light of the obstacles he knew they faced, along with the recommendation of US Assistant

Attorney John Ott, brought her on board. Ott had originally opened the case for the US attorney's office and met periodically with Langford, Fleming, and Assistant District Attorney Roger Brown to keep up with the investigation.

In September 1997, the Clinton administration appointed G. Douglas "Doug" Jones, a local attorney, to replace Caryl Privett as the US attorney for the Northern District of Alabama, which included Birmingham. Jones took an immediate interest in the case. As a student at Samford University's Cumberland School of Law, he had cut class to watch Bill Baxley try Robert Chambliss. Like Caryl Privett, he watched the case from the balcony with intense interest.

Every time Jones appeared on television, Herren's dad would say, "Your *friend* Doug Jones is on TV again." The edge in the word "friend" disclosed his unspoken disapproval. Jones was a dyed-in-the-wool Democrat, and Herren's father "didn't have anything much for Democrats."

Herren was surprised when his father expressed concern over his safety. His dad, who was in his seventies now, had grown up in rural Walker County, north of Birmingham. "You don't want to make these folks mad, or they'll come burn you out," he often said. After all these years, the Klan still had deep claws.

"Daddy, I don't worry about those guys," Herren told him. "My name, phone number, and address have been in the telephone book since I've been a police officer. If they want to come talk to me, they can. I ain't ever worried about any people in my police career, except one person. And thanks to a Kansas City police officer, he's dead."

One of the most colorful characters of the Eastview #13 Klavern was Don E. Luna. On the day of what was the first of many visits, Luna greeted Herren and Fleming from the reclining Naugahyde chair that was his throne. The chair and his bed were the only two places where he could find any kind of comfort for his four-hundred-plus-pound body. He lived with his wife in his mother-in-law's house. His office was that chair set in the living room, surrounded by a fax machine, a telephone, a shredder, and a walker.

Luna's aunt was Mary Lou Holt, the beautiful wife of Bill Holt, a well-known Klansman. Though she probably knew a lot, Mary Lou had not given Bob Eddy any information during his investigation. Herren and Fleming had tried to interview her, but she was now in a nursing home, and her son would not allow them to talk to her.

Luna was the only Klansman who talked freely to Herren and Fleming, though after their first meeting—when Luna hinted that he knew where Jimmy Hoffa's body was and offered an opportunity to invest in a ground-penetrating radar device so they could find him—they realized everything he said could be inflated or an outright lie. Fleming branded him a "con of cons." "You could run a college for future con artists," Fleming told him.

Luna's full-moon face lit up at the compliment. "When I die, I'm gonna con Saint Peter himself." Then, in the next breath, he complained, "Now, I never tried to cheat anyone. My worst problem is I am too trusting of people, and I'm just always trying to help them."

Gregarious and friendly, he was the most educated and well spoken of any of his contemporary Klan members. He had been indicted on over a hundred counts of fraud in another federal judicial district, but because of his health and his agreement to cooperate in the church bombing case, those fraud charges were being held in abeyance.

In a 1964 interview, Luna told the FBI he joined the Klan in 1962 because he felt integration was "being pushed down the South's throat." Fleming and Herren were able to verify he had been the intelligence chief for the Eastview #13, which met in Woodlawn, a small suburban area east of downtown Birmingham. "My job was to make sure no FBI pimps got in and that applicants would make good Klansmen."

"Who would those be?" Herren asked.

"There were three types of people that joined the Klan in the 1950s and 1960s," Luna told them. "There were bums with nothing else to do with their lives, generally low income, poorly educated types, who found acceptance by like-minded folks. Then there were those prone to violence. And there were those who strongly supported the Klan and used it for their political ends, but couldn't become official members because of their standing in the community."

Herren thought of the estimates he and Fleming had heard, that 40 percent of the Birmingham Police Department had been part of or sympathizers with the Ku Klux Klan during the 1960s. In one of his early reports to Baxley's office, Eddy wrote, "The more I get into the bombing, the more aware I am that certain police officers, present and past, were close to the suspects in each bombing." In fact, in the 1960s, the Eastview #13 Klavern met in the lodge of the Fraternal Order of Police. Many influential people, including judges, wore the white robes in secret. It was no wonder the FBI director, J. Edgar Hoover, had decided the chances for a conviction were remote.

At the same time, ironically, some of the Birmingham police felt it was the FBI who was protecting the suspects. From their perspective, leads given to the feds disappeared into the federal maw. No reports or information came back. The lack of reciprocity and the failure of the government to file charges fueled the mistrust. Birmingham law enforcement also received threats from the Klan and hate groups, including black radicals. Aware that some of their members were informants for or members of the Klan and/or the FBI, a selected group met secretly in homes to discuss the case.

Luna told Herren and Fleming about the Klan meetings. They would last about an hour and a half, opening—like so many civic club meetings—with a pledge and a prayer. New and old business would be discussed, mostly anti-Jewish and anti-Kennedy talk, but never violence, Luna insisted. According to Luna, Robert Shelton, the Imperial Wizard and national leader of the Klan, did not support violence and had directed anyone with information regarding the church bombing to cooperate with the investigation.

As the intelligence officer in the Eastview #13, Luna conducted the Klan's own investigation of the bombing. In 1964 he told the FBI he had interviewed Blanton and that Blanton told him "the FBI had a witness who could place his [Blanton's] automobile at the Sixteenth Street Baptist Church the night before the church was bombed." Blanton also complained he had to "fix his story with his girl." It was Luna's impression that Blanton, who was "visibly shaken," was using his girlfriend Jean Casey, whom he married shortly thereafter, as an alibi for his whereabouts on the evening of September 14, 1963.

Luna also claimed that he had worked in an undercover capacity for Al Lingo, the director of the Alabama Department of Public Safety, informing Lingo of Klan activities, including those of the notorious white supremacist J. B. Stoner and his National States Rights Party. Luna told the FBI he felt the Klansmen were not smart enough to plan bombings of the type that occurred in Birmingham in 1963. "An unknown individual has been furnishing support through technical and organizational assistance," he said. Other sources also told the FBI that J. B. Stoner had, along with others, come to Birmingham to give Klansmen instruction in how to put together bombs and timing devices.

Stoner believed Hitler had been too moderate, that blacks were an extension of the "ape family," and that Jews were "vipers of hell." He had run for political office in Georgia—for governor, lieutenant governor, and the US Senate. In 1960, the National States Rights Party moved their headquarters to Birmingham. Stoner had been on the FBI's original list of suspects for the Sixteenth Street Baptist Church bombing, but his alibi had checked out.

When Bob Eddy was digging into the FBI files in 1977, he ran across surprising information concerning Stoner. The story began with a report from the Birmingham Police Department. Eddy reported what he found to his boss, Attorney General Bill Baxley. Despite Baxley's instructions to Eddy not to get sidetracked from the Sixteenth Street bombing, Baxley said, "We need to follow up on that."

Eddy made contact with the officer who had written the report, to hear the story firsthand. An attempted bombing of a Birmingham synagogue in 1958, along with six other bombings in Jewish communities across the Southeast, prompted Jewish business leaders to approach Mayor (and president of the commission) James W. Morgan and Public Safety Commissioner Bull Connor and demand they take action. Efforts through Alabama congressional representatives to get the FBI involved failed. Hoover did not want to get the FBI involved in local law enforcement affairs.

Connor, probably through his contacts with the Klan, had information that linked J. B. Stoner to that particular bombing and probably others as well. In addition to pressure from the business community, Connor's motivations included the fact that he didn't control Stoner, and that wasn't to be tolerated. Connor had Sergeant Tom Cook and Captain G. L. Pattie pose as representatives of businessmen interested in setting off bombs in targeted places. The undercover officers shared a target list with Stoner, but told him they were waiting for the funds to come in and instructed him to wait for word on which location to hit before doing anything.

Stoner, however, was an entrepreneur with initiative and did not wait for further instructions. On June 29, 1958, he bombed Bethel Baptist, a small church in north Birmingham where Reverend Fred Shuttlesworth galvanized the local civil rights movement. One of Shuttlesworth's body-guards, Will "John L." Hall, grabbed the sizzling bucket of dynamite left outside the church. He ran with it to the street's edge where he deposited it and dashed to safety just before it detonated, raking the houses across the street with shrapnel and blasting out windows. Stoner then called Sergeant Cook (whom he believed was an out-of-town businessman) and demanded his payment.

The local district attorney's office, concerned about the entrapment aspects of the case, refused to prosecute. Cook had given the report of this incident to the FBI, hoping they could make a case, but neither local nor federal charges had ever been brought against Stoner.

Eddy sent the information to Baxley, who immediately opened the case. Stoner was indicted at the same time as Robert Chambliss, but skipped town prior to arrest. He was not brought to trial until 1980, when John Yung, an assistant attorney general who had been a key member of the prosecution team on the Chambliss trial, tried and convicted Stoner of the 1958 Bethel Baptist Church bombing. The church had been unoccupied, but the damage to the occupied dwellings across the street allowed the prosecution to charge Stoner with conspiring to a felony. For three years after his conviction, Stoner dodged prison. When his appeals ran out, he was a fugitive for four months and then served time in prison until 1986.

Stoner was not a member of the Klan, and thus an outsider, but Luna claimed to be an informant to everyone—the Klan leadership, the FBI, and the state. It would not have been out of character for him to play all sides, and his antics eventually got him expelled from the Klan for what he termed "financial difficulties." One of his scams had been an attempt to convince his fellow Klansmen to invest in the idea of a gated community near Lake Purdy, an unincorporated area in Shelby County, just south of Birmingham. The development would be only for Klan members and their families, a protected area, a safe haven where people of like minds could live together and not be integrated with the "trash." Ironically, the area later became home to many posh, gated communities.

Over the course of several meetings with Herren and Fleming, Luna agreed to wear a wire and call some of the old Klansmen. Nothing of any value came from those wired conversations.

Fleming and Herren asked Luna about various members of the East-view #13 who were suspects or persons of interest in the bombing case. Luna remembered Bobby Frank Cherry, Tommy Blanton, and Robert Chambliss—the three major suspects—as members of the Cahaba River Bridge Group and "violent mental cases."

Gary Thomas Rowe was another member of the Eastview #13 whom Luna remembered as being an instigator of violence. Recruited as an FBI informant, Rowe was a controversial player in the civil rights drama of the 1960s. Herren read of an incident in which Rowe reported shooting and killing a black man on his way home during a 1963 riot. Rowe claimed an agent told him "not to talk about it." A Birmingham policeman also told him to "go home and forget about it," though it was unclear whether that was because he knew Rowe's status as an informant or simply because Rowe was white and his victim was not, or because they assumed he had actually missed, since both the police and the FBI had searched unsuccessfully for a victim. The man later showed up at a hospital and recovered from his injury.

A little over a week after the church bombing, the double shrapnel bomb went off in a black neighborhood near civil rights attorney Arthur Shores's house. Just after the explosion, an FBI agent saw Rowe in a phone booth near the location. Rowe claimed he was calling the FBI to report information about that bomb. His presence there remained a mystery. Was he following the Klansman who planted the bomb, or had he been part of the operation? Was he, like Luna, playing both sides?

Rowe had, by his own admission, been a participant in many of the Klan's acts of violence, including wielding a baseball bat when Freedom Riders were dragged from a bus and beaten in Birmingham on Mother's

Day in 1961. The Freedom Riders were testing federal law forbidding segregation on public transportation.

Rowe said that as an undercover informant he was directed by the FBI to get information any way he could, including sleeping with Klansmen's wives. He claimed to have given the FBI a heads-up about the Freedom Rider melee. He also warned that the Birmingham Police, under Commissioner Bull Connor's orders, had promised the Klansmen fifteen minutes of free rein. Rowe testified before a congressional hearing in 1975—the Church Commission—that his FBI handler's response to his warning had been to "go and see what happened." Nothing was done to stop the Klan from beating the Freedom Riders. In response to questions about why the police were absent during the melee, Bull Connor said simply it was Mother's Day, and his officers were with their mothers.

FBI headquarters' official instructions regarding Rowe were to make certain that he did not "direct, lead, or instigate any acts of violence." While Rowe apparently adhered to the letter of those guidelines, he did participate in the violence. Herren knew from working closely with Birmingham's Narcotics Unit that the best informant walked a narrow line. His information was only good if he were trusted, and if he held back, he would lose that trust. Rowe's FBI handler echoed that when he testified at the Church hearings: "If he [Rowe] happened to be with some Klansman and they decided to do something, he couldn't be an angel and be a good informant."

A report in the files quoted a Birmingham policeman as saying Rowe showed him documentation that he was with the CIA. Bob Eddy had a contact check that out, with negative results. "If he was, he'd never have said he was," the contact told Eddy. Eddy didn't doubt Rowe had CIA documentation, but he believed it was fake—something he had dummied up. "Rowe," Eddy said, "was a master at putting the truth together with a lie."

Rowe was a slippery character, but he saved Agent Brook Blake's life on one occasion, stopping Agent Blake from walking down a road where Rowe knew Klansmen were waiting to kill him. Rowe's deep-cover position as an FBI informant was shattered in the murder trial of Viola Gregg Liuzzo. Liuzzo was a civil rights volunteer killed on a remote stretch of road while taking a young black man home after the Selma bridge march. Rowe was in the car with the men who shot Liuzzo.

Although some doubted his claim that he had not fired his weapon, Rowe told the FBI he had handled the situation by emptying his bullets out the window while the others were firing, and then reloading and doing the same thing. A search of the area revealed all the unfired bullets from Rowe's gun along the stretch of highway where the murder had taken place.

Rowe's testimony at the Congressional hearings was pivotal in the Church Commission's conclusion criticizing the lack of guidelines and oversight on FBI informants' behavior, and eventually led to reforms.

Shortly after Rowe's testimony in 1975, Robert Chambliss, who had not yet been indicted, showed up at police headquarters. When he was asked if he knew who might have bombed the church, he said, "Well, they arrested me for having that dynamite. I got it and gave it to Rowe and them." Was there any truth to this, or was Chambliss, who had surely heard the case had been reopened, just trying to divert suspicion to another target? Herren remembered reading a report where five years earlier, shortly after one of Luna's arrests for fraud, Chambliss told Birmingham investigators that Luna had told him to get some dynamite "to blow up some stumps."

The Birmingham police investigators assigned to assist Bob Eddy's 1977 investigation of the Sixteenth Street bombing case—Jack LeGrand, especially, and Ernest Cantrell (who had been an intelligence officer in the 1960s and attended Klan meetings) to a lesser degree—were convinced Rowe was responsible for the church bombing. Bob Eddy was suspicious of Rowe, but Herren and Fleming never found any evidence supporting the notion that Rowe had a role in the church bombing.

Agent Neil Shanahan, who had arrived in Birmingham early in 1964 and inherited Blake's informants—both Rowe and Mitch Burns—said he never had any concerns about Rowe being involved in the church bombing, primarily because the Klansmen of the Eastview #13, and particularly the Cahaba Boys, did not like Rowe. Rowe was among the young dandies that went out drinking and carousing after the Klan meetings. The older, more serious Klansmen, like Blanton and Chambliss, called the group Rowe hung out with "a bunch of pantywaists." They didn't trust him. Half the Klan thought he was a government pimp, and they spent a good deal of time arguing with each other about that and about whether other members were on the Bureau payroll as well.

Though each official Klavern had an action squad or "klokan," the Cahaba Boys were a separate group. Elizabeth Cobbs, Chambliss's niece, wrote in her book, *Long Time Coming,* that the core members of the Cahaba Boys were "a tight knit, secret society" that had been together in various forms for several years—Rowe was never a member.

Rowe's picture was not included in the Klan photos shown to Kirthus Glenn, the witness who saw a car of white men behind the church at 2:00 AM the morning of the bombing. Some people saw the failure to include Rowe's photo as a plot to protect Rowe; others as simply that the FBI knew Rowe was an informant and not involved in the church bombing.

Rowe insisted a police dispatcher friend called him to tell him about the church bombing, but records showed that dispatcher was not working that morning. When Bill Baxley opened the case in the 1970s, he told Bob Eddy they were going to take a hard look at Rowe.

They arranged to meet him for an interview in a hotel in San Diego. Baxley arrived first and told Eddy to join them. When Eddy arrived, he found there was a hardware convention in town and all the hotels were full. He had to sleep in the lobby.

In his book *Until Justice Rolls Down,* Frank Sikora reported that when Eddy met Rowe, Rowe was "of medium height, with a bullish chest—he had once worked as a bouncer in a bar, and he looked the part. His reddish hair was close-cropped, his face square, the eyes narrow." Eddy brought all his skill to bear in the interview, but couldn't get much out of Rowe other than wandering stories about how great Rowe was.

When he reported this to Baxley, Baxley said, "Put him on a polygraph." Rowe failed the first polygraph. Rowe and his attorney agreed to take another test if they could pick the examiner. They chose a retired FBI agent. After the test had been administered, the polygraph examiner commented that everything Rowe said was a lie. "Is his name even Rowe?" he asked in exasperation.

Baxley next instructed Eddy to put Rowe under hypnosis. Eddy took Rowe to a specialist in hypnosis and waited outside the door. Eventually, the hypnotist came out the room, shaking his head. "There is no way I'm going to be able to put that man under hypnosis," he said.

Until he died in 1998 at age sixty-four, Gary Thomas Rowe and his actual role remained an enigma. He was buried under the name of Thomas Neal Moore, the identity the FBI gave him as a protected witness.

Don Luna told Herren and Fleming that Al Lingo, the director of the Alabama Department of Public Safety, was obsessed with making an arrest in the church bombing before "Kennedy's boys did." Lingo met with several Klan members, offering them a guaranteed sentence of three years in prison if they confessed the bombing to him. According to Luna, Robert Chambliss was a participant at one of those meetings, but Cherry refused to meet with Lingo. (Cherry, however, made a statement to the FBI that he had, indeed, attended such a meeting with Lingo at the request of Tommy Blanton.) Apparently, no one took Lingo up on his offer.

Luna also claimed he had arranged with Lingo for the October 8, 1963, arrest of three Klansmen—Robert Chambliss, Wesley Hall, and Charles Cagle—for possession of dynamite allegedly obtained before the church bombing. Purchasing and possessing dynamite was illegal inside the city limits, although it could be readily purchased in the county. Chambliss had often purchased dynamite at Negron's store in north Jefferson County.

The misdemeanor charges were dismissed on appeal, possibly because evidence indicated the box of "found" dynamite had been planted. In a letter dated April 10, 1964, to President Johnson, Hoover said that the investigation (i.e., attempts to elicit confessions) had been "greatly hampered when premature arrests were made by the Alabama Highway Patrol." If not for that arrest, however, and the subsequent article in *Jet* magazine in which Gertrude Glenn recognized Chambliss as the man she had seen in the early morning hours behind the church, Robert Chambliss might not have been convicted in 1977. Glenn was a strong witness for the state, the only witness who was able to put Chambliss at the scene the night the bomb was placed.

A document found in papers of Mayor Albert Boutwell lists Luna, Al Lingo, Art Hanes, Imperial Wizard Robert Shelton, and several others as meeting at the Saint Francis Motel on September 29, 1963. That evening, Luna accompanied State Investigator Posey to knock on Chambliss's door and make the arrest.

Despite Fleming's designation of Luna as the "con of cons," there were enough truths in his stories that Herren and Fleming followed up on his assertions. Luna's love for telling tales included a few on himself. "Once," he said, shifting his bulk on the reclining chair, "I got up to use the bathroom and my mother-in-law, thinking she'd do something nice, decided to clean my chair. She sprayed Armorall all over it and polished it up. When I came back and sat down, I just slid out of it, right onto the floor!" He laughed. "Couldn't get up. 'Course she couldn't lift me."

"What happened?" Herren asked.

He chuckled. "She had to call the fire department. Paramedics had to haul me up and put me back in the chair." His heavily padded palm patted the chair's arm. "She doesn't do that anymore."

15 | WILLIAM "BILL" JACKSON

BILL JACKSON WAS "a piece of crap." That was Herren's opinion, and he'd seen many examples in his career as a police officer. Jackson liked his wives young, between twelve and fourteen, and preferred to pick them out from the local skating rink. His reputation with younger children was worse. By one account, he had used a belt to whip a crying baby still in the crib.

Jackson owned Paradise Barber Shop in Vestavia, a small suburb south of Birmingham, and professed to be a man of God. It was said he liked to quote scripture while he cut hair. The Klan tolerated him, allowing him to hang around. He shared many of their views and wanted to belong, but they wouldn't allow him official membership because he was Catholic.

The Klan's historic aversion to Catholics was indelibly stamped on Birmingham's history with the shooting of Father James E. Coyle. Coyle, the longtime priest of Saint Paul's Cathedral, was killed in 1921 by a Klansman irate that Coyle had married his daughter to a Puerto Rican. The trial was infamous, in part, because the shooter's attorney was Hugo Black, one-time member of the Klan and a future Supreme Court justice. Black later denounced the Klan and became known for his support of civil rights, but his early involvement was an example of the general acceptance of the Klan's values and the pervasiveness of its influence as a requirement for social mobility.

Jackson admitted to the FBI that he was at the Modern Sign Company with Blanton and Chambliss on the Friday night before the church bombing. He later changed his story to say it was Saturday night. In one of Cherry's statements to the FBI in 1963, he said Jackson brought a "very pretty young girl that looked about fifteen" to the sign shop.

In the 1960s Jackson had lied to the FBI, and he had called Baxley asking about rewards on more than one occasion in the 1970s investigation. Now, he wanted to give information to Herren and Fleming.

Jackson told them that Blanton called him on September 14, 1963, and asked him to come to the sign shop to help them make signs and do silk screenings in preparation for a rally. Jackson did so and saw Blanton and Chambliss and other people he didn't know there. He worked at the shop until midnight. Jackson saw Chambliss and Blanton moving things Saturday night into and from the backseat and trunk of a car parked outside the shop. He claimed he didn't see Cherry or know who he was. The Modern Sign Company was owned by Merle Snow, a known Klan sympathizer, and was only three blocks south of the church at the corner of Third Avenue and Fourteenth Street North.

The Modern Sign Company was located where Johnston Welding and Supply (at #1526-1528 Third Ave. North) is shown in this 1940 photo.

Jackson had told one of his wives (his fifth) that he knew who had bombed the church. He also said he had attended a meeting under the Cahaba Bridge with Chambliss, Blanton, and Troy Ingram after the bombing, but couldn't remember anything else, only that about eleven people were there.

In 1977, he agreed to be hypnotized by Hilda Tant, a Birmingham psychologist. Under hypnosis, Jackson produced more details about the meeting, remembering that the people present all signed a piece of paper, but he couldn't recall what anyone said and grew agitated at the questions. Dr. Tant told Bob Eddy she thought Jackson couldn't remember because it was too traumatic. Herren and Fleming thought he remembered just fine but didn't want to admit he had known anything about what was discussed.

On several occasions, Herren and Fleming tried to get information from Jackson. He had to know more than he was saying if he'd been privy to those important meetings, but Jackson kept denying he knew anything more. Frustrated, they decided to go talk to him at his barbershop. When they arrived, there was no one at the shop except Jackson. They began with small talk, and then asked him about his current relationship with the Klan. Jackson denied any association. "I'm a lamb of God," he said, throwing up his hands.

Fleming reminded him he had admitted to being at the Modern Sign Company shop with Chambliss and Blanton the Friday evening before the bombing. "What were you doing?"

"We were silk screening some Confederate flags."

"What did you do afterward?"

"Nothing," Jackson said. "I don't know anything."

Fleming stepped closer and pressed him. "You're lying."

The protestations grew in fervor. Fleming closed the gap between them. Herren could see the anger on his partner's face. Fleming had told him about his encounter with his neighbor when Fleming was eighteen, how much he had looked up to the man as a true Christian until he heard a heartless, racist remark from his lips. The more Herren came to know Fleming, the more he respected him. Fleming did not flaunt his religious beliefs and values, but he practiced them, and Herren shared the anger he knew was boiling in his normally mild-mannered friend.

Violence was brewing in the room, and he readied himself to back up his partner. Thinking of the crying baby whipped with a belt by this man and the young girls whose lives he had ruined, he hoped Fleming might provoke Jackson.

Fleming moved even closer, almost nose-to-nose. "You're lying," he said again, pressing him intentionally, wanting him to break and tell them what he knew or make an aggressive move.

"I'm not lying; I'm a preacher!" Jackson declared. It was evident at that point Jackson was not going to admit to any knowledge about the Klan or the bombing or, unfortunately, take a swing.

Fleming glared down at him, disgusted. "You ain't any more a preacher than that telephone pole over there!"

16 | CHARLES CAGLE AND "QUICK DRAW" YARBROUGH

CHARLES A. CAGLE LIVED in the boondocks of Winston County, Alabama. A member of the Eastview #13, he was one of the Klansman arrested for possession of dynamite. In the mid-1960s, influenced by the unrest and violence in the South, the House Committee on Un-American Activities took a hiatus from its focus on communism to investigate the Ku Klux Klan. Cagle was one of the Klansmen called to testify.

As they had in the past, Herren and Fleming sought out a post office for directions to Cagle Road.

"Lord, we don't even deliver mail that far out," the postal worker said when they gave her the address. "They have to come to the main road to get the mail."

Following her directions, they wound through the countryside. Herren remarked, "This country reminds me of where my grandmother and granddaddy Herren lived."

"Where is that?" Fleming asked.

"In Carbon Hill, Alabama, up on the Walker/Fayette county line. My granddaddy was a miner during the night and a farmer during the day. He worked two jobs, having so many children to feed. He was married on the tenth day of the tenth month in the tenth year and had ten children. He had a neighbor ask him one time, 'Frank, why do you have ten kids?'

"'Well, it's the railroad's fault.'

"'Frank, you never worked on the railroad,' the neighbor said. 'How is it the railroad's fault?'

"My granddaddy said, ''Cause the railroad comes behind the house at 3:30 AM. It's too early to get up, and too late to go back to sleep.'"

With a snort, Fleming pointed to a dirt road turnoff. "I think that's Cagle Road."

The entrance to the turnoff was framed with a potpourri of parapher-nalia—webbed Indian dream-catchers, foxtails, spears, and a deer's skull.

"What are we getting into?" Herren muttered.

Fleming agreed. "Thank goodness there are two of us."

Herren touched the subtle bulge of his gun, glad they were both armed as well. He wondered if Fleming were wishing he had a bigger partner. Herren wasn't as small as he had been years ago when he first applied to be a police officer at the Jefferson County Civil Service. Back then he had a twenty-nine-inch waist and weighed in at 120 pounds, ten pounds less than was required. He chuckled to himself. For the weigh-in, he'd eaten as many bananas and milk shakes as he could, strapped ten pounds in quarters to his legs, and carried three guns. They found two of them, but he still passed the weigh-in because they didn't find the quarters.

He glanced over at Fleming, wanting to assure him he might not be a big man, but he was scrappy and wouldn't let his partner down. He would always have his back. Herren and his old patrol partner, "Cookie Monster," had survived plenty of tight spots together.

About a quarter of a mile down the dirt road, the house appeared, and to Herren's surprise it was a normal-looking home. He'd expected something like a black paper shack or, at the least, a log cabin. Cagle met them on the porch, never asking or allowing them inside. He was about six feet tall with his mostly gray hair combed back, and he wore a plaid shirt and jeans. When they asked him about the church bombing, he told them the FBI blew up the church, using their "pimp," Tommy Rowe.

This wasn't the first time Herren and Fleming had heard such a the-ory. Some Klansmen and wives they'd interviewed blamed the bombing on the church storing ammunition and firearms in their basement. Oth-ers insisted the Negroes did it to get sympathy on their side or to cre-ate such disorder that federal troops would be called into Birmingham, bringing to mind a statement Governor Wallace made while running for president—"It looks mighty funny to me that there have been forty-seven such bombings in Birmingham in the last ten or fifteen years and yet no one has been hurt. . . . And these bombings have led to the raising of millions of dollars for civil rights causes."

They didn't get anything more from Cagle, but sometime later, Herren returned to his house with Agent Jeff McDonald to serve Cagle with a grand jury subpoena. This time, Cagle refused even to come to the door, most probably recognizing the car and Herren. They knocked several times and from inside, Cagle's dog raised Cain with every knock. They knew Cagle was inside, and he knew they were outside. It was an old game, but it had been a long drive out to the house, and it annoyed them to just turn tail and leave.

Jeff said loudly, "I've got all day, how 'bout you?" and Herren replied, "Yeah, I do too." So, they went back and sat in the car, and every five minutes hit the car's siren button, and the dog would go crazy. When the dog quieted, they hit the siren again . . . for three hours. Cagle didn't get served the subpoena that day, but it wasn't a restful afternoon for him.

Fleming hadn't been available the day Herren scheduled an interview with Levie "Quick Draw" Yarbrough, so Herren took Mark Sawyer with him. Sawyer was a young "first office" agent, meaning the Birmingham office was his first assignment.

Many of the old Klansmen now made their homes in the deep backwoods of Alabama. Quick Draw Yarbrough had retreated to Cullman County north of Birmingham.

Herren and Sawyer stopped at the Hanceville Police Department to ask for directions. Herren knew they were out in the sticks, where law enforcement was not particularly enamored or impressed with the big city police or the "FB&I."

Agent Sawyer chuckled under his breath at the dispatcher's bright green fingernails. At that moment, the police chief strode in, and Herren realized his nametag sported the same surname as the dispatcher's. He hoped Sawyer kept his mouth shut, or they might be spending the night in the Hanceville jail. Fortunately, Sawyer kept his amusement to himself, and they headed out, following the directions that took them down endless dirt roads, far out into the woods. It reminded Herren of the visit to Cagle's house.

Herren told Sawyer, "Listen, just follow my lead. I'm going to introduce myself as Ben Herren, sergeant in the Birmingham Police Department, which I still am, and I'm going to say 'This is Mark Sawyer,' because these people don't want to have nothing to do with a federal agent. They're more likely to talk to us if they don't know you're FBI."

"OK."

Yarbrough's dirt drive did not sport Native American paraphernalia as Cagle's had, but the couple that answered the door—Yarbrough's brother and sister-in-law—were, Herren quickly decided, "country with a capital C." They invited Herren and Sawyer to sit on the front porch to wait for Yarbrough and freely talked about Yarbrough being part of the Klan "back in the day." The woman's teeth were as green as the Hanceville dispatcher's fingernails. When Mrs. Yarbrough invited them to supper, Herren glanced at Sawyer. The young agent's face turned a pale shade of the same color as he probably imagined a meal of possum or raccoon.

They excused themselves before Yarbrough showed up, deciding to return another day.

On another occasion, Herren and Fleming hunted down an elderly man named Thompson who had been a teenager in the late 1950s and early 1960s. His father was a close companion of Dynamite Bob Chambliss. Informants had related a story to the FBI: Thompson was driving with his father in the front passenger seat and Chambliss in the back. Chambliss got out of the car to throw a stick of dynamite under Reverend Shuttlesworth's house. Young Thompson got nervous and drove off before Chambliss could get completely back into the car. Chambliss hung onto the back door, the toes of his shoes literally burning off before Thompson stopped to let him get in.

Thompson was an elderly man by the time Herren and Fleming interviewed him. Like so many of the old Klansmen, he had a huge family Bible on his coffee table and denied everything, except that his father had known Chambliss.

"Well," Herren said, "let me ask you: Is there any truth to the story about Chambliss losing the toes of his shoes and being dragged by a car?"

Thompson struggled to keep from laughing, but finally managed, "I don't know anything about that, sonny."

17 | PARTNERS

WHEN HERREN'S FULL CLEARANCE finally came in, they gave him a code number and a card he could swipe to open certain doors, including the restroom. He could even park in the garage and finally felt like less of a stepchild. The relationship with Fleming had warmed considerably. They ate together now almost every day. Fleming liked to go to places where he was comfortable. Although Niki's West had great food, Fleming hated it because they rushed you down the cafeteria line. He would get on a kick and eat at one place until he got burned out, but his favorite spot was Courtney's at Sixth Avenue and Twenty-Fourth Street South, a hangout known as the Pitt Grill when Herren and his partner had patrolled the south side of Birmingham.

One day at lunch while Herren and Fleming waited for their food, Herren looked around at the diners and thought about the agents in the 1960s going to the restaurants where Klansmen were known to hang out. The G-men would have stuck out like sore thumbs. He wondered if he could pick them out today. "When did agents stop having to wear white shirts?" he asked.

"Oh, it wasn't just the shirts," Fleming said. "We had to wear a suit, a white shirt, and shoes that tied—no loafers."

"You mean shoes with laces?"

"Yep. If you didn't have handcuffs, at least you had laces."

"I never thought about using shoelaces," Herren said.

"The Bureau was late getting started with the hats and late getting rid of the hats, I always thought, but by the time I came on we didn't have to have hats, thank goodness. To answer your question, until the day Hoover died, you wore a suit and a white shirt."

Herren grunted.

"Now," Fleming added, "the very next day after he was gone, the office looked like a rainbow. There was a guy in Philly that came in one day with yellow pants, *yellow* trousers, and they were very sheer. You could see his polka-dot underwear through them."

Not expecting this, Herren, who had just taken a swallow of iced tea, almost choked. When he recovered, he said, "Some guy was waiting all his life to become an FBI agent and wear that polka-dot underwear—talk about fulfilling a lifetime's ambition!"

"What about you, Ben?" Fleming asked. "Did you always want to be a police officer?"

"No, I think the first thing I wanted to do was be a dentist."

"A dentist?"

"When I was a youngster, I broke out my front teeth and spent much of my time in a dental chair. The dentist was the son of my daddy's boss at TCI, Tennessee Coal & Iron."

Fleming looked puzzled.

"That was a big steel company here. It originated in Tennessee, but moved to Birmingham in the 1800s. Anyway, I just thought dentistry would be something I would enjoy, but after I got to about the seventh grade, I got to thinking about law enforcement." He took another swallow of tea. "Had I not gone into law enforcement, I'd probably have been a truck driver. I don't know why that correlates. But I probably would have drove a truck."

"It doesn't seem to match up."

"Well, I put myself through college driving a school bus. My first year, I think I was paid sixty-five dollars a month. But, you know, I had to go to school anyway, so might as well get paid for it. I got married in September '75 to a girl I met on my school bus at Minor High School."

Fleming stirred his tea. He liked it sweet. "Where did you go to college?"

"Got my associate degree at Walker Junior College. Then I went to Jacksonville State and finished up my degree in law enforcement."

"Didn't I see somewhere you had a master's?" Fleming asked.

Herren nodded. "Years later, after I was with the police department, I went back to Jacksonville and got my master's in public administration. My goal, after I retired from the PD, was to be a chief of police somewhere in a little twenty-man department."

Fleming nodded. "You'd make a good one."

"Maybe, but after I made sergeant, I got to looking around and saw a lot of lieutenants I'd respected when they were sergeants, but as lieutenants they kind of went crazy, issuing dumb policies and stuff. I started thinking, I can't help the guys on the street if I get promoted and start making dumb decisions too. I never did take the lieutenant's test. I just decided upper management of law enforcement was probably not the place for me. The place for me was down in the trenches, helping the guys get their job done."

"So you worked as a detective?"

"First I was the sergeant over the Technical Surveillance Unit in Vice and Narcotics, then I became a detective."

"Ever work a homicide before this one?"

Herren leaned back in his chair. "Not as a detective, but as a patrolman." He knotted his fingers over his stomach. "My first homicide was a very interesting one."

The waitress set down their plates, and Fleming started eating, knowing Herren was launching into story mode.

"We got a call," Herren said, "and there was definitely a dead body on the floor behind a chair in an empty house. Nobody else was there except two children asleep in the back bedroom. We left them asleep, and about that time people were coming up, so we started asking them questions, trying to find out what happened."

Fleming nodded and stirred more sweetener in his iced tea.

"And somebody said, 'Well, Yolanda was here at the house with the kids.'

"I asked, 'Well, where's Yolanda now?'

"'We don't know.'

"So, I went back into the house. A few minutes later, I hear someone call out, 'Yolanda's here!' I run outside, and there's a black female about eighteen years old who has come up on the porch. She's hysterical, screaming, 'I shot him, I shot him!' And she's waving a gun up and down.

"I finally grabbed the gun, and she just latches on and hugs me tight, just out of fear, while I'm holding the gun up over my head, trying to keep it away from her."

Fleming's eyebrows lifted, but he didn't interrupt.

"About that time Sergeant Andy Willis walked up on the porch and lifted the gun out of my hand."

The waitress put more tea in their glasses. You couldn't run out of tea in a southern restaurant.

"Go on," Fleming said, tipping his fork at Herren. "What happened?"

"Well, come to find out, Yolanda had been watching those two children in the back for her sister. Her daddy gave her a .38 snub-nose revolver to take over to the house while she was babysitting. And she had gone to sleep in a chair in the living room and had stuck the revolver down on the right side in between the arm and the cushion.

"She woke up with a man's gloved hand over her mouth and something cold and metallic pressed against her neck. So she reached into the cushion for the gun and fired one shot over her shoulder. She k-ringed him, nailing him right in the heart. He died instantly, falling onto the floor behind the chair. And she ran out of the house."

"My word," Fleming said.

Herren speared a pork chop and began sawing at it. "Well, this guy had a stocking over his face, one glove, one screwdriver—which is what he had held against her neck—and was wearing a T-shirt, and that's all he was wearing. His pants were outside the back window where he crawled in. His intent to rape her was evident by the lack of pants and the . . . condition of his anatomy. In fact the coroner said, 'I've never seen this before . . . but it's self-defense to me.'"

It was Fleming's turn to sputter his tea.

18 | WYMAN S. LEE AND PERSHING MAYFIELD

Thomas Blanton spends nights alone in a weedy, dirt lot in Fulton-dale, locked inside a chain link fence topped with barbed wire. As a watchman, he guards four old vans, several rusting trailers, and the contents of a locked shed from whatever dangers ride through the night. "At that time [1963], he was pretty wild and crazy," says former Klansman Wyman S. Lee, the man who has given Blanton his job, but warns him not to say hateful things to black customers of Lee's sewer-cleaning business. "He has a lot of hate, anger and resentment built up in him," Lee said.

Herren put down the *Birmingham News* article by John Archibald and Jeff Hansen and rubbed his eyes. Two days after the reporters had talked to Wyman Lee, he and Fleming had paid their own visit. Lee wore the same dark green uniform shirt and trousers with a tear in the right arm he had worn on previous occasions. He operated his business, B & L Sewer, out of a small trailer.

A former Klansman and member of the Cahaba River Bridge Group, Lee knew Blanton and Chambliss. He was acquainted with Bobby Frank Cherry from going on missionary operations with him. Cherry had acknowledged Lee as well in the interview in Texas, calling Lee a sissy. Lee claimed to be Blanton's closest friend since the days of the church bombing. People working near the business told Herren and Fleming that Lee and Blanton used to take showers together outside.

Although Blanton acted as a night guard for Lee, he had held other jobs, particularly as a security guard. At one place Blanton, who was short and stocky, was known to his fellow workers as a gung ho guard who liked to hide behind doors to check on employees. They called him the inch-high spy.

Lee seemed to have dealt with his own past by becoming a Mormon. He had invited Herren and Fleming to the temple, claiming he possessed a card that would allow him access to the holiest inner sanctum. They declined his offer.

Herren turned the newspaper to the back section to check the obituaries, a nightly habit he had acquired to see if anyone on their interview list had died.

The following day, he headed to Roebuck, an area east of Birmingham, looking for a person he did not expect to find alive. William H. "Jack" Cash was the brother of Herman Cash, one of the original suspects. Herman Cash probably had been in the car when the bomb was planted. Jack Cash was in his nineties. Back in the day, he had owned a barbeque and beer joint off the Bessemer Super Highway, a hangout for the Klan. Herren remembered Cash's BBQ, having eaten there on occasion with his father, who loved a good barbeque and a beer.

Cash had been arrested with a group of white men who assaulted Reverend Shuttlesworth in 1957 as Shuttlesworth attempted to integrate Phillips High School in downtown Birmingham by enrolling his daughters. After the Sixteenth Street Church bombing, FBI agents interviewed Cash and asked him about the incident at Phillips School. He claimed he was arrested because he had "accidently bumped into Shuttlesworth."

Herren knocked on the door of Cash's house. There were no signs of life anywhere, though it was about 3:00 PM. After a few minutes, he heard a faint rustle inside, then the shuffle of feet and the *clunk . . . clunk . . . clunk* of three deadbolts unlocking. The door opened and a tiny ghost of a man with a bald head and a face drawn up in wrinkles stood before him in his pajamas. Herren introduced himself, and the wizened little man slammed the door in his face.

It was impossible to be angry at him.

"Well," he told Fleming later. "At least he had enough energy to walk to the door, open the door, and slam the door in the FBI's face one last time before he died."

Another elderly Eastview #13 Klansman on the list was Pershing Mayfield. He was of special interest because he had worked at DuPont, a dynamite manufacturing plant south of Birmingham. Mayfield now lived in Mount Olive, a community about fifteen miles due north of Birmingham. His house was a pleasant country home with big shade trees on a large lot. Small white pillars supported the front porch roof. The first thing Herren noticed was a wheelchair ramp. He knocked on the door, and a lady a little older than him answered the door. He introduced himself and asked if Pershing Mayfield was there.

"Yes," she said, "but he's very sick."

"I'm sorry, but I would like to talk to him for a few minutes if I possibly could."

She tilted her head. "What's this about?"

"Well, it's about something that happened a long time ago in the 1960s. We're not accusing him of anything; we just want to ask him a few questions and get some information from him."

She turned and hollered, "Daddy! This is Mr. Herren from the FBI."

From back in the house, a raspy voice shouted, "I don't want to talk to him! Tell him to get outta here!"

"OK, I heard that," Herren said. "Could I just talk to you a few minutes?"

"Well, if you'd make it quick. Daddy don't want you here."

They sat down at the kitchen table, and Herren asked, "How old is your father now? He must be in his eighties."

"Yeah, he is. I was a teenager during those times. I remember them well."

"What do you remember?" Herren asked.

"Well, every time I went out on a date, the FBI was following me around. And I always knew it was the FBI, 'cause they was wearing hats, even at night they wore them hats. I couldn't go nowhere without them knowing where I went." She frowned. "Almost lost a boyfriend over them."

Herren could imagine the FBI in their white button-down shirts, suit coats, and fedora hats trying to blend into the background in Mount Olive.

"Get him outta here!" Another shout from down the hall: "He still here? Get him outta here!"

"So, your dad's in bad shape now?" Herren asked on his way out the door.

"Yeah, he's confined to bed. He has a black hospice nurse that comes in every week. She bathes him and gets his medicines and makes sure everything's OK with him."

The image startled Herren. What irony. He didn't know specific things Pershing Mayfield might have done or said out of the hatred that fed the Klan, but he wondered what went through the man's mind now, near the end of his life, having to be bathed and taken care of by a black nurse.

19 | WILLADEAN BROGDON CHERRY

MIKE GOWINS—THE WITNESS WHO heard Cherry boast about bombing the church when Cherry cleaned carpets in Texas—was slowly dying. Fleming and Herren visited him when they could, watching him put together his intricate little model cars and keeping an eye on his health. He had good days and days when he struggled to breathe, but he enjoyed their visits. It didn't take much to brighten his day.

"I'd like to bring him one of those model cars he loves," Fleming said.

"Yeah, that would make him happy," Herren agreed, but they decided not to, even though it would have been a very inexpensive gift. If they ever made it to trial on this case, a defense attorney might try to make it look like a bribe. There were no second chances with this case. Their suspects were old; their witnesses could die at any moment; somebody could recant on a story. One little legal error, and they could lose the evidence that had been so painstakingly put together.

As a ten-year-old, Herren had thought of the Klan as a bunch of grown men running around in white sheets and funny-looking hats. They were a fixture at the annual Alabama State Fair—handing out Klan literature, applications, and tiny Confederate flags on sticks. He remembered riding in the car with his mother to shop at a new shopping center in

Midfield, a small community west of Birmingham. Music played and a crowd of men gathered in the A&P Grocery parking lot around the flatbed of a truck that served as a stage. When she saw them, Herren's mother hastily turned the car around. "Aren't we going to get groceries?" he asked. "No," she said, "not today."

Now, working this case, he found himself the repository of odd bits of information about the Klan. He was surprised to find they had a revered book, the Kloran, where much of their values were written. It was like their Klan Bible, and it was set out like a Bible with books, chapters, and verses. The Kloran laid out how a good Klansman was supposed to act, what the Klaverns' bylaws should be, even how the meeting room was to be set up. Klan members followed Klanlore, which established the practices of Klan brotherhood, calling on members to watch out for each other, to raise bail or legal expenses if necessary, or even to see that a fellow Klansman's widow and children were cared for. The document asserted that the "prime purpose of this great Order is to develop character, practice Klannishness, to protect the home and the chastity of womanhood, and to exemplify a pure patriotism toward our glorious country."

Almost every home of an aging Klan member had a family Bible on the coffee table, not a normal-sized one, but a huge volume Fleming referred to as "the ten-pound family Bible." All professed they were good Christian people. Some, like the FBI informant Mitch Burns, had become Klan members because their fathers and grandfathers had been. It was a family tradition.

Klansmen believed the institution served a useful purpose in the community but—like others Herren had known who loudly professed their religion—their actions often belied their words. Klan policy called for punishment for those who didn't provide for or abused their families, often tying them to trees and whipping them with belts. Yet many abused their own wives. The same kind of discipline was to be applied to men who "messed around" with black women, though Tommy Blanton talked freely to Mitch Burns about having sex with black women.

It was no secret in Elizabeth Cobbs's family that Chambliss tried to molest the children. In her book, *Long Time Coming*, Cobbs said her mother warned her not to ever be alone with him. Cherry's family had reported the same kind of behavior of him. Perhaps the violations of their own codes of conduct were related to other cult phenomena where the inner circle engaged in the very behavior they forbade to others.

The wives of some of the Klansmen, now elderly women, seemed even harder than the men. Fleming and Herren knew from information in the original files that some had been abused by their husbands, but the women would not say a word against them. Perhaps it had been so ingrained in them for so long never to talk about what happened, never to trust any outsider, that it was just impossible for them to speak, even now. Or maybe they just stood behind their men. Bob Eddy had waited with an arrest warrant in hand while Chambliss's wife had combed her husband's hair.

There was one woman Herren and Fleming desperately wanted to talk to. She was the third wife of Bobby Frank Cherry, but the old files, in the custom of the day, only referred to her as Willadean or Mrs. Bobby Frank Cherry, and despite all their searching and the resources of the FBI, they couldn't find her. The only clue they had about her identity was that an agent in the 1960s had noted she had fiery hair as "red as the clown Bozo's."

They had good reason to believe she might talk to them. She and Cherry moved to the northeast after the bombing, and Willadean lost a daughter in a fire she blamed on her husband. Cherry had not held back his violent side in their relationship, but she outsmarted him. One day she had loaded up the kids in the car and before Cherry could get in, she'd just driven off.

One morning, Fleming was at the Sixteenth Street Baptist Church talking to the pastor when he got a call from the office. "Bill, we got an agent out in Montana that needs to talk to you. He's got some woman with information about the church bombing."

Fleming hurried to the office and got on the phone to the Montana agent.

"A lady just came in yesterday," the agent said. "Says she saw an article in the paper, and started telling us this story. I don't know what she's talking about; she sounds crazy to me. But she says she's got some information on some old bombing in Birmingham."

"Well, who is she?" Fleming asked.

"Claims she was married to a Bob Cherry."

"What's her name?"

"Willadean. That mean anything to you?"

"Oh Lord have mercy sakes!"

Fleming found Herren sitting at his desk. "Go home, get your suitcase, and get back here."

"What?"

"We're going to Billings, Montana."

"OK . . . Why?"

"Willadean has surfaced. She read a little news article on Cherry, got in her car, and drove two hundred fifty miles to the nearest FBI office in Billings. They had no idea what she was talking about, but they called us. Thank the Lord they did."

———

Two hours later, Herren and Fleming were sitting in a plane headed to Billings. Normally the nearest agent would handle an interview with a subject, but nobody had the background Fleming and Herren possessed on this case, and there was general agreement at the local office and headquarters that they should go.

Herren gazed out the window at the clouds forming below them. "Do you remember much about the 1960s?"

"Oh, I remember it," Fleming said. "I was eighteen. I grew up with the colored and the white water fountains and bathrooms. It wouldn't be COLORED MEN and COLORED WOMEN; it would just be COLORED BATHROOMS."

"I do remember that."

"One thing my mother did, I'll never forget," Fleming said. "We were at the bus depot in Albany, Georgia—which was not a real good place to be—but my momma came from a lower economic situation, and she was waiting for my grandmother who was coming for a visit.

"A black lady got off the bus, and her suitcase broke open. Everybody just stepped on her clothes and ignored her, but Momma rushed over to help the lady pick everything up."

Herren nodded. "She sounds like a good person."

"That always stuck with me," Fleming said. "I remember watching the protests around Phillips High School on TV with their signs and hatred, and I would think, How can people go to church on Sunday and then do this on Monday?"

"We had a lot of what we called caravanning in the suburbs," Herren said. "People would tape rebel flags on the side of their cars and ride through the neighborhoods, blowing horns and hollering at people."

"It was the same in Georgia, but the worst thing—" Fleming shook his head. "I was a teenager and working construction, and I had a real good friend who was black. He was a little older than me. We went to lunch one day, and I pulled into a pay phone near the curb at a restaurant. I had my back to the car while I was on the phone. Well, when I finished, I turned around, and a woman and a very large man were marching towards the car, yelling, 'Get off my property!'"

"What did you do?" Herren asked.

"I'd forgotten all about being there with this black guy while I was making a phone call. And so they came and threw him off the property, and they were fixing to throw me off the property, because I brought a black guy on the place." He paused. "That stuck with me too."

Herren knew they had been descending and was trying to look down through the thick clouds to get a glimpse of the airport below when the wheels hit. The knuckles on his hand went white. "What the—?"

Only when they exited the plane did he realize the airport was on a plateau a distance from the city. They had landed while he thought they were still several hundred feet up in the air. He took a deep breath. He hadn't expected this case to add so many white hairs to his head.

It was October 1997. They rented a car and started the 225-mile drive through Montana to Glendive, where Willadean Cherry lived, passing windblown tumbleweeds and Sinclair gas stations. Fleming drove.

Herren had long ago decided riding in a car with Fleming was more nerve-racking than flying. His partner's brain worked faster than he talked, and he often jumped subjects without warning or just started a conversation out of the blue from the previous day. Herren appreciated his partner in many ways, but not his driving. Sometimes Fleming was so deep in thought, he simply forgot what he was doing, and if someone were in the backseat, he would turn around to carry on a conversation. Yet, despite all Herren's polite offers to drive, Fleming insisted on taking the wheel.

At a rest stop, Herren pointed out a sign that looked like the deer crossing warning signs in Alabama—except it read "Rattlesnake Crossing."

"Oh my goodness!" Fleming said.

Montana was a spacious land, the colors and foliage austere compared to the verdant green that crowded every available space at home, but it was beautiful country. Several times they saw ranchers on horseback—complete with chaps and cowboy hats—herding cattle back down from the pastures in preparation for winter. It was like being inside a Western movie.

At one restaurant they stopped at, a family sat nearby, and one of the younger boys looked out the window. "Daddy, you can see snow on the mountains. I know it's terrible, but I sure think it's pretty." Snow was terrible, Herren realized, because it was so harsh on these people. They spent most of the summer getting ready to survive the winter.

Fleming nudged Herren. "That guy should take off his hat at the table."

Herren snorted. "Bill, his hat probably cost more than our suits."

When they reached the town of Glendive, they first stopped and spoke to Willadean's daughter, Gloria LaDow. Gloria's hatred for her stepfather was evident. When she was young, she said, Bobby Frank Cherry forced her to have sex with him—and with his son, Tommy Cherry, while Bobby watched.

"I hate him and I wish desperately I could tell you I knew something about the bombing, but I don't know anything about the case."

"Well," Herren said, "if you ever come to Alabama and you want to press charges against Bobby Cherry for molesting you, I'll put you in touch with the right people to help you."

She said she would think about it.

"One more thing," Fleming said. "What kind of shape is your mom in, mentally?"

"Oh, OK. She takes a few pills here and there," she said with a shrug.

When they finally arrived at Willadean's, they found her hair was no longer the blazing red the agent from the 1960s had reported. It was a dull gray-auburn color, but there was still an element of steel in the large woman—the woman who had driven a bus and a truck for a living and left Cherry on the side of the curb. She had been his third wife; they were married from 1970 to 1973.

"I thought Cherry had been tried and convicted for that bombing a long time ago," she told them. "I saw this article in the paper, and I was confused, because I thought this was all done with." She explained that in 1977 her sister told her she didn't have to worry about Bob Cherry anymore. He had been tried and sent to prison; her sister apparently had gotten him mixed up with Robert Chambliss.

Willadean showed them the piece from the newspaper that had led her to drive the long way to Billings to talk to someone in the FBI. The article was only about an inch and a half long, just a mention of the case being reinvestigated. It could have easily been overlooked.

Willadean told them about her life with Cherry. Their marriage was rocky and violent. In 1971 after he beat her, she had him committed to Bryce Hospital, the state mental institution. The hospital kept him for five or six weeks and then released him.

Fleming asked her if Cherry had ever talked to her about the church bombing.

She nodded. "He told me he would kill me if I ever said anything about it, but once when we were living in Birmingham, the car broke down about a block away from the Sixteenth Street Church, and he pointed to it and said, 'That's where we bombed the church.'"

"Did he say he had put the bomb there?" Herren asked.

"He said he was there when the bomb was put together; it was made with dynamite, and he said he lit the fuse."

That surprised Herren. They were convinced the bomb had some kind of delay device. If so, Cherry would not have literally lit a fuse. Perhaps he meant that figuratively, or perhaps he was just bragging. No physical evidence remained as to what kind of timing device was used, but consensus in the 1960s investigation was it was either a drip or acid device. Chambliss was known to have used and experimented with both, trying unsuccessfully to get the timing right. An acid method would entail putting acid into a gelatin capsule and dropping it into another kind of acid, such as sulfuric acid. When the sulfuric acid ate through the gelatin, the chemical reaction of the two acids would start a fire, which would light the fuse.

The water-drip method worked in something as crude as a coffee can with a hole in the bottom. Inside the coffee can were a series of fishing floats or bobbers and some metal connections. As the water dripped through the hole, the float would lower until it made a connection. There were two clues that pointed to a drip-method timer. Chambliss once rambled to the police about how "a fellow told me once how to make a drip method bomb. Use a float, a fishing bobber, a weight, [and] a bucket full of water with a hole in it." Also, not long after the Sixteenth Street tragedy, on September 25, another bomb, referred to as the shrapnel bomb, went off on a public street and pieces of fishing tackle were recovered from the area.

All of this flew through Herren's thoughts, but Willadean snatched his attention with her next statement: "Bobby would have terrible repetitive nightmares," she said. "I even tape recorded him. He kept saying he didn't snore, so I taped him snoring and then I played it back. The cat was sitting at the end of the bed, and the cat jumped in the air and took off, because it couldn't take snoring on both sides of the bed. And then he started mumbling in his sleep. I was trying to wake him up to let him listen to this snoring. He kept mumbling in his sleep. So I advanced the tape and started asking him some questions."

Fleming and Herren exchanged quick glances. A tape of that would be a gold vein.

"Do you still have the tape?" Herren asked.

She shook her head. "No, it was destroyed when my house burned."

"That's OK," Fleming said. "Tell us about the nightmares."

"He kept having these nightmares, and I would ask him, 'What's wrong? What are you dreaming about?' Then he would mutter, 'The girls, the little girls . . . the little girls shouldn't have died.'"

Herren met Fleming's eyes.

"He wouldn't talk any more to me about it," Willadean said, "except one time after he had been awake for a bit, he said, 'Well, it's a pity that they died, but at least they can't breed.'"

Fleming glanced over at the tiny piece of newsprint. If that had not found its way into Willadean Brogdon Cherry's hands, they would not be here in Glendive, Montana, hearing this, and a vital piece of the puzzle would not have just fallen into place.

20 | SANBOMB

"CONGRATULATIONS ARE IN ORDER, Ben," Fleming said. "You are now an official Bureau employee."

The day before, Monday, October 13, 1997, Herren had retired from the Birmingham Police Department. Today, Tuesday, October 14, was his first day employed as an FBI intelligence analyst, not just a loaner from the PD.

"You think you're going to like it?" Fleming asked.

Herren grinned. "If I can ever figure out what the hell everyone is saying. I've never seen an organization that has more acronyms. It still takes me a while to figure out what you people are talking about. But, I'm not complaining." He chuckled. "Today, my new supervisor was showing me around up on the fourteenth floor. Those folks have hardly seen me and don't have a clue who I am or what I've been doing. A woman rushed down the hall and stuck out her hand, saying, 'Nice to meet you. I'm the T&A lady here.'"

Herren glanced over at Fleming, expecting a laugh.

Fleming nodded, "Time and attendance."

"Uh, well no," Herren said. "I worked in Vice and Narcotics a long time, and T and A had a different meaning."

Still nothing from Fleming.

"You ever heard of a T and A film?" Herren ventured.

His partner looked at him blankly.

Herren cupped his hands on his chest. "Tits and ass, Bill."

"Oh my goodness."

Fleming, as usual, had insisted on driving, talking animatedly about his plans to acquire more photos of Confederate generals' graves, his personal hobby. Then, with a mental bounce Herren was finally getting accustomed to, Fleming asked. "Well, Ben, how does retirement feel?"

Herren took a deep breath and thought about the question. "I got kind of mixed feelings. I've been waiting and waiting to get my twenty years in, and that feels good; still, there's a lot of folks I'm going to miss." He hesitated. "But the PD's not the same as it used to be."

"I know what you mean," Fleming said. "The Bureau was different in the old days. It was more formal then; there were a lot of rules. Everything had to be just so, but if you had a baby or someone died, you'd get a card signed by Hoover. That kinda gave it a family feeling. And I think for the five seconds it takes to sign a name on a piece of paper—that would up morale, you know?" His voice turned wistful. "But they don't do it anymore."

"You ever regret choosing to go with the FBI?" Herren asked.

"No, not really, but yes . . . in some ways. It'd been so much better if I were a brick mason. At least I could drive by and see a building where I had laid the brick. I could point to it and say, 'I did this.' In law enforcement, there's nothing you can point to and say, 'I did that.' It's just history that's passed."

Herren agreed. "You're right. Unless you do something extraordinary, nothing's written about it. It's all just your memories. You can remember how you helped people; but it's not something your kids can say, 'That's what my daddy did.'"

Three months later on January 29, 1998, yet another bomb went off in Birmingham, Alabama, this one directed at an abortion clinic. Like the church bombing, it left a woman blinded in one eye. It also took the life of an off-duty policeman, Robert "Sandy" Sanderson. And it effectively halted Herren's participation in the Bapbomb investigation, exchanging it for Sanbomb.

A student from the University of Alabama in Birmingham was standing nearby when the bomb exploded and noticed a man who did not react to the explosion, as if he knew what was going to happen. The man calmly walked away—with the student following him and getting a partial tag number.

The crime tore up the community, especially the law enforcement community, and a tremendous effort went toward solving it. Herren and Fleming were snatched off the church bombing case, Fleming for about a month and Herren for over eighteen months.

When Fleming came back to the church bombing case alone, he felt handicapped without Herren's detailed recall and steadying presence and didn't think he could work it satisfactorily without him. Even the US attorney, Doug Jones, relied on Herren if it had to do with the church bombing case. Fleming often referred to Herren as "Doug Jones's encyclopedia."

Herren worked the Sanbomb case seven days a week for twelve-hour days. After six months, they reduced his schedule to six days a week and only ten-hour days. He focused on telephone analysis, studying the patterns in calls from the suspect's friends and relatives. It was an intense and grueling effort, fueled by a united determination to find the man who had left such devastation in his wake. Based on all he had read of the 1960s investigation of the church bombing, Herren believed the agents working that case had felt the same way.

By February 1998, evidence tied the Sanbomb suspect with the Atlanta Olympic Park bomber, Eric Robert Rudolph, who had fled to the mountains of North Carolina. After almost two years, Herren was allowed to return to the church bombing case, first only part-time and then eventually back on the case full-time, though Sanbomb rocked on as a manhunt.

21 | WAYLENE VAUGHN AND GLORIA LaDOW

BY THIS TIME, HERREN and Fleming were convinced the killing of the girls had not been part of the Cahaba Boys' plan. The dynamite was supposed to have gone off earlier while the church was empty. They based this on an accumulation of facts.

The FBI investigators in the 1960s had reached the same conclusion, believing the crude timer—either a water drip or acid detonator—had not functioned as intended. In the case of the water drip, the hole for the drip possibly had been contaminated by dirt. A former Klansman that Herren had spoken to in the Fultondale area commented, "I just didn't think Chambliss was smart enough to make a water timer."

Bill Holt, another Klansman, told Bob Eddy a man named "Brown" from Tennessee, an expert in timing devices, came to Birmingham to show the Klan how to make an acid detonator. They tested it in a field but could never anticipate the timing. Cherry had explained how to make an acid timer in detail to an FBI agent in the 1960s.

All the other bombings had been done at night, not in broad daylight in areas with people about. Herren and Fleming felt the suspects placed the bomb in the mimosa shrubs under the stairs in order to keep it hidden, and it was unlikely they had any idea the nearest wall was the ladies lounge.

However, two white men were seen fleeing on foot just before the explosion. Also, a young boy had seen a Rambler station wagon with two white males pass by the church and then speed off just before the explosion. Herren and Fleming (and the FBI in the earlier investigation) had considered whether someone had just used a fuse as the timer and thrown it out of a car. They rejected that theory because the amount of dynamite needed to create the damage done to the church would have made it very awkward to throw out the window. A short fuse would have been very dangerous. A longer fuse would have produced smoke and an odor.

One of the church members, Buddy Kelly had walked into the church by the stairs five minutes before the explosion. He noticed no smoke or odor. It was possible the two white men who were seen fleeing the scene on foot and in a vehicle just as the bomb went off may have been checking on the device or even possibly had come to disarm it, though that would have been extremely dangerous. No evidence of their motivation existed.

It was mentioned in the files that a person answered a phone call in the church shortly before the explosion where a man gave a warning, minutes before the bomb exploded. Carolyn Maull McKinstry, who was fifteen at the time, said she had answered that call. It is possible someone who knew about the bomb wanted people to get out of the building. The church, however, had received several such threats since May 1963.

Herren and Fleming didn't credit the Klan with a lot of intelligence, but it didn't take much to know that bombing a church full of people during Sunday services would not have earned their cause anything. It would be more likely that they wanted to time it so the damage to the church that was headquarters for the local civil rights movement would have greeted the Sunday churchgoers. Also, it seemed likely James Edward Lay had hindered the original plan when he interrupted the suspects two weeks earlier on a weeknight, although that also could have been a trial run.

Among the many family members Herren and Fleming interviewed was Bobby Frank Cherry's daughter from his first marriage, Sue Cherry, who told them that Cherry said the bomb was supposed to "put a scare into them; no one was supposed to get hurt." Cherry voiced his regret to Herren, or as close to regret as he could come, with the words, "Once the bullet leaves the gun, you can't call it back," and with the nightmares his wife reported where he would cry out, "The girls! The girls!"

Chambliss's first shocked reaction watching television footage had been, "We never meant to hurt anybody." Days later, Klansman Hubert Page said the bomb went off hours later than it was supposed to, and it was not meant to kill the children. Chambliss retorted, perhaps in bluster, "I meant for it to kill someone."

"The Klan is mean," Fleming said, "I don't say anything good about them, but they didn't intend to kill the girls. And they couldn't have admitted that if Jesus was at the other end of the table."

Another theory, and the one the prosecution attorneys believed, was that the bombers knew Sunday was Youth Day—a large sign announcing it had hung outside the church all week—and the Klan was sending a warning message about school integration. The latter was almost certainly true, apart from whether they intended specifically to kill children.

Regardless of their intent, the men who planted the bomb were responsible for the tragic outcome. In addition to intentionally causing the death of another, the legal definition of murder in Alabama included: "Under circumstances manifesting extreme indifference to human life, he or she recklessly engages in conduct which creates a grave risk of death to a person other than himself or herself, and thereby causes the death of another person."

It was also possible that Cherry's regret had more to do with the consequences of the little girls' deaths—the sudden withdrawal of sympathy for the Klan and the reaction of outrage and sorrow that lifted a local protest into the national spotlight and galvanized the civil rights movement. The 1964 Civil Rights Act passed the following year. The Sixteenth Street Church bombing was the beginning of the decline of the Klan. Few people wanted to be associated with a group that killed little girls and was being investigated and watched all the time. That was certainly not part of the Klan's plans.

In any case, there was a reason murder carried no statute of limitations. In Herren's and Fleming's minds, a murderer needed to suffer the consequences, regardless of how long he'd gotten away with it or how old he was.

US Attorney Doug Jones and Agent Fleming flew to south Alabama in a small Bureau plane to meet Waylene Vaughn, Tommy Blanton's old girlfriend. It was the first time Fleming had ridden in a Bureau plane, a privilege normally only granted to the director or VIPs.

Herren referred to Waylene as Blanton's go-to girl. His relationship with her was no secret. His wife, Jean, knew of it and was openly jealous.

Waylene now lived in a tiny shack. The years had been unkind to her, Fleming observed. She looked bad. He wondered where her life had taken her since the days when she would meet Blanton at the Blue Bird Hotel on the old Bessemer Highway.

Vaughn told them she had joined the army to get away from Blanton. She had seen him do horrible things to black people. She did not think much of him, though she had dated him long ago. "He bragged to me that he'd had sex with a man—Wyman Lee." Fleming was quite sure this was not acceptable Klan behavior, but neither was dating black girls, a topic of discussion between Blanton and Mitch Burns recorded by the tapes in Burns's trunk. Though she did not want to testify, they told her how important she was to the case. They needed her to help establish Blanton's hatred toward blacks and thus his motivation for bombing the church. She finally agreed to come.

Gary A. Tucker had surfaced as a suspect as recently as 1988. Tucker was a mental patient at Bryce's Hospital in Tuscaloosa, Alabama. On his deathbed, he claimed he had helped make the Sixteenth Street Baptist Church bomb. The reports Herren had read dismissed Tucker as a possible suspect, but Herren didn't completely rule him out until he tracked down the agents who had interviewed Tucker. That convinced him that the man was either delusional from the pain medications he was taking or motivated by some psychological affliction. There was no evidence he had ever been involved, and the person Tucker claimed had been his accomplice had been in prison at the time of the bombing.

Another loose end was one of the most intriguing documents in the files, an AIRTEL teletype from Dallas FBI headquarters to Birmingham. On May 5, 1980, the Dallas field office had received an anonymous phone call that sounded like it was from a black male. The caller said he worked at Wyatt Industries in Dallas, and he and other employees at Wyatt had heard Bobby Frank Cherry make statements claiming responsibility for the church bombing in Birmingham that happened in 1964. That date, of course, was incorrect, but there could be no doubt what the caller was referring to. He gave a description of Cherry as a white male about fifty-three or fifty-four years of age, six foot two to six foot three, about 210 pounds, and a member of the KKK, now living in Grand Prairie, Texas.

In Herren's interview with Cherry, Cherry had mentioned working at Wyatt Industries, which gave the call credence. From 1980 to the day they discovered the AIRTEL in the files, no one had pursued it further, since it was an old, closed case by that time—but for the last year and a half Herren and Fleming and Dallas Special Agent Strauss had looked for that man.

Agent Strauss subpoenaed Wyatt's old employee records, which had to be dug out of a warehouse, and he sent the files to Birmingham. Herren spent hours digging through them, finding the payroll records of Cherry's employment and matching the dates to find out who was working with him. While he and Fleming were in the Dallas area interviewing Cherry, they talked to several people who had worked at Wyatt. They had made a side trip to Gunbarrel, Texas, looking for a person named Bonds who seemed the best prospect for their mystery man, but they couldn't find him.

One evening, after almost a year and a half of trying to determine the identity of the anonymous caller, the FBI night dispatcher called Herren at home and said he had a guy named Bonds on the phone. Furious at himself for not having paper close at hand, Herren grabbed a napkin and any scrap of paper he could find while the dispatcher forwarded the call to his cell phone.

Bonds told Herren he had been a welder's helper back them. "I am black and he [Cherry] didn't like me," he said. "Cherry said, 'I'll tell you how we treated the black people back in Birmingham; we blew up their church.'"

Herren scribbled as fast as he could. This was just what they needed. A real break! But Bonds talked for over an hour, and his statements started to sound off the wall. He referred to Bill Clinton as his best friend and said his information would solve the Olympic bombing case and the James Earl Ray case. Herren asked him where his information came from. Bond replied gravely, "God gave me the information."

Herren sighed and put down his pen. Bonds may have actually heard Cherry say what he claimed, but he could never take the stand to testify.

22 | TOMMY FRANK CHERRY

THE DARK PICTURE GLORIA LaDow painted of her stepfather, Bobby Frank Cherry, who had sexually abused her as a young girl, was confirmed in other interviews. A daughter-in-law claimed, "All the Cherry family hate blacks and have no respect for women. Bobby refers to women as whores." One daughter later told Fleming, "I wanted to be a nurse. My whole goal in life was to be a nurse, and then Momma died and I had to take care of the kids. I had to iron, and I had to cook, and Daddy would ridicule me for trying to be a nurse. He'd say, 'There's no need for a woman to be going to school.'"

Bobby Cherry's son, Tommy Frank Cherry, was fifteen, the eldest of seven children, when his mother, Virginia, died of cancer, and his father put him and his siblings in Gateway Orphanage in Birmingham before marrying again and taking on his new wife's children. Herren, Fleming, and Doug Jones flew to Austin, Texas, to talk with him.

They had some wait time on their hands. Herren and Fleming spent it checking out President Lyndon Johnson's library and the tower on the campus of the University of Texas where Charles Whitman, a student and former Marine, had barricaded himself with a rifle and randomly killed over a dozen people in 1966. Two policemen and a citizen had climbed the tower and finally succeeded in shooting Whitman. It was a fittingly gray, somber day to be there.

Whitman's autopsy had revealed a brain tumor that possibly played a role in his actions. That made it all a little easier to understand, but

Herren was accustomed to the idea that people were capable of anything and sometimes just went crazy or sometimes were just mean, and there was not really a good explanation for what they did. You would go crazy yourself trying to figure out why people did what they did.

After that, they headed to a cemetery where Fleming hoped to pursue his personal hobby, or "affliction" as Fleming himself termed it—photographing the graves of Confederate generals. A graduate of North Georgia College, Fleming had majored in history, and the Civil War was his passion. He would only photograph those graves confirmed by the Southern Congress. There were 425 confirmed sites, and Fleming had 332 of them. Whenever he traveled, he made a point of looking to see who was buried nearby. It was a magnificent cemetery with beautiful old oak trees, but it had begun to rain—not a drizzle, but a soaker.

Herren held the umbrella over Fleming so he could take pictures of the tombstones, a favor he would make certain his partner remembered in the future. While they were hunting around the cemetery, Herren found an interesting grave of a Texas Ranger who had died in the early 1900s. Inscribed on his headstone was a verse entitled, "The Texas Ranger's Poem." Perhaps a bit infected with Fleming's affliction, Herren snapped a shot with his camera.

Fleming, Herren, and US Attorney Doug Jones met Tommy Cherry in a hotel in Austin. At that time he lived near his father and did not want him or his family knowing he was talking to the FBI. When the bomb at the Sixteenth Street Baptist Church exploded, it rattled the frames on the walls at the sign shop where eleven-year-old Tommy had accompanied his father and several other Klansmen. It had also rattled his world, as rumors about his father's part in the crime followed him all his life.

Tommy had always denied having heard anything directly from his father about his participation in the bombing, but when Fleming interviewed Tommy's ex-wife, Marsha Gale Cherry, she said Tommy told her, "The less you know about it the better."

From interviews with Tommy's daughter, Teresa Stacy, the investigators knew there had been bad blood between Tommy Cherry and his father over her. Things had even gotten physical. Teresa told them her grandfather, Bobby Frank Cherry, had put his hand on her breast. Jones didn't mention the subject directly, but it was in his voice when he said, "We know you've had some problems with your dad."

Tommy was hesitant, as if torn between loyalties. Jones wanted to play a tape for Tommy. During Herren's interview with Bobby Frank Cherry, Cherry mentioned busting Reverend Shuttlesworth with brass knuckles when he attempted to integrate Phillips High. Jones tasked Herren and Fleming to find footage of the incident. At WBRC, a local television station, they found Jimmy Parker, the videographer who had taken the original video. In 1957, he worked as a cameraman for WBIQ Channel 10, an educational television channel.

One day, he went to Phillips High School to pick up his transcript, and as he was leaving the school, he saw a crowd of about fifty white people jeering at a cluster of four or five black people, adults and teenagers. A group of white men rushed from the crowd as Parker grabbed his camera from his car. To get a better angle, he jumped on top of a police three-wheeler motorcycle to film what became an important part of the era's records.

Now a slim, graying man, Parker was happy to retrieve the film from the station's archives and show it to them in a video editing booth. The black-and-white footage replayed history. Several men converged on Shuttlesworth and his wife, forcing them to flee back inside their car. Both were wounded, as were some of the youth with them. Because Herren and Fleming had seen several photos of Cherry as a young man, it wasn't difficult to pick him out, especially when he reached into his back pocket for the brass knuckles and struck Shuttlesworth. Parker made them a copy of the tape.

In the Dallas hotel room, Herren showed Tommy Cherry the film footage and asked if he could identify the man with a cigarette in his mouth who pulled an object from his pocket and hit Shuttlesworth.

"That's my dad," Tommy said flatly. Tommy had stood at his father's side during the press conference Bobby Cherry called after the interview with Herren and Bob Eddy in Athens, Texas. Now, though he refused to say he'd ever heard anything from his father about participating in the church bombing, he talked about the wedge between them, how they had even come to blows. When he was younger, his father had beaten him and Tommy's mother, Virginia Cherry. Tommy's round face tightened when he spoke of his mother. He stood abruptly and walked over to the balcony ledge, pulling out a cigarette.

Fleming followed. "My mother died of cancer too," he said, putting a hand on Tommy's arm. Both men, lost in their memories, had tears in their eyes, but didn't speak further. They just sat together sharing their sorrow. It was a moment Fleming would always remember—the irony of two men from such opposite sides of life finding a common grief that bound them, if only for a few moments. When they walked back into the room a few minutes later, Fleming wondered if Tommy would open up more, but he didn't—or couldn't—condemn his father.

Tommy Cherry later told Pamela Colloff, a writer for *Texas Monthly*, that as a child he knew his father was hotheaded and mean, flying into a rage at any provocation, but that his dad was a hero to him. "He was a protector and a charmer, the toughest guy on the block." When asked if he had told the FBI everything he knew, he replied bitterly, "I've answered their questions, but I'm not going to help them hang him."

That conflict between loyalty to his father and doubts about the role his father had played in a terrible crime showed on Tommy's face in the Dallas hotel room. Fleming believed Tommy hated the association with racism and the bombings with which his father had tainted him and the entire family. Some part of Tommy Cherry wanted to tell and wipe it all away, but maybe he knew it would never go away, no matter what he said, or maybe he clung to his loyalty to his father with the desperation of a son who always wanted to please but never could.

As they left, Tommy turned to them, his words burdened and heartfelt. "Tell them [the families of the little girls] that we—our family—are sorry for their loss."

23 | MARY FRANCES CUNNINGHAM

AN ENDURING MYSTERY REMAINED from the 1960s and 1970s investigations. It centered around one woman—Mary Frances Cunningham. She was the sister of Flora "Tee" Chambliss. Tee was married to Robert "Dynamite Bob" Chambliss. The sisters were close, and Tee and Mary Frances spent a lot of time together.

Fleming found a report in the secret informant files dated December 7, 1964, of two people telling the FBI an amazing story. They said they were at the Sixteenth Street Baptist Church around 2:00 AM on September 15, 1963, and they observed the church bombing suspects in the act of placing the bomb. The FBI gave the informants the cover names of "Dale Tarrant" and "Abington Spaulding" to protect their identities, and for years that was how they were known.

Their story was believed because the two informants were Mary Frances Cunningham, the sister of Robert Chambliss's wife, and Elizabeth Cobbs, Robert Chambliss's niece. Cunningham had been an ongoing source of information to the FBI even before the bombing, through John Hancock, a Jefferson County sheriff's deputy.

When Bob Eddy was sitting in the Birmingham FBI office in 1977, reading the file documents, he knew nothing of this, but he kept running across Elizabeth Cobbs's name on interview summary files. When he asked specifically for Elizabeth Cobbs's file, his request was denied. Since he was not allowed to see informant files, he realized that had to mean Cobbs had become an informant at some point.

Eddy went to Jack LeGrand, his contact with the Birmingham police and asked if LeGrand could locate Cobbs. LeGrand came through, and Eddy called her from the FBI office. At first, she hesitated to speak with him, but then she came to the office.

Cobbs naturally assumed Eddy was with the FBI and had read her file, and the first thing she said to him was, "I wasn't there." Bewildered, Eddy just nodded. After they spoke for a while, he believed that she preferred to speak with him outside the FBI offices, so he made an appointment to meet her. Later, when Eddy went out to talk to her again at her apartment, he sat at her kitchen table and asked her about that statement. "Well," she said, "you've read all about it, haven't you?" He still had no idea what she was talking about, but was afraid she would clam up if she knew that. "Tell me about it," he said.

Over the course of several interviews, Cobbs explained that her aunt Mary Frances Cunningham, frustrated that Deputy Hancock had done nothing with the information she gave him, decided to go to the FBI herself. She asked Cobbs to back up the story about what had happened the night the bomb had been placed, even though Cobbs had not been there.

"Who *was* there?" Eddy asked.

Cobbs said she believed it was Cunningham's sister, Tee Chambliss, the wife of Dynamite Bob Chambliss. In order to protect Tee, Cunningham asked Cobbs to go with her to talk to the FBI and tell the story as if she had seen what Tee Chambliss actually saw.

It seemed far-fetched that two women would have put on wigs and floppy hats and ventured out in the wee hours of the morning, exposing themselves to great danger, to witness such a thing. Eddy learned, however, this bold and brave foray was not unusual behavior for the two sisters, as both women disapproved of the Klan and Chambliss's bluster and actions. Tee and Mary Frances often chided Chambliss about what he was doing, saying he and his fellow Klansmen were "picking on helpless people." The two sisters had once taken a clock from Tee's house to Deputy Hancock and an FBI agent so a wire could be placed inside it.

The Friday before the church bombing, September 13, 1963, Chambliss put something in a room and told his wife not to go in there. Of course, as soon as he left the house, Tee and Mary Frances opened the door and found a container the size of a shoebox. Inside were ten to twelve sticks of dynamite wrapped in brown paper with a four- to six-inch fuse.

The following evening, Saturday the fourteenth, there was a lot of activity around the house and the auto parts store on the corner next door where Chambliss met with Gafford in the backyard. Klansmen came and went. Blanton arrived in his Chevrolet. Tee and Mary Frances knew a bombing was being planned and decided it was going to be the church—something they had heard Chambliss and others talk about on previous occasions. Chambliss told Tee he was going to Troy Ingram's and, if anyone called, to tell them. Late that night, after everyone had left, Tee and Mary Frances looked in the room where the box of dynamite had been. It was gone. They decided to go to the church and see for themselves.

Bob Eddy asked Cobbs to introduce him to Mary Frances Cunningham, which she did, and Eddy interviewed Cunningham on several occasions. Although she would never directly admit it, he strongly believed she had been at the church. He learned her indirect responses were answers shadowed in denial. For example, when he asked why Cunningham didn't go alone that night, she responded, "Tee and I did a lot of things together." He asked why they wore wigs, and she said, "Someone who was trying to hide their identity would do that." "Why would anyone go to that intersection [behind the church]?" he had asked. Cunningham replied, "If someone were in that position, they could see all the way down the alley." If Eddy asked her a direct question she didn't want to affirm, her repeated response was not denial but, "I don't want to hurt my family."

Documents showed a detailed report was given to the FBI in 1964 about the foray to the church: The witnesses spotted Blanton's blue and white Chevrolet on Sixth Avenue North, which runs east-west in front of the church, with Tommy Blanton at the wheel and Robert Chambliss in the backseat with two others the witness felt certain were Bobby Frank Cherry and Herman Cash. Blanton drove north on Fifteenth Street to the alley and stopped at the corner of the alley that ran behind the church. Blanton and Chambliss remained in the car. The two other Klansmen, Bobby Frank Cherry and Herman Cash, got out of the car; then one of them got into the backseat with Chambliss, and the other began walking east down the alley toward the side of the church where the bomb was placed, "carrying something by a handle." Cunningham later told Bob Eddy that Cherry had been the one carrying the object, but the FBI report said Cunningham only knew it was not Chambliss or Blanton.

Blanton started his car and drove north, still on Fifteenth Street, turning right onto Seventh Avenue North where he went out of the women's sight. Four or five minutes later, the women saw Blanton's car parked at the intersection of Seventh Avenue and Sixteenth Street, a half block north of the church, with Blanton, Chambliss, and a third person inside. The fourth person was walking from the rear of the church toward the car. The women became frightened and quickly drove off.

The report also said Cunningham saw a "dark-colored car, make and model unknown, which appeared to have several white men in it cruising the area around the Sixteenth Street Church."

This was critical, detailed evidence and matched Kirthus Glenn's story in terms of time, the location of the car, and the position of Chambliss in the backseat. The two women, for obvious reasons, did not want to testify.

After interviewing them in 1964, Agent Alexander sent a teletype about their eyewitness accounts to headquarters. The memo read, "Our concentration on coverage of the Cahaba River Group . . . has produced a significant breakthrough in the form of live sources who may eventually be in a position to furnish testimony in this matter." He added neither would "testify at this time, since they are literally fearful of their lives."

The FBI requested permission from headquarters (undoubtedly J. Edgar Hoover) to discuss the evidence with the US attorney "in order that full appreciation of the prosecutive problems involved are known, so that solutions or alternative courses of action may be kept under active consideration." Headquarters responded, "Any discussion with the US Attorney at this time appears to be premature. . . . When we have witnesses ready and willing to testify in state and/or federal court, the matter will be taken up with the [Justice] Department."

As Herren and Fleming read the old files, the already complex plot surrounding the two women thickened. Mary Frances Cunningham also told the FBI in the 1960s that she warned Deputy Hancock of the bomb *before* it went off at the church. When agents questioned the deputy, he said his informant, Cunningham, had called him around 2:30 AM on September 15, 1963, about eight hours before the explosion, but he told her to call back and hung up on her. He received another call from her the next morning about 8:30 AM saying there was a bomb at the church. He told no one about it.

In interviews with Bob Eddy, Hancock said at first that he never received a call, that his informant called the office in the wee hours, and that he didn't receive the message until he went in at 8:00 AM Sunday morning. Phone logs of Chambliss's home phone verified that a call had been made from there about 2:30 AM Sunday morning, which would have been just shortly after the two women reported observing Blanton's car at the church. Hancock finally admitted to Eddy that he hung up on Mary Frances and didn't take her report seriously, because she was always coming to him with information about Chambliss's plots and bombs. He said there was a bombing weekly in Birmingham and many false warnings about bombs, and it was hard to keep up with them.

To both the FBI agents in the 1960s and Eddy in the 1970s, Hancock claimed he was "headed toward the church" around 10:00 AM when the bomb exploded at 10:22 AM.

Why the hour-and-a-half gap?

Herren and Fleming learned that Hancock later admitted to Eddy that he had met with Mary Frances that morning and had delayed going to the church because he'd been "distracted," claiming they were having an affair. Mary Frances denied this.

Fleming read the story Elizabeth Cobbs related in her book about the incident:

For many months, Dale [Mary Frances Cunningham] had been in and out of the Chambliss home—helping Tee serve coffee at meetings, stuffing envelopes with political literature, visiting—and listening, and watching. Everything she had heard and seen, she had passed on to the deputy. She had even helped him place a bug in the house . . . but he would not talk to her that night when she called him.

Later that night, they spoke again and met at their usual area (north of Tarrant City) about 6 o'clock Sunday morning [the morning of the bombing]. Hancock asked Dale [Cunningham] many questions, teased her, and drove around town and the rural areas for several hours, even stopping for coffee. She was frustrated that he apparently did not believe her. During the many months she had been giving him information about Robert's [Chambliss's] Klan activities, nothing ever seemed to be "enough" for him to bring charges against Robert and his buddies.

Before 10 o'clock that Sunday morning, Hancock dropped Dale [Cunningham] back at her car, telling her he would "check it out." He later reported that as he drove back toward town, the bomb at the church exploded. He had not called in any alarm or bomb threat in the four hours he had Dale's information, and what's more, he had effectively kept Dale isolated so that she could not give her information to anyone else until the expected time for the explosion had passed.

Cobbs commented in her book that Hancock "neutralized Dale's role as an informant," and this was a "pattern repeated with other law enforcement officers and their informants on Klan activity." Was that true? Had Hancock deliberately thwarted Cunningham's efforts to report what she knew? Other than his delay on the day of the bombing and Elizabeth Cobbs's statement in her book—which was surely taken from what her aunt told her—there was no supporting evidence of this. The FBI files referred to information from a county deputy, information that most likely came from Chambliss's wife through Mary Frances Cunningham to Hancock. Also, Hancock took Cunningham and Cobbs to the FBI to tell their story in 1964.

Cunningham and Cobbs had good reason to believe in conspiracies—they provided information to law enforcement for five years at risk to their lives with no results. On the other hand, their refusal to testify had handicapped efforts to take a case to court. In spite of that, the FBI agents in Birmingham wanted to move forward. Cobbs and Cunningham saw that the agents who had worked closely with them were almost as frustrated as they were. Like Baxley, they were stymied by the top administration.

Another question remained. Cunningham and Cobbs were flown to Savannah by Baxley in 1977 for a polygraph exam. Did a polygraph administered to Cunningham, which reportedly revealed deception, reflect what happened during those four hours or what happened behind the church when the bomb was placed there? Despite the fact that the polygraph reportedly showed deception on the part of both women, Eddy never wavered in believing Cunningham and probably Tee Chambliss were at the church that night. He knew polygraphs did not measure lies but rather stress—and both women were under a lot of mental stress.

A strong piece of evidence supporting Cunningham's presence at the church was the fact she had called Deputy Hancock in the wee hours of the morning, about fifteen minutes after the suspects were seen at the church. The time she originally gave the FBI that she saw the suspects matched the time Kirthus Glenn gave and also the place—in the alley behind the church. Apparently, Cunningham did not know of Glenn at the time she gave her information to the FBI. It was too much, in Eddy's mind, to be a coincidence.

In an attempt to get at the truth, Herren and Fleming interviewed Agent Alexander, the original FBI agent who had taken the women's statements in the 1960s. They asked if he believed Mary Frances Cunningham and Elizabeth Cobb (standing in for Tee) that day.

Agent Alexander responded, "I had no reason not to, absolutely none. I did believe them, certainly."

Alexander, Eddy, and Fleming believed the women had been at the church that night, but Herren had his doubts about the whole thing. After carefully reading through the old files, Herren felt Mary Frances Cunningham might have made up the story of following the suspects, deciding Chambliss needed to be arrested, perhaps to save her sister from him. Cunningham's recanting of the story and the polygraph in 1977, which indicated the women were not being truthful, added to his suspicions.

Tee had personal reasons, as well as philosophical ones, to hate her husband. Chambliss was known to be a brutal man. One day he told Tee to get canned sardines for his German shepherd while he was out. Tee, who was sick in bed, did not comply. When he returned, Chambliss took out his fury on her for this insubordination, beating her badly. It was not an unusual occurrence. Cunningham was well aware her sister suffered at Chambliss's hands.

During Chambliss's trial, Tee called the courthouse and asked Bob Eddy if it looked like Chambliss was going to be convicted. Afterward, her attorney came by the house and found her lying on the couch, a towel over her head. When he told her that her husband had been convicted, she cried, "Hallelujah!" and threw her towel into the air.

Herren also noticed the old FBI files reported an informant saying Chambliss had been particularly ill-tempered the previous week and "complained that the church bombing did not kill enough blacks." To Herren, it seemed to be the kind of statement that was added in desperation to get the FBI to arrest Chambliss.

By this time, both Elizabeth Cobbs and Tee Chambliss were dead, so the secret of the truth about what had happened that night rested with Mary Frances Cunningham.

Herren and Fleming went to talk to her.

When Bob Eddy met Mary Frances in 1977, she was still an attractive woman. He imagined she had been a beautiful lady in her younger days. Now in her seventies, her blonde hair was gray, and she appeared more of a grandmother to Herren and Fleming. The interview in February 1997 started well, and their impression of Mary Frances Cunningham was of a sweet, elderly lady, but she denied having seen anyone at the Sixteenth Street Church on the night of the bombing. She said she had lied to the FBI.

Fleming asked her if she had been seeing Deputy Hancock during the time of the church bombing. In reaction to his question, she exploded, working herself into a fit, throwing herself on the couch, and rolling on the floor, as if she were being tortured by the question.

As the instigator of her extreme reaction, Fleming felt he should remove himself and left the house. Herren, abandoned by his partner and left alone with a hysterical woman, followed Fleming as soon as she had calmed down.

If Mary Frances Cunningham truly went to the church that night, she had risked her life and her family's safety to be an eyewitness to a terrible crime and tried to warn her law enforcement contact. She must, however, have been conflicted about being with him or not being able to convince him of the need to take action. The fault lay heavily on Hancock. As a law enforcement officer, it was his duty to respond to her information in a timely manner. Throughout the years, the heartrending speculation weighed on all the investigators—had Deputy Hancock taken Cunningham's warning seriously, the deaths of four young girls and the serious injury to another might have been avoided.

Herren and Fleming didn't see Cunningham again until sometime later, on an evening when Herren had plans to take his wife out to dinner for her birthday. He received a call that Doug Jones and Assistant US Attorney Robert Posey, who had been brought into the case in 1998, wanted him and Fleming to join them for an interview with Mary Frances Cunningham. If her statement to the FBI in the 1964 was true, it was a bombshell, and they wanted to hear her story or her denials themselves.

Herren groaned silently. The birthday dinner was one of many family events neglected while working this case. He would try to make it up to her, but missing his wife's birthday was going to be a tough one. Fleming shrugged. His own wife knew the system and was reconciled to lost nights and weekends.

With trepidation, Herren and Fleming met Jones and Posey. At least there would be witnesses if she reacted again with hysterics. Herren sat on a dining room chair across the room from Cunningham. She repeated her denials, and in the middle of the conversation, she suddenly got on her knees and made her way over to him, putting both hands on his legs and calling him her angel. Herren was mortified. The attorneys decided she would not be a prosecution witness.

A few days later, Herren found a statuette of an angel sitting on his desk, a gift from Fleming.

24 | FEDERAL GRAND JURY

IN MAY 1965, THE Birmingham FBI determined "it is apparent that the bombing was the handiwork of former Klansmen, Robert E. Chambliss, Bobby Frank Cherry, Herman Frank Cash, Thomas E. Blanton Jr., and probably Troy Ingram." The May memo further stated, "Delay in prosecution progressively decreases the chances of effective prosecution of this case." It urged the case be tried by state authorities "due to the climate of public opinion favoring prosecution." The memo indicated Macon Weaver, Birmingham's Northern District US attorney, shared that opinion. Weaver later told Bob Eddy he had never been given any evidence in the case, though he may have supported the idea that public opinion favored prosecution. The memo made clear that the specifics of the case had not been discussed with the US attorney, and recommended that he be fully briefed.

It is clear from this memo that the Birmingham FBI wanted to proceed with the case, believed there was a strong case, or at least the potential for a strong case, and felt the community (i.e., a jury) would support the prosecution of the men who had murdered four innocent girls. The Bureau's response, six days later, was all of one paragraph:

> From an evaluation of the evidence received thus far in this investigation, the chance of successful prosecution in state or federal court is very remote. In view of this, the Bureau disapproves at this time of the conference you recommend with the US Attorney.

151

In other civil rights violation cases, the FBI based their jurisdiction on a Reconstruction-era civil rights law that had a five-year statute of limitations. However, that statute expired on the church bombing in 1968. The federal law concerning transportation of dynamite, however, had no statute of limitations when a death was involved. Ironically, Hoover had rejected that legal theory when he was asked to have the FBI investigate the bombings that occurred in Birmingham prior to the one at Sixteenth Street Church.

In March 1965, green boxes full of dynamite were found at various locations across the city, reigniting the investigation under the name Greenbomb, and the investigation plodded on for several more years. In fact, internal documents indicate that even as late as 1971 the Birmingham police submitted a suspect's fingerprints to be compared against a latent print found in association with Greenbomb (with negative results), and files indicated the FBI considered the Bapbomb case still under active investigation.

Hoover responded to a letter from a citizen asking why the FBI never made any report to the public on their investigation. His reply of April 20, 1970, was simply: "There was no FBI report made public concerning the Birmingham church bombings because information in our files must be maintained as confidential pursuant to regulations of the Department of Justice."

Although federal jurisdiction ended in 1968, the Birmingham office continued to send monthly reports to headquarters. The Bapbomb case was finally officially closed in July 1973.

Years later, in 1980, a judicial committee investigation determined J. Edgar Hoover had blocked evidence going to the Justice Department that could have led to prosecution of the suspects. The official story from the FBI was that prosecution was remote, in terms of the evidence—the key witnesses did not want to testify—or perhaps the possibility of a fair trial in 1960s Birmingham. Another theory proposed a trial and conviction would give the civil rights movement and Hoover's "enemy," Martin Luther King, a win, and that wasn't to be tolerated. Hoover's antipathy toward organizations like King's Southern Christian Leadership Conference (SCLC) was well known. In fact, the SCLC was subjected to FBI surveillance as part of the COMINFIL (communist infiltration) program. It was unknown whether those who voiced such opinions had knowledge of the degree of effort and resources put into the 1960s investigation. Such an effort would seem to indicate a sincere desire to solve the case and prosecute the wrongdoers; however, it was also possible Hoover wanted to know who did it for the sake of knowing. Knowledge was power in his world.

Perhaps in response to the judicial committee conclusion, the church bombing case was reopened briefly in 1980 by the Jefferson County District Attorney, David Barber, and again in 1988 by Alabama Attorney General Don Siegelman, but no new evidence came to light.

———

Fleming and Herren shared the highs and lows of the investigative roller coaster with Doug Jones, who kept close tabs on the case. "I've never had a US attorney actually take my opinion seriously," Fleming said and added, "I've also never spent so much time in anyone else's office." In fact, Fleming and Herren jokingly referred to having the "Jones Office Blues," because they never left his office without more things he wanted them to do. But even when they came to discuss their frustrations or lows, they always left feeling better, pumped up and ready to dig deeper. There was no question Jones was as committed to the case as they were.

Organizing the case was a daunting task. One day, Fleming asked for extra clerical help, and two young women in their early twenties were sent down to assist them. Herren was poring over a file and Fleming was on the phone, talking about Hoover. One of the girls turned to the other, "Well, who is this J. Edgar Hoover he keeps talking about?"

The other replied, "Don't you know anything? He was an old SAC [Special Agent in Charge] around here."

It was all Herren could do to keep from laughing aloud. He couldn't wait to share the story with his partner once Fleming got off the phone.

———

Because there was no applicable federal law in effect at the time of the crime, the church bombing needed to be tried in state court. However, the prosecution team used the federal grand jury as a tool for investigative purposes and to get witnesses' statements on record. Grand jury testimonies were secret. Jeff Wallace, the deputy district attorney assigned to the case, had to get clearance from the FBI to be able to read the grand jury transcripts. Herren and Fleming had access to the information through a federal 6-e rule, which allowed prosecutors to share information important to the investigation disclosed in the grand jury. Investigators had an obligation to keep it secret.

On October 27, 1998, a federal grand jury was called, and many people were subpoenaed, including every Klansman that Herren and Fleming could find still alive. And almost every one arrived with a cross on his lapel or a Bible in hand.

Among the subpoenaed was Jessie Benjamin "J. B." Stoner, the infamous Atlanta attorney and the leader of the National States Rights Party. Stoner had defended James Earl Ray, the assassin who killed Martin Luther King in 1968. Stoner had been out of prison for the Bethel Baptist Church bombing since 1986. He arrived with drama, a large white Panama hat over his gaunt face. He walked with a pronounced limp, supported by a cane. Fleming was sitting in the witness room when Stoner settled himself and tried to verbally spar with Doug Jones. In Fleming's opinion, Stoner was "trying to be a smart lawyer like Jones, but he [Stoner] was just an idiot."

One of the Eastview #13 members subpoenaed was Levie "Quick Draw" Yarbrough, the brother-in-law of the green-toothed woman Herren had met in the backwoods of Cullman County. In an old photo Herren found in the files, Yarbrough, who was a big, heavily muscled man, stood with his thumb and little finger tucked into his side pocket, leaving the three middle fingers extended on the outside—one of the Klan's secret hand signals. He was rumored to be handy with guns and had worn a pistol when Bob Eddy had interviewed him in the 1970s.

When Yarbrough answered the summons to the federal grand jury, Herren was shocked that the small, shrunken man was the same person as the one in the photo. Before he took the stand, Herren and Fleming interviewed him, and Yarbrough started talking about spaceships. He was excused from testifying, although they suspected his attorney had suggested to him that if he were to act crazy, he wouldn't have to testify.

To his surprise, Fleming found the national Klan leader, the Imperial Wizard Robert Shelton, to be a "gentleman from top to bottom." The irony was not lost on him that this was possibly the man who ordered the bombing, but at the grand jury and in the witness room, he was polite and respectful.

The investigative team wanted to bring in Willadean Cherry's brother to testify at the grand jury. Charley Wayne Brogdon had been a serious alcoholic since leaving the navy. His criminal record listed over fifty arrests, all for alcohol-related offenses with the exception of one car theft case. At one point, about fifteen years after the bombing, Brogdon lived for several months with Willadean and Bobby Frank Cherry in Washington. Cherry was working as a security guard and made the comment to Brogdon, "Can you believe it? They let me carry a gun after what all I did?"

It was not an incriminating statement in and of itself, but it was one of the pieces that became meaningful when put together, and that was what they were doing—piecing together a puzzle.

Fleming called the nearest FBI agents in Florida, where Brogdon now lived, and told them, "We got a guy we've never seen we need to bring up to Birmingham to testify. He's an alcoholic. Can you deliver him to the bus depot? Just pick him up and take him to the bus depot."

The agents agreed. When Brogdon's bus was due to arrive, Fleming went to the depot to pick him up. He waited for three hours, thinking Brogdon might have had to catch a later bus. Finally he went home and called the Florida agent. "What's the story, guys? He didn't get off the bus."

"Yeah, yeah," the agent said. "We left him at the bus depot, but we found out later he just went home. Apparently, he had some kind of attack or something. He tore off all his clothes, threw his stuff out in the backyard, and . . . um . . . he's sitting in a chair in the backyard now, stark naked."

They tried again. This time—with the help of Brogdon's wife—they got him on a plane.

Fleming called the Florida agents who reported Brogdon actually got on the plane. "Hey guys," Fleming said, "I've never seen him. What does he look like?"

"No problem, you will recognize him."

"How?"

"Don't worry about it, Bill, you'll understand when you see him."

Fleming wondered if the agents were going to accompany Brogdon, but as soon as a man stepped off the plane wearing his circa-1943 Hawaiian shirt with pleated pedal pushers and a Walmart bag for his cleaner going-to-court clothes, Fleming understood.

"How was the flight?" Fleming asked.

"Great," Brogdon said, "after the fifth vodka."

Fleming shook his head, but had to admit, if anyone could handle it, this guy could. He took Brogdon to the men's room where he changed into his circa-1952 Hawaiian shirt and a pair of pants that almost went to his ankles.

With great trepidation, Fleming delivered him to the grand jury, where he did a surprisingly decent job testifying.

25 | POLICE FILES AND STATE GRAND JURY

WHILE THE GRAND JURY testimonies proceeded, Herren chased rumors that old files existed somewhere in Birmingham Police Department, including secret surveillance reports on Martin Luther King. Two of Herren's assignments—one as a police sergeant and one as a case investigator with the FBI—provided answers to the role the police department had played in collecting intelligence during the civil rights era.

In the mid 1980s, when Herren was working Vice and Narcotics, his lieutenant, Dennis Blass, wondered what was in the large black fire safe set in a corner. He had it opened and found surveillance files and photos from the 1950s and '60s. The rumors were true—all the subjects were African American. Birmingham Police Chief Arthur Deutsch authorized donating the files to the Birmingham Library archives.

Other files, supposedly stored in an attic at a fire station, were destroyed by a leak in the roof. In April 2000, however, Fleming and Herren, accompanied by Blanton's attorney David Luker, responded to a report from the police department that some bombing files had been found. By this time, a new building closer to downtown housed the administrative headquarters. The old jail—which had served that purpose—now sat empty.

The files were discovered in an abandoned downstairs room of the old jail used as a storage closet. There were several file cabinets. Papers and boxes were strewn about on the floor. They found some interviews of LeGrand and Cantrell's—Birmingham policemen assigned to the case in the 1960s and '70s—but, to their disappointment, little related directly to the church bombing. The files did reveal two other black youths were killed that same day.

After the church bombing, the city exploded into riots and violence. Martin Luther King warned President Kennedy that "unless immediate federal steps are taken" Birmingham would see the "worst racial holocaust the nation has ever seen." At the request of Police Chief Jamie Moore, Governor Wallace sent 150 troopers into the city and had the National Guard standing by.

On instructions from the attorney general's office, federal marshals escorted Negro children to school the day after the church bombing. Headquarters instructed agents, "No interviews should be conducted after dusk unless absolutely necessary and dictated by pertinent information." Law enforcement tensions were fueled by a report four days after the bombing of a burglary where four cases of dynamite were taken from a DuPont manufacturing plant in nearby Walker County.

The two additional homicides occurred the day of the bombing. In the aftermath of the chaos, sixteen-year-old Johnny Robinson was exchanging stones with white teens and throwing bricks and stones at police officers. He fled down an alley and was shot in the back by police when he refused to halt.

Virgil Ware, a thirteen-year-old African American male, was riding double on a bicycle with his brother on Sandusky Road between two communities north of Birmingham. They had not participated in any of the violence but were simply headed home when two sixteen-year-old white males rode by on a red motorcycle and shot Ware with a .22 rifle. The boys were Eagle Scouts who had been to a Klan rally and purchased a Confederate flag for their motorcycle. The suspects were tried and convicted in juvenile court, so—even though they received only seven-month suspended sentences—reopening the case was not possible.

Both of these tragedies seemed lost in the public's mind, perhaps paling against the drama of the four young girls killed while attending church, but they equally depicted the violence that had simmered and boiled over on September 15, 1963.

When Fleming and Herren interviewed Willadean Cherry in Montana, they spent time with her daughter, Gloria LaDow, who told them about her molestation as a child by her stepfather, Bobby Frank Cherry. As soon as she was old enough to escape him, LaDow joined the air force. Fleming followed up on her account. Her military health records established injuries that supported her story. Since the incident had occurred in an area south of Birmingham, Fleming called Jill Lee, an assistant district attorney in Shelby County. He told her the situation and asked, "What can y'all do?"

Lee told him the difference in ages at the time of the incident made the crime statutory rape. Even though it happened in 1971, in Alabama, the statute of limitations did not apply to any sexual offense against a child under the age of sixteen, and it could still be prosecuted if the victim wanted to come forward. LaDow was in jail in Florida on a misdemeanor charge. She was released under a writ, and a US marshal brought her to Shelby County where she signed an affidavit. A rape charge was filed against Bobby Frank Cherry. At the time, May 2000, Cherry was in Texas. He was picked up there on the felony warrant and jailed.

Despite the walls Herren and Fleming encountered trying to interview Klan wives—with the exception of Willadean Cherry—there was one they felt almost sure they could make some headway with. She had been badly abused by her husband, Augustus Cash, a friend of Bobby Frank Cherry. When Helen Cash opened the door, Herren and Fleming introduced themselves, but before they could explain why they were there, she said, "Is this about the church bombing?" She clasped her hand to her chest. "My husband told me everything, but he would kill me if I told anyone." Augustus Cash was an old man, twenty-seven years older than his wife, confined to a wheelchair and hooked to oxygen, yet she still feared him. And her husband, she said, feared Bobby Frank Cherry.

They left without anything more than they had to begin with. Herren shook his head. "I don't understand it. Even if their husbands beat the devil out of them, they won't talk against them."

"Even if their husbands are dead, they won't talk," Fleming said.

It was hard to know what motivated the wives to such silence. Herren suspected it varied. In some cases, they shared the values of their husbands, although not always. Tee Chambliss had not approved of her husband's doings, though that did not mean she was in favor of desegregation. There were many in the South of the 1920s to 1960s who were appalled at the violence of the Klan but who believed strongly in segregation.

Southerners' positions on the issue of race made for a complex landscape. Many stoutly defended what they felt was the South's cherished way of life. Others, black and white, supported and embraced the civil rights movement, and many, black and white, thought change needed to come gradually, not with protests and demonstrations. If, however, the women of the Klan whom Herren and Fleming interviewed had private opinions that differed from white supremist ideology, they kept it to the inner sanctums of their hearts. Some may have felt loyalty to their husbands or families or feared retaliation from them or the Klan. Even now, the Klan's code of silence held them in an iron grip.

The prosecution team met periodically to discuss the status of the case and review the evidence available on both Blanton and Cherry, the prime suspects. The breakthrough they had hoped for—finding a Klansman who wanted to clear his conscious—had not happened. Although they all believed Blanton was guilty, the case against him was especially weak, and most were hesitant to go forward with the indictment on him.

Jeff Wallace, the Jefferson County deputy district attorney represented the state. He disagreed. "We've waited thirty-seven years to prosecute this case, and we've got to do this right." He had their attention, if not their concurrence. "We need to end this," Wallace insisted, "to bring some resolution to it. Blanton has been a suspect in the minds of the community since the beginning. We can't just not prosecute him. There's not going to be another chance. We need to indict him and present what we have to the court and the people." District Attorney David Barber supported Wallace's position, and Jones agreed to go forward with Blanton's prosecution.

The team decided, however, to test the waters and see if Blanton and Cherry would negotiate over a plea of guilty, and they got word to the defense attorneys that if Cherry and Blanton would give the community the truth about what happened, the prosecutors were willing to talk about a possible plea bargain. Neither defendant responded, and Cherry continued to deny any involvement in the bombing. On May 4, 2000, his attorney told the media Cherry was offered a deal to receive probation if he pleaded to transporting explosives over state lines—a federal offense.

In fact, no probation deal was ever discussed. Either the news media got it wrong, or this was a strategy on the part of the defense attorney.

With concurrence from both US Attorney General Janet Reno and Alabama Attorney General Bill Pryor, the prosecution team moved forward with the next step—calling a state grand jury and asking for indictments on Bobby Frank Cherry and Thomas Blanton. The job of the citizens called to sit on the grand jury was to determine if enough probable cause existed to issue indictments on the suspects. "Probable cause" was not as demanding a standard as "beyond a reasonable doubt," which would be the standard of proof required of the trial jury.

At a grand jury proceeding, only the prosecution would offer evidence about the case. The defense would not be present. Because there was no federal nexus in this case, it was officially handled as a state murder trial. The federal grand jury had been an investigative tool—getting possible suspects and witnesses to testify under oath, but for the state grand jury, only Herren and Fleming and the prosecutors would testify.

They presented what all the witnesses they had interviewed had stated they heard Cherry and Blanton say. Satisfied that enough probable cause existed, the grand jury indicted Cherry and Blanton on May 16, 2000, on four counts of felony murder each and four counts of universal malice murder, meaning the intention to kill was not directed at any particular individual. That part of the indictments read that Thomas Blanton and Bobby Frank Cherry did unlawfully kill the victims "while perpetrating an act greatly dangerous to the lives of others, and evidencing a depraved mind regardless of human life, although without any preconceived purpose to deprive any particular person of life."

The felony murder charge was actually a charge of causing a death while committing an arson and read, "[Thomas Blanton and Bobby Frank Cherry] did unlawfully, intentionally and with malice of forethought perpetrate or attempted to perpetrate an arson . . . by willfully burning or causing to be burned the Sixteenth Street Baptist Church in Birmingham, Jefferson County." Prosecutors were worried they had no evidence to prove any part of the church actually burned, but they had been able to include that charge on the indictment.

The next day, May 17, 2000, Blanton and Cherry turned themselves in. Within forty-eight hours they appeared before Judge Pete Johnson, a formality during which the judge informed them of the charges against

Thomas Blanton (left) and Bobby Frank Cherry (right) at their initial hearing.

Birmingham News/Landov

them and their rights. At that time Charlie Melton, a retired Birmingham homicide detective, was working as Judge Johnson's bailiff. Just before the hearing, he brought the two suspects into the holding room separately. Melton recalled that at first, they did not react to each other. Cherry appeared calm, but Blanton seemed confused and agitated. After some time, Cherry turned to Blanton and said, "You're Thomas Blanton."

"Yeah," Blanton grunted.

"I ain't seen you since then."

Blanton said, "I don't know what the hell I'm doing here; I ain't done nothing."

"I've called headquarters," Cherry said, as if to reassure him.

"What are you talking about?" Blanton asked.

"The group; you remember the group. I've called, and they're sending help."

Melton also recalled Judge Johnson talking about a chair Martin Luther King had sat in when he was arrested. Johnson had taken care to have the chair preserved and placed in the new criminal justice building when the courts were moved. Melton quipped, "Judge, I got the chairs these fellows [Blanton and Cherry] sat in; you want to keep them too?"

Johnson declined.

Prosecutors had hoped to have the additional rape charge on Cherry, but Gloria LaDow failed to show up for court on the case, and the charges were dropped.

It was the prosecution team's intention to try both Blanton and Cherry together. They were worried about the strength of the cases. The evidence against Cherry seemed to hang mostly on statements by family members who might have motivations other than good citizenship. Also, they worried Cherry's tendency to brag might be seized upon by the defense with the theory he had not actually participated in the bombing, but only bragged later that he did. They felt the evidence made a stronger impact when heard together. That strategy fell apart in November 2000 when Cherry's lawyers presented a psychiatric evaluation that claimed Cherry had dementia and was incompetent to stand trial. Judge

Garrett indefinitely postponed Cherry's trial. The news shook up the prosecution team and the community.

Lack of physical evidence was a gnawing concern for the prosecutors, but nothing had been found in the debris that had been sent off. They explored the possibility of pulling up tile in the church basement and trying to run tests for the presence of nitrates, which would indicate explosive residue. When the FBI lab said it had been too long ago and would be a waste of time, they abandoned the idea.

The prosecutor's case on Blanton depended primarily on testimony from the informant Mitch Burns and what they had been able to glean from the tapes. But Burns was still refusing to testify. On a hunch or inspiration, Fleming contacted the FBI agent who had first shown Mitch Burns the autopsy photos of the four girls and had convinced Burns to befriend Thomas Blanton. After ten years, with constant threats on his life, Agent Blake had retired from the FBI. Now in his eighties, the aging agent answered the call and flew to Birmingham to talk to his old friend and former informant. Mitch Burns agreed to testify.

One of Burns's grown daughters wanted to attend the trial. Burns was not happy about her hearing what was on the tapes. Many surprising revelations had come out on those "Trunk Tapes." The conversations of Blanton and Burns were full of violence and prurience.

Herren offered to talk to Burns's daughter to explain what she would hear her father say on the tapes was not "real." He had been acting a part, doing a very brave thing to help solve a terrible crime. It was not the most comfortable job Herren had ever been called on to do.

26 | THE KITCHEN TAPE

THE THREE REEL-TO-REEL TAPES Fleming had sent to the lab in 1997 had been returned, along with cassette copies. They couldn't risk subjecting the fragile originals to the constant stopping-starting process involved in trying to transcribe them, but they could use the cassettes. When the tapes came back from the lab, they were designated Q1, Q2, and Q3. Despite the noise of the road on the Burns/Blanton tapes and of dishes being washed and other background noise on the Kitchen Tapes, they were able to make out bits and pieces, but so far, they had not found the elusive conversation between Blanton and his wife about a meeting and the planning and/or making of a bomb. Herren, in particular, spent a great deal of time listening to the cassettes. But that, like everything else, went on hold during the Sanbomb investigation of the Birmingham abortion clinic.

When he finally returned to the case, Herren reviewed the background of the making of the Kitchen Tapes. In 1964 John "Slim" Colvin was an electronic technician with the FBI. That June, nine months after the church bombing, he rode by Thomas Blanton's house in an area called West End and noticed a FOR RENT sign on one side of the duplex. He reported it, and SAC Ray Faisst instructed him to lease the apartment. Thomas Blanton still lived with his wife and his father in half of the duplex. Colvin rented the vacant attached apartment. In order to cover his absences, Colvin "explained" he was a long-haul truck driver.

In 1997, federal wiretap or electronic eavesdropping laws required a court order—in 1964 when the bugging took place, there were no such laws or court cases. The authority to grant permission for a wiretap rested with the executive branch of government. Prior to, and especially after, the church bombing, the struggle for civil rights engendered violence and the threat of violence, prompting Attorney General Robert Kennedy to issue an order giving permission for the FBI to proceed with electronic surveillance on Blanton for national security purposes.

To cover the sounds of installing the microphone, Colvin asked permission to put up shelves in the closet in his apartment. The closet wall was a common wall between that apartment and Tommy Blanton's residence. Colvin and Ralph Butler—the same agent who had set up the tapes in the trunk of Burn's car—removed the baseboard in the closet and placed the bug against the outer wall of Blanton's kitchen, near a small existing hole. What they didn't realize at first was the microphone was right under the kitchen sink. Herren and Fleming dubbed them the Kitchen Sink Tapes.

Agents had transcribed a short section of one of those tapes with a very interesting conversation between Blanton and his wife. This was the tape Fleming dearly wanted to get his hands on. But after listening to the tapes he had found—Q1, Q2, and Q3—he realized that conversation was not on any of them. The ELSUR (electronic surveillance) clerk had looked twice and reported there were no more tapes in the evidence room. But there was a transcript, so there had to be more tapes somewhere.

The inventory paperwork documenting the existence of the tapes was dated 1981. At that time electronic surveillance evidence was kept in the SAC's safe, but at some point, an ELSUR evidence room had been set up, and the tapes were moved there. On July 19, 2000, Fleming decided to go look himself.

The evidence room was not the orderly place Fleming had hoped for; but on the other hand, the disorderly piles of boxes gave rise to the hope the treasure he sought could indeed be somewhere within. Perhaps—like the Ark of the Covenant in *Raiders of the Lost Ark*—it lay there lost in government bureaucracy over the past thirty-seven years, misfiled or mislabeled or perhaps just moved aside. Fortunately, the FBI's evidence room was not nearly as massive as the government warehouse in that movie. The tapes should have been in a round folder tied with a string and stored in the metal cabinet where the first three tapes had been found. There were no more such tapes in the cabinet.

Fleming carefully went through everything he could find that would be the necessary size for the large reel-to-reels, regardless of what the label said. He finally gave up and was leaving when he spotted an unmarked cardboard box in the corner near the trash bin. It looked at home there, a discarded box waiting for its turn to be taken out with the garbage. When he opened the dusty box, he found fourteen reel-to-reel tapes.

"You are a bulldog," Herren told his partner. "Once you get on a pant leg, you won't turn loose."

It was a breakthrough moment, weighty with potential. In the unlikely event they could find something useful on them, they would be gold—if not, they were as useless as the dust coating them.

The fourteen tapes were sent to the FBI lab immediately. On November 11, 2000, Fleming received an official opinion regarding the tapes from general counsel in Washington, DC. As Fleming had worried all along, the Bureau's attorneys confirmed the tapes were inadmissible based on a 1967 US Supreme Court ruling, *Katz v. US*. In *Katz*, a bug had been placed on the outside of a phone booth to record the phone conversations. In ruling on that case, the Supreme Court set the standard of expectation of privacy and established the requirement of a warrant to authorize a bug. No warrant had been issued for the bugs in either Mitch Burns's car or against the wall of Thomas Blanton's kitchen, because four years prior to the *Katz* decision, warrants were not required.

In addition to the official legal opinion, the Washington attorneys told Fleming there wasn't a snowball's chance in hell of getting the transcripts or tapes admitted as evidence. Fleming relayed to Doug Jones that the DC counselors said the Birmingham office was wasting their time. Jones didn't seem surprised at the news. "Let's see if we find something first, then we'll worry about getting it into evidence."

The fourteen reel-to-reel recordings covered a substantial period of time. As soon as the lab returned cassette copies of the tapes, secretaries from the steno pool and clerks were corralled to help with the massive job of transcribing them. Herren spent weekends and holidays listening to the tapes, playing them over and over, trying to fill in words the stenos couldn't make out. It was tedious and frustrating work.

Herren and Fleming had reached a point where they were ready to admit defeat finding the Kitchen Tape recording that matched the transcript when an excited lady in the steno pool called Agent Fleming: "You've got to hear this—come down now!" Fleming joined her immediately. She was literally bouncing with anticipation and had him put on the headphones to listen. He was elated. She had found the conversation they had been looking for! It was on a section of tape the lab labeled "Q9." Fleming heard the words himself and immediately called Doug Jones.

Jones's reaction startled Fleming: "Oh God, tell me you didn't hear it." Then he started warning about building a Chinese wall. Neither Fleming nor Herren knew what he was talking about. The tape excerpt was a critical piece of evidence that would confirm Blanton's connection in the bombing, regardless of whether it could be used in court or not. Their elation was dashed when they learned they could have been "tainted" by hearing the evidence. The tapes had been made in the 1960s under national security authorization. Herren and Fleming were listening to them for a criminal investigation. Jones's concern was they may have breached the Chinese wall that divided the two interests.

When they met with Jones, he said, "Don't tell me what was on the tape," obviously not wanting to be tainted himself. "But was it good?" he asked eagerly.

"It's good," Herren replied.

"Really good?"

"It was really good."

"Did he mention the word?"

Herren knew Jones meant "bomb." He nodded. "He mentioned the word."

"What kind of clearance did they have to plant the transmitter?" Jones asked, wanting to make sure the bugging was lawful. "It wasn't a black bag job, was it?"

"They didn't have warrants," Fleming said, "but they had authorization from Robert Kennedy."

Jones wanted the paperwork in hand. "Get it from Washington."

"Jones, we can't use any of the tapes," Fleming reminded him. "You know they couldn't use them in '63. Headquarters says there is no chance of using them."

"You watch," Jones said.

27 | ENHANCING THE TAPES

US ATTORNEY DOUG JONES told Fleming to send the original reel-to-reel tape containing the pertinent Q9 Kitchen Tape conversation and a few other promising sections to Forensic Audio in Los Angeles, California, to see if they could enhance the tapes and pick out any more words. Anthony Pellicano, dubbed the detective to the stars, owned Forensic Audio. He was known for his expertise in enhancing tape recordings. "Pellicano is the best," Jones said.

On January 8, 2001, Fleming sent the original reel-to-reel tapes and transcripts to Forensic Audio with a request to digitize the audio and enhance the recordings. Aware of the importance of this evidence, Pellicano videoed every step of the process, beginning with the moment he received the reel-to-reel tapes, so there could be no accusation he had tampered with them. He returned the original tapes, along with the enhanced versions on CDs, and a transcript of what he had heard.

The transcript Pellicano sent back for Q9 did not differ much from what they had sent him. He did note, however, that there was a third voice on the tape, something they had not realized. Once they knew, they could distinguish the separate voice. It was an exciting development, because it raised the possibility they might be able to overcome one of the legal challenges to getting the tape introduced as evidence—the husband-wife privilege. The presence of a third person during the communication eliminated confidentiality and eradicated the privilege.

Jones also wanted a third party—with no connections to the FBI and no knowledge of what they were looking for—to listen to the Q9 Kitchen Tape and see if the same words would be heard. The Internal Revenue Service's criminal division often sent tapes to Belle Mills, a blind woman with particularly sensitive hearing, to get objective transcripts. Fleming and Herren tracked Mills down and had her listen to Q9. She confirmed what they had heard and was able to pick out a few more precious words.

At the time of the church bombing, Carolyn Jean Casey (or Jean Casey) was a young teenager and Blanton's girlfriend. He married her shortly afterward to make sure she wouldn't testify against him. She was Blanton's alibi to the FBI in 1963. He claimed they were sleeping on her sofa the night the bomb was placed. "Jean won't testify against me," Blanton told a fellow Klansman, not knowing he was talking to a government informant.

After the investigation was closed, Blanton divorced Jean Casey. When Bill Baxley reopened the case in the 1970s, Blanton remarried her, presumably to be able to claim the spousal testimonial privilege; Jean Casey, as his wife, could not be required to testify against him. He divorced her again after the state closed its investigations and possibly would have married her a third time when the FBI opened the case again, except she had married someone else.

When the media released the news of this new investigation being opened, Blanton told one of his former employers, "I hope my alibi is still good, because my alibi is [now] my ex-wife. But she is the mother of our child."

When Herren and Fleming brought Jean Casey into Doug Jones's office to interview her and play the tapes for her, they were set to confront her about the third voice. She confirmed the voices they heard were hers and Blanton's, and unasked, she also mentioned one voice was that of another person who had been present, although she couldn't remember who it was. This was a gift for the prosecution.

Jean Casey told investigators she was aware Thomas Blanton had married her to prevent her testifying against him in the church bombing. She said she had not been out with him on Saturday night before the bombing as he claimed. "And," she added, "he did not fall asleep with me on our couch until 2:00 AM. That would never have happened, because my daddy wouldn't let it happen."

On the Friday night before, Blanton stood her up, calling about 5:30 PM and canceling his date with her. She thought he went out with his part-time girlfriend, Waylene. That put into context what Herren and Fleming had heard on the Q9 Kitchen Tape.

After setting up the microphone in the wall of the duplex apartment a few months after the bombing, the FBI paid a visit to Jean Casey, who was now Blanton's wife, hoping to spur the very conversation later caught on tape. When Blanton came home, she told him the FBI had been by, and he, of course, wanted to know what she told them. The first voice was Jean's complaining in a high-pitched, whiney tone:

"You never bothered to tell me," Jean says, "what you went to the river for, Tommy."

"What did you tell them I did?" Blanton asks.

"You didn't even—"

"What did you tell them I did at the river?" Blanton asks again. "What did they ask you I did at the river?"

"They asked me what you went for and I told them I didn't know."

"They were interested in that [other] meeting I went to. They know I went to the meeting. OK? So they knew I was at the meeting."

"What meeting?"

"The Big One."

"What meeting?"

"The meeting where we planned the bomb."

"Tommy, what meeting are you talking about *now?*"

"We had to have a meeting to make a bomb."

"I know that."

"I think I'll wear this sh— I'm going to wear this shirt."

"Is that what you were doing that Friday night when you stood me up?" Jean asks.

". . . Oh, we were making the bomb."

"Really? Modern Sign shop?"

"Yeah."

"I think what got me is when they told me at Modern . . . some people at Modern Sign Company said you weren't there."

"Who said I wasn't there?" Blanton asks.

"Jean," a third person says, ". . . don't you learn anything with the FBI? Every breath they utter is a lie."

"I know," Jean says, "but I didn't know that then and I didn't know whether to think you stood me up to go out with somebody else. That's the first thing that hit me. . . . You stood me up to go out with Waylene."

"That's what they want to do, to make you mad," the third voice says.

Herren, Fleming, and the prosecutors believed the bomb was made, or at least finished, the night of Friday, September 13, or Saturday, September 14. In 1963 Cherry told FBI agents he was at the sign shop on Friday night. When Herren and Bob Eddy interviewed Cherry in Texas in 1997, Cherry said it was Saturday night. Waylene Vaughn (Blanton's girlfriend) said Friday night Blanton was out with her—just as Jean Casey had feared. Waylene Vaughn remembered that particular Friday night, because it was her last date with Blanton. She left for the military a week later.

Despite the tangled knots in the web woven by the differing stories, the significance of the tape was the admission out of Blanton's own mouth that he had participated with others in planning and making the bomb, the "Big One," shortly before Bapbomb.

28 | PREPARING FOR TRIAL

GEORGE W. BUSH REPLACED Bill Clinton as president of the United States in January 2001, but at the time Bush did not exercise the tradition of replacing the local US attorney with an attorney from his own political party. He kept Doug Jones as US attorney while the case was being pursued. The other federal members of the team were Assistant US Attorney Robert Posey; Robin Beardsley and Amy Gallimore, Jones's law clerk and assistant, respectively; and Andy Shelton, a trial consultant. John Ott, who had been the original US assistant attorney on the case, had retired in April of 1998.

Once a distrusted outsider, Herren was now redacting informant files to be given to the defense attorneys during the process termed discovery. It took several weeks to go through it all, blacking out the names of confidential informants or other information not to be specifically presented in trial. Additional copies of the tape recordings had been ordered for the defense.

To their relief, Jones's concerns about Herren and Fleming hearing the evidence on the tapes did not become an issue. The challenge to admitting the tapes would primarily be whether the original taping had violated Blanton's constitutional rights, specifically his Fourth Amendment protections against unreasonable search and seizure. The general counsel attorneys had already given their opinion that there was no chance of getting the tapes introduced. Jones and the prosecution team would have to come up with a compelling argument to the contrary in order to get the tapes admitted as evidence. It was sure to be a battle.

Herren and Fleming kept busy lining up witnesses and any other evidence to be presented, and made a return trip to the public library. The trial would be the culmination of all their work, but Herren cautioned himself not to get his hopes up too high or get too caught up in the desire to get a conviction. There was a lot going against them. He heard his own voice instructing the new detectives in his unit: "Your job is to get the best evidence you can and get it ready for court. Just get your evidence in a legal way, so it doesn't get thrown out or create a problem with testimony. Whatever the prosecutors do, or the judge, or the jury, that's out of your control."

He had seen cases lost that should have been won. If you put your heart in there, you were going to end up bitter. This was an important case, but he and Fleming had done their best and given it a chance to be heard by the people.

It did chafe him, however, when he was asked if he believed Blanton and Cherry were really guilty. His answer was always the same: "If I didn't believe it, they'd never go to court. Yes, they were guilty." Attorneys had to look at their jobs differently; they represented both the innocent and the guilty. But a law enforcement officer's job was to pursue the guilty and exonerate the innocent.

Some people had the perception that political pressure drove the investigation, but to the contrary, the position of the legal department at headquarters had always been of the not-a-snowball's-chance-in-hell-you'll-ever-be-able-to-get-this-to-court-or-convict variety. Once they had followed all the leads, he and Fleming could have killed the investigation if they felt it was stymied. There had been plenty of times when it felt that way, but then a witness would step forward and get them all excited again . . . if only they could keep them all alive to testify.

One very promising witness in the Chambliss case had died in a hotel only days before an interview with Bob Eddy. Fleming and Herren worried especially about the health of Mike Gowins, who was dying of asbestos poisoning, but any of their elderly witnesses could die at any point.

Blanton's defense filed several motions that could have stopped the proceedings or hindered their case. Circuit Court Judge Garrett held hearings to decide on each one. One of the first claims was that the delay of a trial "intentionally garnered a tactical advantage" for the prosecution and denied Blanton due process. The defense claimed their case was hindered by the deaths of exculpatory witnesses, who would have been able to provide testimony favorable to Cherry. Also, they claimed the prosecution gained an advantage because of the cultural changes over the years. In other words, the defense claimed the state decided to prosecute now because "the jury pool was predisposed to its case." The prosecution countered this by arguing the long delay did not produce an advantage to the prosecution, because key witnesses for their side had also died.

Not surprisingly, the defense filed a motion to suppress the Q9 tape. In a criminal proceeding in Alabama, spouses could not be compelled to testify against each other, but could choose to do so. Alabama law also gave spouses a confidential communications privilege, which meant a person could refuse to testify, or *prevent their spouse* from testifying about any confidential communication made during the marriage. If a communication was made privately to a spouse and not intended for disclosure to any other person, it was considered confidential. The third voice on the Q9 Kitchen Tape—coupled with Jean Casey's testimony there was another person present when she had the conversation with her husband—negated any objection on the grounds of spousal confidentiality.

But the legality of all the tapes was hotly contested by the defense on other grounds as well. The current governing law concerning wiretaps, which required court approval (a warrant), was not passed by Congress until 1968. In 1963, however, the executive branch of government could approve electronic surveillance for national security purposes. The prosecution team set about establishing the legality of the tapes by first showing the national security need for intelligence. They presented evidence about the social unrest and violence of the time, the grave concern over communist influence, the assassination of the president, and the church bombing and subsequent riots. The evidentiary problem remaining was the fact that wiretaps at that time were only allowed for intelligence gathering purposes, not for evidence in a criminal case. Hence, the tape was not legal for the purposes of the trial.

The prosecution team overcame this daunting legal challenge by bringing to the court's attention the evolution of the interpretations made by the US Supreme Court over the years. The 1968 law called for the exclusion of evidence if the law was not followed. If police illegally taped a conversation, the court would throw the evidence out, considering it the poisoned fruit of the poisonous tree. Over the years, however, the Supreme Court began to make exceptions to that fruit of the poisonous tree rule. Exceptions were granted for good faith—when law enforcement operated under the mistaken belief their actions were legal—and for inevitable discovery, that is, when the evidence would have come forth regardless of law enforcements' actions. The exclusionary rule was not meant as punishment or to allow the guilty to go free, but to deter law enforcement from disregarding the legal rules of obtaining evidence. It should be balanced by the need to seek the truth. In this case, the prosecution argued, there was no preventative value in excluding evidence obtained many years before the law even existed. The court should, therefore, rule in favor of the truth-seeking process. Judge Garrett agreed and allowed the tape to be submitted as evidence.

Another hearing was held to determine whether the prosecution could show the 1957 film footage that depicted the attack by Cherry and others as Reverend Shuttlesworth tried to integrate Phillips High School. Normally such a thing would not be allowed on the grounds it would prejudice or inflame the jury, but prosecutors argued the purpose of playing the film was to show Cherry's motivation and his mindset at the time, and Judge Garrett allowed it into evidence for that purpose.

It was during these preliminary hearings that David Luker, Blanton's lawyer, came over to speak to Herren. Luker had been a Birmingham police officer, and they knew each other, though not well. "Ben, you done good on this one," he said.

"We're just bringing a case to trial," Herren replied.

"No, you've hit a home run."

Shortly after, for unknown reasons, David Luker stepped down as Tommy Blanton's defense attorney.

29 | THE TRIAL OF THOMAS BLANTON

IN FEBRUARY 2001, JUDGE Garrett appointed John Robbins to represent Blanton. Robbins was a respected defense attorney, an alumnus of Cumberland School of Law like Doug Jones. Robbins complained about the limited amount of time he had to prepare for the case, which was scheduled for trial in April. He spent only two days, however, with the discovery evidence Fleming and Herren had painstakingly put together.

In April 2001, only one week before the selection of jurors was scheduled, Judge Garrett held another hearing on Cherry's inability to aid his defense. Lacking evidence to the contrary, he put Cherry's case indefinitely on hold.

Originally, the prosecutors thought their strongest case was against Cherry, but the development of the Q9 Kitchen Tape segment reversed their assessment. Now the Blanton case appeared the stronger of the two. Jeff Wallace, the assistant district attorney assigned to the case, particularly welcomed this exciting development, as he had pushed for Blanton's indictment in spite of the weakness in the government's case.

Jury selection for Blanton's trial began April 15, 2001. Eight white women, three black women, and one black man were selected, and the trial began April 25, 2001. Judge Garrett, who had presided at the pretrial hearings, was also the trial judge. He had served on the bench for twenty-eight years. Herren believed his first testimony in court as a police officer had been before Garrett, and he thought well of him. They had been very fortunate in his rulings so far.

Garrett chose to hear the trial in the Mel Bailey Criminal Justice Building, referred to locally as the old courthouse because a newer one had been built across the street. The courtroom was larger than the new one, providing a balcony level and a lower level. Three stories below the courtroom, on the walls of the building's lobby, were two large murals. One displayed an elegantly dressed white woman looking down over black slaves toiling in fields. On the other a white businessman overlooked black workers in an iron mill.

At the trial, the families of the four young girls sat in the front row. Herren knew each one—Chris and Maxine McNair, the parents of Denise McNair; Alpha Robertson, mother of Carole Robertson; Sarah Collins Rudolph and Junie Collins Peavy, who were Addie Mae Collins's sisters; and Dr. Shirley Wesley King, Cynthia Wesley's adopted stepsister. Witnesses, other than victims, were normally not allowed in a courtroom except when they took the stand, under the presumption their testimony might be influenced by what they heard. The defense agreed to allow an exception to that rule, perhaps acknowledging the families were all victims and deserved to hear the proceedings.

The investigators sat at the prosecutor's table when they could. Herren and Fleming's duties would call them in and out of the courtroom, preparing witnesses and organizing evidence. This was the prosecutor's show, but there was still much work to be done behind the scenes. Herren would be required to be in court when the recordings were played, to queue up the tapes.

For the prosecution, US Attorney Doug Jones began the opening remarks. As planned, he painted a picture of the time when struggles to desegregate schools and lunch counters met with violent resistance from the Ku Klux Klan.

Ladies and gentlemen, it's been a long time, thirty-seven . . . almost thirty-eight years.

There were people, and Thomas E. Blanton was one of them, who saw their segregated way of life dissolving and couldn't stand it.

What is important about '63 was not just the political and social changes, because in a bitter sense, 1963 in Birmingham was about killing. It was about youth. It was the youth who marched in the spring of '63. And they met at the Sixteenth Street Baptist Church.

A photo of a children's march was displayed on the screen.

And later it was again the youth in September that had to walk into what had been segregated schools. The youth were on the front lines in Birmingham. The two most powerful things in Birmingham in 1963 were not just the leaders that we've all heard about over the years. The two most powerful and constant things in 1963 were the youth and the churches. And most importantly, the Sixteenth Street Baptist Church. And that's what was attacked. . . .

The evidence will show that . . . for a whole week prior to this explosion, the bombing, there was a marquee outside advertising youth services. Whoever, I submit, planted that bomb knew that this was going to be a youth service. That is a reasonable inference. . . . The church was a target. The youth was [sic] a target. The people that perpetrated this terrible tragedy knew exactly where they were going and who they wanted to kill.

On the screen Smith had set up, the 1957 film rolled and then photographs of the girls—whole and beautiful, posing in pretty dresses. Photos of the explosion's raw aftermath followed. One photo showed a clock hanging on the wall in the Social Cleaners store across the street from the church. The bomb had stopped the clock at 10:24 AM.

"When the bomb went off, the clock stopped and time for Birmingham stood still," Jones said.

It was dramatic, but it was true.

Jones laid out what he expected the evidence to show, giving the jury a road map.

For the defense, John Robbins said in his own opening remarks, "Mr. Blanton's segregationist beliefs did not prove he was a bomber. The prosecution's case against Mr. Blanton is utterly circumstantial." He emphasized the jury should not be swayed by the emotions evoked by the girls' deaths. "This case is not a popularity contest pitting Mr. Blanton against four young innocents. . . . They want you to decide this

The clock in the store across the street stopped at moment of the bombing.

Larry Harris

case on the emotion of the moment. They want you to not analyze this case. They want you to decide it on a gut level, because they know every human being, if you decided a case on a gut level, you would decide in favor of those four girls. But the court of law can't operate that way no matter how much we try. . . .

"You're not going to like Tom Blanton. You're not going to like some of the things he said. He was twenty-five years old. He was a loudmouth. He was annoying. He was a segregationist, and he ran his mouth about that. He was a thorn in the FBI's side. He was annoying as hell. But just because you don't like him and the views he espoused, doesn't make him responsible for this tragedy." He cautioned the jury, "It's not about closure. It's not about removing the tarnished image that Birmingham has, or you may feel Birmingham has, because of what happened here in the '60s."

The prosecution began the presentation of their evidence, calling Reverend Cross, the pastor of the Sixteenth Street Baptist Church in 1963. He described that Sunday morning as he remembered it, how he searched through the rubble of the basement. "We discovered a fresh body and removed that one and then a second body. They were all stacked on top of another . . . in that same pile, as if they were clung together after the bombing."

Alpha Robertson, Carole Robertson's mother, testified from her wheelchair about rushing to the church. Her shock relived at seeing the devastation before her and realizing her child was dead was obvious to Fleming and, he was sure, the jury.

"When Carole left for Sunday school, was she going to participate in the youth service that day?" Jones asked her.

"Oh yes, she was. . . . She was going to be an usher. She had on a little white dress and a new purse and little black patent leather pumps."

"And when she left for Sunday school that morning, did you see her alive again?"

"No."

Jones asked, "Did Carole have a Bible with her that day?"

"Yes, she had a Bible with her that day, and I have that Bible now. From the rubble came her Bible and wallet and billfold with pictures of school."

Maxine McNair struggled with her emotions. "We heard this loud noise and everybody was taken aback, didn't know what it was all about. We had been accustomed to hearing loud noises. But the first thing I said was, 'My baby, oh, my baby.' I don't know why I said that."

Junie Collins Peavy took the stand. "I got there [to the church] a little early because I was . . . playing the piano for the youth department. . . . When it was over with, everybody went to their Sunday school class. And for some reason, Carole Roberston came up to me and we started talking. . . . She had on her white dress and black shoes, I believe. Looked real pretty. We were talking about the Youth Day program. And she was telling me about how she was going to participate in that program, and she was real nervous, and she couldn't wait until it was over. So I tried to kind of encourage her, you know? It will be OK."

It had not been OK, Fleming thought. Not for Carole Roberston or her friends or their families.

In 1963 Jack Owens worked with the Birmingham Fire Department. The explosion shook Fire Station 1, a few blocks from the church. A cloud of dust rose from the church and covered the street as they arrived at the scene.

Richard Harris, a field supervisor with Alabama Gas, had checked the gas lines and found them undamaged.

Outside the jury's hearing, a battle raged over a video. The FBI had recorded an explosion on the Marine explosives range at Quantico, Virginia, to show the jury what a high explosive shockwave did to vehicles, so that the jury could compare the effect on the vehicles with the photos from the scene. Ten pounds of dynamite were used in the taped explosion. The prosecution also wanted the jury to note the size of the crater left in the ground, which was considerably smaller than the one at the church.

In arguing why the prosecution should be allowed to show the video to the jury, US Assistant Attorney Robert Posey told Judge Garrett he anticipated the defense would claim the bomb was thrown out of a passing car. Establishing the amount or weight of the dynamite was relevant to counter the practicality of this argument. Although the FBI experts had privately given estimates in the range of forty to fifty pounds, they refused to testify as to the weight of the dynamite. There were too many unknown factors, such as the strength of dynamite used and the effect of the concrete stairs over the bomb, which concentrated the blast down and to the sides. The prosecution attorneys were hoping the jury would reach their own conclusions.

The defense argued, "What the prosecution wants to do is just blow up something because, you know why? Because we're in the Sixteenth Street bombing case."

The judge allowed the video without the sound or the slow motion segment.

Special Agent Mark Whitworth with the FBI Explosives Unit took the stand. Whitworth had worked bombing scenes in Pakistan and Saudi Arabia and was the coordinating examiner for the forensic evidence from the USS *Cole* bombing in Yemen. The rippling effect on the cars at the scene, he said, was due to the shockwave of expanding gas. Punctures in the sides of the cars were "high energy and impact damage from projectiles that the explosives picked up." He laid out the differences between types of explosives. "In a high explosive, the detonation wave or shockwave . . . is faster than the speed of sound in that material. The material is entirely consumed, and it converts this solid material into a very large volume of gas which produces a shockwave." He explained that the shockwave emanates from the explosive like a giant bubble of super dense air, slamming into whatever it meets. The creation of the ground hole outside the basement window was caused by the shockwave of the explosive hitting the ground below it and ejecting all of that material out of that area. The concrete stairs over the bomb would have increased the force that went downward and to the sides.

Another expert witness, retired special agent Charles Killion, explained it was not unusual to be unable to find the detonation device. "The material can just simply be consumed in the blast. . . . It may be traveling at eighteen thousand feet a second . . . [and it] might be unfindable."

On the defense cross-examination, Killion stated it was very dangerous to use a fuse, because "it will appear . . . not to be lit and in fact it is." When Robbins asked him if it were possible for a bomb to be lit and thrown, Killion agreed it was.

When Waylene Vaughn, Blanton's old girlfriend, was called to the stand, Deputy District Attorney Jeff Wallace questioned her for the prosecution. Vaughn said she first met Blanton at the Greyhound bus station where she worked at the lunch counter. She was not a member of the KKK, but she had gone with Blanton to social functions and meetings. He never told her he had participated in the bombing, but twice Blanton drove to the Safeway Grocery Store on Finley Avenue in front of the Farmer's Market. The store was frequented by black people. Blanton poured a substance that would burn skin, but not fabric, on the seats of several cars in the store parking lot.

She didn't know what the substance was, but he called it acid and let her smell it. She said, "It's the type smell that you jerk your head away from it once you smelled it."

On another occasion, he wrapped the bottle of acid in a handkerchief and took it inside the grocery store. When he came out, he said, "They'll be closing this damn place in a little bit, because I just put it in the meat counter." He then added, "This damn store is ran [sic] by Jews that wait on nobody but damn niggers."

Blanton started talking to her about dynamite and fuses once, but she didn't understand what he was saying and wasn't interested. Referring to instances of bombings reported in the newspapers, Blanton's response was, "They should kill more of them."

One night on the way to her home, he threw a bottle of the acid at a group of men and women standing outside a black nightclub. To their consternation, a car immediately followed them, pulling in front of Blanton's vehicle at an intersection and blocking their path. Vaughn remembered seeing a black woman in the backseat of that car. "She looked as frightened as I was at the time."

The men got out of their car and approached. "They said they were going to beat the hell out of both of us." Blanton pulled a .45 automatic he always kept under the dash, held it out the window, and chambered a round. One of the men approaching them warned, "He's got a gun!" They hastily returned to their car and left.

On another occasion, Blanton tried to run over a man who was crossing the street. "And the black male jumped, bodily, dived for the curb. . . . I screamed, and he [Blanton] says, 'All I want is a chance to kill one of those black bastards.'"

Waylene Vaughn testified Blanton had taken her out on September 13, 1963, the Friday before the Sunday explosion at the church. They had gone to a drive-in theater, and he had taken her home after midnight.

Fleming watched as Robbins rose to cross-examine Vaughn, remembering the first trip to south Alabama to see her, the tiny run-down place she lived in, his impression of how hard life had been on her. He and Doug Jones had gone to convince her she was needed. She did not want to testify and still feared the Klan, but she had come.

Robbins began the cross-examination with disbelief evident in his voice. "You professed you're not a segregationist, not a racist, but you attended two Klan rallies and a Christmas party sponsored by the Klan?"

"That's true."

"You didn't break the date off," Robbins pressed, ". . . and say, well, why don't you take me home?"

"That's correct."

"You didn't report this to the police, did you?"

Vaughn replied, "During that time frame it would have been a waste of time to report that type of thing to the police."

"You didn't find the Klan sexy?" Robbins asked.

"Oh, God, no."

"But you hung out with Tommy Blanton and would shack up in motels around this town with him, right?"

She was silent for a moment. "If you want to put it that way."

"Well," Robbins said sharply, "I'm putting it exactly in your words. You dislike what he stands for, but you didn't dislike him enough not to go to some hotel room during this time and perform oral sex on him, did you?

Sitting stiffly, she met his gaze. "That's correct."

Anger flooded Fleming at how Robbins had pushed her and embarrassed her. At the same time, Fleming was proud of her. He knew what Robbins was doing, trying to get her to lie. And she hadn't lied.

At this point, plans had been to bring James Lay to the stand. Lay was the man who volunteered in the Negro Civil Defense in the 1960s. An important witness, he had seen white men in a black 1957 Ford parked beside the church two weeks before the bombing, possibly scaring them off when he flashed his bright lights on them. One of the white men was outside the car near the bush under the church's back stairs with a black ditty bag.

When Fleming went to the post office where Lay worked to interview him, he found Lay celebrating at his retirement party. Fleming offered to return to speak with him another time, but Lay insisted on talking. He had not testified at Chambliss's trial, a fact that always puzzled Fleming. Lay seemed like the kind of man who would testify without hesitation. He had stood in front of an angry mob after the bomb exploded and voluntarily patrolled the streets at night.

According to Bob Eddy, Baxley tried to get Lay to testify. Baxley even had Denise McNair's father, Chris McNair, invite him to breakfast and try to talk him into testifying, to no avail. Lay's refusal to testify caused Bill Baxley's temper to flare, but even when Baxley called him a coward, Lay still declined, saying alternately that he couldn't remember or that he had told the FBI everything back in the 1960s and they wouldn't heed him, so he wasn't talking to them again almost twenty years later. Baxley had him subpoenaed and kept him in a witness room throughout the trial.

When Fleming interviewed Lay, two decades later, Lay's story was that Baxley refused to let him testify, locking him up in a room. The investigators also learned Paul D. White—the other man who had verified Lay's story to the FBI (although never claiming to identify the suspects)—had not really seen anything. White lived in a boarding room across the street behind the church. Lay apparently saw him arrive home. He knocked on the door and asked White if anyone from the radio station had dropped him off or followed him. White said no.

Lay wanted to call the police that night and report what he had seen, but he knew a single black man's word without corroboration was worthless—or perhaps he wanted a witness for a late-night encounter with the police. In any case, he roused White out of his bed and asked him to back up his story. Even with two witnesses, the policeman's response to his report was, "You ain't seen a damn thing, boy."

When subpoenaed to the federal grand jury in 1998, however, Lay did tell his story. The prosecution team's excitement at his testimony turned into concern when they learned Lay had suffered a stroke and could not appear before the trial court. They preserved his testimony because a statement to the grand jury is under oath, so they asked the judge if someone could read Lay's grand jury testimony to the court. Judge Garrett agreed.

Who should have this man's voice? Fleming was initially going to read the statement, but in a flash of inspiration, Herren asked, "What about Shelly Stewart?" Shelly Stewart had been in the Civil Defense unit with Lay. He was a well-known local black radio host.

Silence reigned in the courtroom as Doug Jones asked the same questions Lay had been asked at the grand jury, and Stewart's deep, resonant voice gave Lay's testimony.

For cross-examination, Robbins called Fleming to the stand. Robbins questioned Fleming about Lay's army records. Lay was diagnosed as suffering from emotional instability, "dramatic behavior," and suicidal tendencies. He had received shock treatments for his condition.

Robbins also asked about what happened when Lay first arrived at the scene after the explosion. A boy about fourteen years old had told him he had seen the white men who bombed the church. Absorbed in rescue efforts, Lay had never discovered the boy's name, but the FBI agents working the initial case thought they had found him, tracking him down from pictures of the scene published in national magazines. Fleming testified that agents had spoken with Eddie Mauldin, a young black man about that age, but Fleming did not know if that was the same boy with whom Lay had spoken.

———

Assistant US Attorney Robert Posey called William Jackson, the Catholic Klansman groupie Fleming had confronted in Jackson's barber shop. Jackson wore no tie, just Dockers, and no socks. He testified to seeing Blanton and Chambliss at the sign shop the Saturday night before the bombing. "Seems like Tommy was getting something out of the trunk, getting something out of the car, taking it in the sign shop."

On an earlier occasion, Jackson had met Klansmen at Cash's BBQ and then gone with them to the Cahaba River. It was his understanding Chambliss was trying to form his own Klavern. Blanton was there. "Him [Blanton] and Bob [Chambliss] was always buddies." Jackson also testified that Blanton had a hateful attitude toward blacks, Jews, and Catholics. "There was always some threats going on. 'Should hang one,' you know. 'Blow one up. Kill one.'"

He admitted lying to an FBI agent who took him to the city jail in the 1960s to identify Blanton. The reason he gave for telling the agent he didn't know Blanton was that "Tommy was shaking his head."

Posey said, "There were a number of occasions in the past when the FBI would come by that you were not truthful with them?"

"Oh, yeah," Jackson agreed. "I would tell you a lie in a minute."

On his cross-examination, Robbins set about attacking Jackson's credibility, pointing out Jackson was a bigamist and had called Baxley three times asking for reward money. At the end, he raised his voice in an accusation that sounded very much like the one Fleming had thrown at Jackson that day in the barbershop. "You're just a big fat liar, aren't you?"

Fleming watched the next witness closely. The court saw an elderly man in a wheelchair approach the witness stand. Fleming saw a retired FBI agent who had brushed death to be here. Frank Spencer, who was in his eighties, had been a co-interviewer of Blanton back in the 1960s. He and Richard Hanes were the only FBI agents alive who had talked to Blanton and could authenticate Blanton's statements. Fleming and Herren located Spencer in Florida, and Fleming had made the call. Spencer's daughter answered the phone. When Fleming told her who he was, and that they needed her father to testify in the trial, she said, "Oh my goodness, this is just what he needs. He needs to come and testify on this case. His son was murdered a year ago, and he's really down. He needs something positive in his life right now."

Fleming kept in contact with Spencer and sent him his original FBI 302 reports, so he could refresh his memory. His daughter drove him up for the trial, but en route, Spencer's aging heart failed him, and they made it only to Montgomery.

In an hour, Fleming was at the hospital. Spencer, at that point, decided not to testify. Fleming called Doug Jones. Remembering how Jones had talked Blanton's girlfriend into testifying, Fleming told Herren, "Jones could make Hitler talk about himself."

Jones drove to Montgomery. It wasn't just Agent Spencer he had to convince. Even after Spencer was released from the hospital, his doctor refused to allow his patient to go. But Jones's power of persuasion lived up to Fleming's prediction. The doctor shut down his office and came to Birmingham with his nurse. He sat in the courtroom so Spencer could see him and vice versa. In the adjacent witness room, in case they were needed, were paramedics, a gurney, and resuscitation equipment. Fortunately, Spencer did not need either his doctor or the crash cart.

Agent Spencer and Agent Richard Hanes testified to interviews with Blanton in 1963 in which Blanton claimed he had broken a date with Jean Casey on Friday, September 13, 1963, to "probably" attend a Klan meeting, but it wasn't the regular Klan meeting (which was held on Thursdays). He couldn't recall what it was about, where it was held, or who was there. Eventually, he remembered he had gone to the Modern Sign Company to make some signs.

The following night, Saturday, September 14, he said he picked up Jean Casey about 6:30 PM. They went to Ed Salem's drive-in, then up to Vulcan Park, and then arrived at her house about 11:15 PM. He fell asleep on her couch, and she woke him up about 2 AM, at which point he went home. In a later interview, he changed his story about who he was with and said he was out that Saturday night with his girlfriend Waylene Vaughn.

In preparation for playing the Q9 Kitchen Tape, John Colvin, the retired FBI electronic technician, told how he pretended to be a truck driver and rented the duplex at Blanton's house. Retired special agent Ralph Butler recalled removing the baseboard in the closet of that apartment and installing the microphone next to a tiny hole in the wall. The wire ran through tongue-and-groove flooring and through a telephone line to the reel-to-reel recording equipment set up in another apartment not far away.

The judge, attorneys, and jury in the courtroom were equipped with wireless headphones to better hear the recordings. There was a heart-stopping moment for the prosecution team when technical advisor Bill Smith attempted to play the tapes, and the jury complained they weren't hearing anything. Everything had tested out fine the previous day and should have been working. Jones shot Smith a look, and Herren thought he was going to fire the man on the spot.

The judge called for a recess.

There was a scramble at the prosecution table. What was wrong? Suddenly, Smith realized the problem was a file Jones had left in front of the sensitive wireless transmitter. Once that was removed, everything worked fine—and Smith kept his job.

When court resumed, the prosecution played the Q9 Kitchen Tape—the conversation where Blanton, his wife Jean, and an unidentified third person were talking in their house. As Herren started the playback of the recording, he thought about the countless hours that had gone into searching the tapes for this small snatch of conversation upon which the entire case might depend, and then the hours trying to decipher missing words. In addition to outside input, he and Fleming had listened to this segment over and over to make sure the transcript was as accurate as possible—then three other people had each gone over it yet again to ensure its accuracy.

Despite the work the labs had done, the conversation was still not easy to discern. It was very fortunate the judge allowed the transcripts as an aid to the jury. When the words were before a person, it clarified what might be difficult to make out with sound alone, similar to being able to see lips moving as a person speaks.

The atmosphere of expectation held the room in a tense silence. Herren put on his own earphones, and the high-pitched, whiney voice of Jean Blanton filled the room and his ears—hopefully for the last time— as she berated her husband for not telling her what he did "at the river." Blanton's voice, amid the background kitchen noises and hiss of deteriorating tape, claimed the FBI was really interested in another meeting, one held at Modern Sign Company where "we" were planning and making the bomb, the "Big One."

The audience did not have earphones, and the voices were difficult for the audience to understand over the speakers. During a recess, Judge Garrett allowed the media and audience to listen to the tapes through the headsets. Many of them, however, had the antennas pointed in the wrong direction, away from the line-of-sight transmitter, and only heard static.

Herren took the stand to testify about the tapes. He had been on the stand many times in his career, but it was always uncomfortable at first; he compared it to the feeling of having to take a few hits in a game of football before settling in. In response to questions from the prosecution, he explained his background in the police department as a detective and supervisor in the Technical Surveillance Unit that provided covert audio and video, primarily for narcotics investigations. Still, it seemed like the tedious questions about how he could identify the tapes, where they sent the tapes, and how the transcripts were made went on forever. It was important testimony, he knew, and he was glad to be able to explain to the jury what enhancement of the tapes meant. "In my profession it's a filtering process. . . . You try to filter out ambient noise, extraneous noise, car engine noise, radio, if it's playing." He also explained that the cassette tapes to be played in court were not enhanced; they were only copies made by the FBI lab to protect the old and fragile reel-to-reel recordings.

Finally, his testimony was concluded, and the prosecution brought Mitch Burns to the stand. Burns was the FBI informant who rode with

Thomas Blanton in 1965 with reel-to-reel tapes running under the spare tire in the truck of his car. One Sunday, shortly before this trial, Burns had listened to all of the tapes, making his own corrections to the transcripts that had been chosen to present to the jury. After he was sworn in, Jeff Wallace handled the direct questioning for the prosecution, asking about Burns's underage enlistment as a marine. Then, to preempt the defense, he asked Burns about his membership in the Warrior Klavern in Jefferson County.

"All my relatives was [*sic*] in the Klan, just about," Burns said, "and a lot of friends." He had agreed to be an FBI informant after Agent Brook Blake showed him the autopsy photographs of the little girls. "It was the most horrible sight I have ever seen," he told the jury. "I told them [FBI] I would do all I could to help."

The prosecution played excerpts from several different tapes where Blanton and Burns's conversations included mention of bombs or violence. Again, the jury heard them through their headsets, while the audience listened over loudspeakers. In addition to the transcripts, a video screen displayed what was being said.

Burns: "All this time I thought you were a clean-cut American boy."

Blanton: "I am. I am clean cut. I like shooting, fishing, bombing, fucking. . . ." [Singing] "Boomingham, boomingham, that's my kind of town."

. . .

Blanton: "They make the things [synagogues] dynamite-proof, we'll have to go out of business."

. . .

Burns: "Bombing churches, huh? You mean you get more thrill out of that than you do from women?"

Blanton: "Hell yeah. They ain't gonna catch me when I bomb my next church."

Burns: "How did you do that, Tommy?"

Blanton: "Oh, it wasn't easy, boy. I'll tell you."

Burns: ". . . put one off in it [Sixteenth Street Baptist Church]."

Blanton: "Well, I haven't got one tonight, have you?"

Burns: "No, I mean a cherry bomb."

. . .

Blanton: "Let's go bomb a church . . . I'm afraid I'll goof it up again."

Burns, now seventy-four, was still spry and alert, until they began playing the tapes. Like the jury, judge, and attorneys, he too wore a headset, and his part at this point was just to verify his and Blanton's voices on every tape. There were several tapes. Herren sat at the prosecution table playing each tape for identification and Burns's authentication. After each one, Wallace asked, "Mr. Burns, is that the tape of the conversation between you and Tommy Blanton?"

Burns had to say over and over again, "Yes, that was my voice; that was Tommy Blanton's voice."

It was tedious for Herren, too—after the initial panic the previous day over why the transmitter wasn't working. He had heard every word on the tapes dozens of times. At one point, Herren looked up and saw Burns was softly snoring on the witness stand. No one heard him because they all had headsets on. Herren twisted around to Jeff Wallace, who was standing behind him and got his attention. "Jeff, he's *asleep!*" he mouthed.

Wallace stepped quickly to block the jury's view of their witness dozing on the stand. "Judge," he said, "I think we need to take a break."

When they returned from a break for lunch, Garrett chastised the media for allowing their camera equipment to block the halls. "If it happens again, it won't happen anymore because I'll have all of the cameras removed off of this floor."

Burns returned to the stand. He testified that when he and Blanton were out driving around they drove by the FBI office and the Sixteenth Street Baptist Church "at least once a week, sometimes up to three times a week."

Wallace asked, "Now, when you talk [on the tapes] about dynamite or those other things, you're not talking about cherry bombs are you?"

"No sir."

Robbins cross-examined Burns about his membership as an officer in the Klan, a Black Hawk (a records keeper), and a position as preacher, known as a Klug. Burns treated his membership in the Klan lightly, saying many of his friends had joined it for a lark. He admitted, however, to watching the Klan's beating of the Freedom Riders in 1961 at the Trailways bus station in Birmingham.

Burns had been a very reluctant witness and then a bored witness, but he saw an opening to address the latter when Robbins cross-examined him. Robbins bore down on him relentlessly, questioning his claim of not being a racist at heart and demanding if Burns thought it was funny to watch the Freedom Riders being beaten.

"I didn't laugh," Burns said.

Robbins asked him about his marriage and two children. Then, "Back then [in the 1960s], you had a little thing on the side with [the waitress] Marie Aldridge, right?"

"I certainly did," Burns replied, catching Robbins off guard with his enthusiasm.

After a pause, Robbins continued. "OK. You were having sexual relations with Marie Aldridge, right?"

Burns leaned forward, staring straight at Robbins and pointing his finger at him. "I did not have sexual relations with Marie Aldridge."

Burns's mimicry didn't escape Robbins or the audience. "You didn't have sexual relations with Marie Aldridge like Bill Clinton didn't have sexual relations with Monica Lewinsky?"

"No," Burns fired back. "I didn't use a cigar either."

The packed courtroom burst into laughter again.

"Well, were you getting the same service as the president was?" Robbins persisted.

"No."

There was more edged banter between Burns and Robbins, with Robbins obvious trying to rattle Burns. He implied Burns's credibility was tainted because he had burned a cross with the Klan and because he had been paid by the FBI for the information.

Burns admitted he spent money on vodka when he and Blanton were out.

"So you wanted to get drunk?" Robbins asked.

"I didn't want to get drunk. I had to drink it to put up with him."

". . . He never told you he blew up the church?"

"He certainly did not."

"OK. You made a whole lot of money to tell us that Mr. Blanton is a racist and a punk."

"I did not say he was a racist."

"But you got paid," Robbins insisted.

Burns eyed the defense attorney and after a pause, said, "You know, sometimes we do things that we don't get money for, and this is one of them. I didn't make no money. I spent whatever I did [make] for booze."

On redirect, Wallace had Burns clarify that his wife died in 1953, long before he met the waitress he had been interested in. Wallace asked about a night when Blanton had picked up Chambliss and Burns had to sit between Thomas Blanton and "Dynamite Bob" Chambliss in the front seat of his car. "Under those conditions can you afford to get real drunk?" Wallace asked.

"I wasn't drunk," Burns replied. "I was scared to death."

When the court broke for the day, Herren stayed late to make sure things were prepared for the next day—tapes were queued up correctly, witnesses were ready, and the prosecutors had all the information they needed. One thing a lawyer was not going to do was ask a question he didn't know the answer to. As usual during this trial, Herren was not home until late.

The next morning, before the trial resumed, he told Fleming, "When I pulled up into my driveway last night, I saw a strange car there. My heart just sank. I thought, Well I've been gone too much, now I done come home a bit too early this time and caught some man here."

"What happened?" Fleming asked, concerned.

"I went in, and my wife was sitting in the living room. I said, 'Whose car is that out there in the driveway?'

"She said, 'Yours.'

"I said, 'What?'

"'Our other car broke down, and I couldn't get hold of you to ask you about it, so I just bought a new one.'"

Fleming laughed. "So, now you have a new car."

Herren nodded. "So now I have a new car."

The last two witnesses were Chris McNair, the father of Denise McNair, and Sarah Collins Rudolph, the sister of Addie Mae Collins. On the prosecution's table was a small chunk of mortar and a pair of pristine shoes.

Jones began the questioning, asking McNair about the day of the bombing. McNair said he had been at Saint Paul Lutheran Church that morning. He hitched a ride to the Sixteenth Street Baptist Church where he learned his family could not find his eleven-year-old daughter, Denise. He went to the University Hospital [Hillman Hospital at that time] where he found her and three other bodies in an area they had made into a temporary morgue.

"Mr. McNair, was there anything . . . was there any debris or anything on Denise?"

"Yes."

"What, if anything, in particular?"

"There was a piece of mortar mashed in her head."

Jones went to the table and picked up a rock-like chunk off the table, showing it to McNair. "Do you recognize that?"

"It's a piece of mortar."

"And that was what was given to you by someone at the funeral home?"

"Yes."

Sarah Collins Rudolph, the sister of Addie Mae Collins and the only survivor from the basement Ladies Lounge, was washing her hands at the sink while Addie was tying Denise McNair's sash when the bomb exploded, raining debris onto them. "I had glass that cut my face. And I had glass to get in both of my eyes, and I was blind in both eyes at that time. . . . I called out to my sister. I said, 'Addie, Addie, Addie!'"

"Did she answer you?"

"No, she didn't."

"Did you ever see your sister alive again?"

"No. I didn't see her again."

Robbins declined to cross-examine either of the last two witnesses, and the prosecution rested its case.

———————

At that point, Robbins put forward a motion to dismiss the case, citing lack of a case against his client, but Judge Garrett ruled enough evidence had been presented to make it a case for the jury to decide, and the defense was required to call its own witnesses and present its case.

Surprisingly, Robbins called Fleming to the stand as his first witness. He had Fleming recall Edward Lay's testimony of seeing a black 1957 Ford at the church one night a couple of weeks before the church bombing. He showed Fleming photos of Blanton, Dr. Edward Fields, and J. B. Stoner, segregationists active in the National States Rights Party. Robbins's point was the descriptions of the men were roughly similar; all were of medium build and height.

"What kind of car did Blanton own?" Robbins asked Fleming.

"A blue-and-white Chevrolet."

". . . Mr. Blanton did not own a black Ford, correct?"

"That's correct."

"And Mr. Chambliss did not own a black Ford, correct?"

"That's correct."

"And in your investigation of the case, was a black Ford seen at Dr. Field's house?"

"It had been seen at his residence, yes sir."

It was a shame, Fleming thought, that Kirthus Glenn, the witness from Detroit, had died in 1985. If she had been alive, she would have been able to testify—as she had in Chambliss's trial—that she had driven by the church about 2:15 AM on the morning of the bombing and seen a car she saw again later that morning and picked from FBI photos. The photo she identified was a surveillance photo of Blanton's blue-and-white 1957 Chevrolet.

Jones briefly cross-examined Fleming to address the damage Robbins had done. "J. B. Stoner and Dr. Field's pictures were among those shown to Mr. Lay by the FBI in 1963, weren't they?"

"Yes, sir."

"Lay did not pick them did he?"

"No, sir."

"He picked Blanton and Chambliss, didn't he?"

"That's correct."

Eddie Mauldin was seventeen at the time of the bombing. He was the defense's last witness. On the morning the bomb exploded, he was a block away on Sixteenth Street, between Seventh and Eighth Avenues, just north of the church. Prior to the explosion, he saw a Rambler station wagon, light blue over dark blue, drive slowly south on Sixteenth Street toward the church. He said the car resembled his father's 1957 Chevrolet, except for side paneling. Two Confederate flags flew from front antennas. Two young white men in their twenties, one with an anchor tattoo on his arm, rode in the car. One had a walkie-talkie, and Mauldin thought they were police.

When they got to the church, they sped off and burned rubber making a turn east on Sixth Avenue North, which was a two-way street at that time. Then the bomb went off. Fleming frowned. Robbins was continuing the implication that Blanton's car could have been mistaken: First by suggesting the black Ford Lay saw had belonged to someone else. It could have; in fact it probably did. Fleming and Herren always assumed another car had been used that night. And second, by bringing this unidentified car into the picture and implying the bomb could have been thrown from that car by the white men who drove by that morning just as the bomb exploded.

It was a surprise when the defense rested its case after calling only two witnesses. The prosecuting team was ready in case Blanton took the stand, but he did not, which was his constitutional right. The judge would instruct the jury that they were to attach no significance or weight to that decision.

The defense made another motion for the case to be dismissed, but Judge Garrett ruled again that enough evidence had been presented for the case to be a jury decision.

30 | BLANTON TRIAL: PROSECUTION CLOSING ARGUMENTS

IN HERREN'S VIEW, CRIMINAL trials often had more to do with theater than evidence. The men and women who sat on the jury were not computers, weighing evidence with cold calculation; they were human beings. Among other things, they made judgments about whether and how much to believe witnesses and if the motivations presented fit with their experience or understanding. On the negative side, sometimes logic did not prevail. On more than one occasion, a jury's logic had eluded him.

The closing arguments or summations gave opportunities for both sides to sway the jury's perspective, to remind or distract from pertinent facts. The prosecution always had two chances—they led off and finished, with the defense giving their summation in between.

Posey went first for the prosecution team. Herren knew Assistant US Attorney Robert Posey, not only through working with him on this case but also from Posey's previous position as a deputy district attorney. Posey had always been a straight arrow. Every now and then you could squeeze a little dry wit out of him, but for the most part he was a no-nonsense, just-the-facts-ma'am kind of guy. So, the power and drama of his closing argument took Herren by surprise, revealing a side of Posey he never guessed was there—but he was glad it was, because it manifested at a time when it was most needed.

Posey began in a low-key, soft-spoken manner. "Thank you for the attention you have given to the presentation of evidence. I want to talk to you about the indictment against this defendant, and about why the evidence proves that he is guilty. There are four indictments for the murder of four little girls: one for Cynthia Wesley, one for Carole Robertson, one for Denise McNair, and one for Addie Mae Collins. Four little girls—in church—on a Sunday morning."

One by one, each girl looked out at the courtroom from the video screen, reminding everyone present that they had been flesh and blood, children whose futures were stolen. The last picture was of Sarah Collins, the only one who had survived in the church basement that turned suddenly into hell.

Posey continued. "There was a shock wave of excruciating pain that swept over Sarah Collins as she lay in the rubble of the women's lounge, blinded in both eyes, crying out for her dead sister, Addie. There was a shock wave of grief that swept over the McNairs, and the Wesleys, and the Robertsons as they learned that their children had been senselessly murdered. There was a shock wave that swept all across the Earth, as the world learned of a horrible crime committed in Birmingham, Alabama." He paused. "The question on so many lips on September 15, 1963, is a question still before the jury today: *Why?*

"The grand jury that returned the indictments charged that this defendant killed these children unlawfully and with malice or criminal intent; and the grand jury also used this language—'by setting off or exploding or causing to be set off or exploded dynamite or other explosive, at, under, or dangerously near the Sixteenth Street Baptist Church, during Sunday morning church worship services.'"

While he read the words of the indictment, photos of the devastation at the scene displayed on the screen. Then Posey began revisiting the testimony of key witnesses, reminding the jury of the conversation between Blanton and his wife. "How do we know that 'the bomb' is the Sixteenth Street Baptist Church bomb? For one thing, 'the bomb' could have only one meaning in Birmingham, Alabama, after September 15, 1963. We also know that it was around September 15, 1963, that Blanton was seen with Chambliss and other Klansmen at the Cahaba River bridge and at the Modern Sign shop.

"Why would anyone bomb a church? Who would have a motive to commit such a crime? The grand jury's indictment touches on this question. The grand jury charged that this defendant killed these children 'by perpetrating an act greatly dangerous to the lives of others, and evidencing a depraved mind regardless of human life, although without any preconceived purpose to deprive any particular person of life.' This defendant didn't care who he killed, as long as he killed somebody, and as long as they were black."

He took a deep breath and asked, "Who would do such a thing?" Answering his own question, Posey said, "The same man who rode around Birmingham committing random acts of violence against black people. The same man who we hear on tape saying, 'They're not gonna catch me when I bomb my next church.' The same man who, even a year after the horror of September 15, 1963, can be heard on tape cursing the name of the church where these children died. The same man who lied to the FBI about the Klan, and about what he was doing that Friday and Saturday night before the bombing. The same man who, when his wife asks, 'What did you go to the river for?' says three times on tape that he was at a meeting where they made a bomb. That same man is seen at the church with Chambliss, in the middle of the night, with a satchel in his hand, at the very spot where the bomb exploded that killed these children. Ladies and gentlemen—" he pointed at Blanton, "*this* is the man who committed this crime."

Once again the girls' pictures appeared on the screen.

"This is Cynthia Wesley.

"This is Carole Robertson.

"This is Addie Mae Collins.

"This is Denise McNair. This defendant killed this beautiful child because of the color of her skin." Posey's voice began to rise. "He murdered these four worshippers in God's house on a Sunday morning, because he was a man of *hate!*"

Posey went through the important points of witnesses' testimonies:

"[Mitch Burns] was a crusty old former Klansman. But he was also a man with two daughters. And he saw photographs of four little girls laid out on a slab at a morgue, and he told us that it was the most horrible thing he had ever seen. He agreed to do a brave thing. He agreed to help the FBI investigate a murder suspect. As he rode around night after night, he must have wondered what would happen if this murder suspect discovered the tape recorder in the trunk of his car. But he kept doing it, and he collected evidence that tells volumes about the mind of this defendant."

No one in the room moved as Posey finished. "The deaths of these four little girls must not be in vain. Don't let that happen. Don't let the deafening blast of his bomb be what is left ringing in our ears. Don't let it drown out the voices of these children. On behalf of the State of Alabama, and on behalf of these four little girls, I ask you to find this defendant guilty as charged."

31 | BLANTON TRIAL: DEFENSE

JOHN ROBBINS LAID OUT his defense summation by challenging the credibility of the state's witnesses. The first person he aimed at was Blanton's girlfriend, Waylene Vaughn. Fleming regretted the way Waylene had been treated on the stand, though he knew this was the defense attorney's job. He understood she would be in fear for her life either way after testifying, but especially if Blanton were acquitted.

Waylene Vaughn "comes here and says some really bad things," Robbins said, addressing the jury. "She says Tom Blanton is a bad man. OK. But she continued to date him. If he is such a bad man, I mean, come on. You saw pictures of him. He's not that good looking. And, by God, he didn't have any money. I mean . . . she wants to come out on one side of her mouth and say he's such a bad person doing all these things to black people. Never reported one. Never been corroborated. Not one of those claims has ever been corroborated."

He turned his attention to Mitch Burns, pacing in front of the jury box. "You probably knew people like Mitch Burns," he said. "Turned informer for money. Two hundred bucks a month.

". . . This is my favorite witness, I guess. William Jackson. Now if you believe William Jackson is anything but a liar, then raise your hand and say, let's stop now, go back and convict my client. If you believe he's anything but a liar. . . . He gave numerous statements in the 1960s and said that it was Friday night the thirteenth that he saw Blanton and Chambliss at the Modern Sign shop. He didn't change it to the fourteenth until he checked himself out of a psychiatric ward in the 1970s to meet with Bill Baxley. Well maybe I'll move to the fourteenth—because he really wanted that reward money. He's still P.O.'d to this day that he hasn't gotten any reward money.

"What did they do [at the Modern Sign Company]?" Robbins asked. "Make a bomb [Friday], then unmake it, so they could put it together again [Saturday]? . . . It makes no sense."

Lastly, he raised the idea that it could have been other people who bombed the church. He showed photographs of two other virulent racists at the time, including J. B. Stoner of the National States Rights Party, who had been convicted in a bombing of the Bethel Church. Blanton's dark hair and medium build could have been mistaken for another white supremacist, like Stoner. The two white men in a Rambler Eddie Mauldin saw drive by the church right before the explosion could have thrown out a bomb. Also, Robbins pointed out, James Lay said he saw a black 1957 Ford, like the car belonging to Ed Fields. Blanton's car was a blue-and-white Chevrolet.

All these things, Robbins said, should raise significant doubts in the jury's mind about the state's case.

———

Doug Jones gave the final closing summation for the prosecution. He spoke about the pieces falling into place:

"Planning the bomb. The Cahaba River. The meetings that were held. The Modern Sign shop. Robert Chambliss. September the second. James Lay. They all come together." He paused.

> Are there some pieces missing? Yes. Can we see clearly the picture? We can see clearly the picture from Blanton's own mouth.
>
> . . . And ladies and gentlemen, we come here, in this time and place, to do justice. And it's not cheapened. It's not been thrown out. It's real. And we come here because there were four children who died, and the world changed and we changed. And we come here because a mother's heart never stops crying. And we come here because we do remember. And every day that passed and every year

that passed and Tom Blanton gets older is a mockery of the death of those little children. Every year that passes, bigotry and hate proliferate. And every year that passes, some child can cringe in fear that maybe if I go to Sunday school today, I won't come home.

Ladies and gentlemen, there are a lot of people looking. There are a lot of people, but only four matter: Denise, Cynthia, Carole, and Addie. Those four are the people that look down for the hope and inspiration. Those are the people that look down for justice. Because, as Sarah called out, "Addie, Addie, Addie" in cries of pain, today let us call out to Addie, let us call out in joy and happiness to Addie and her friends . . . that today, in this time and in this place, we did justice. And at long last—and it has been a long time—but at long last, they can rest in peace, because it is never too late for that. And Tom Blanton can finally be held accountable for the crime he committed in 1963.

32 | WAR ROOM

IT WAS AFTERNOON WHEN the judge instructed the jury on the law, and the jury retired for deliberation. Herren and Fleming took all of the materials from the courtroom to the FBI building across the street into a small room they were using as a staging area and command post for the trial. They called it the War Room.

A little more than two hours later, Herren was packing up everything into boxes to take back to the office when Jones received a call: the jury had reached a verdict and was returning to the courtroom. It was a fast verdict—too fast, Herren worried. He had expected about three days of deliberation. His heart sank. The jury must not have believed anything. They bought the defense line and thought they couldn't convict because the evidence was circumstantial—no DNA, no fingerprints. Despite his pep talks to himself that it only mattered that he had done his best, he couldn't help feeling disheartened. With Cherry being declared incompetent to stand trial, this had been their last chance. The jury was just going to let Blanton go . . .

He walked with Doug Jones back to the courtroom, wanting to tell him what perhaps he wanted to hear himself: that no matter what the outcome, he had done a very good job and worked hard.

"Be quiet," Jones said. "Don't say a word; just be quiet."

Later, Jones confessed it was a bit of superstition that made him want silence on the walk back to the courthouse.

The courtroom, which had been packed shoulder-to-shoulder, still had quite a few people there. Word had spread quickly. Everyone waited for the defense team to return and for Blanton to be brought down from his holding cell. Other than the members of the jury, only one person knew what the verdict was—the bailiff, whose duty it was to check the paperwork after the jury made a determination.

Finally, everyone was in place. The jury foreman, an African American woman, stood to read the verdict. Through the media, the world watched. An emotion-laden silence in the room reflected the understanding of what the next spoken words would mean—to the city and the state, to history, to the families of the four young girls.

The foreman's voice cracked as she pronounced the verdict. So primed was Herren to hear "not guilty" that it wasn't until the second count of guilty that he realized what the foreman was saying. At the last "guilty," the bailiff put handcuffs on a stunned Blanton. Herren was stunned himself. *We have just convicted the Sixteenth Street Baptist Church bomber. It took five years, but we did it.* It seemed surreal.

Media reps scrambled for the door, trying to get on the phone and be the first with the story, but Carol Robinson, a local crime reporter for the *Birmingham News*, made a beeline for Fleming. "I can tell this affected you," she said.

For the first time since Herren had known him, Fleming seemed to be at a loss for words.

Camera crews and reporters from across the country waited outside the courthouse. They converged on Doug Jones, thrusting microphones and questions at him. Herren and Fleming stood behind Posey and Wallace, who stood behind Jones. After Jones gave a statement, Herren and Fleming walked through the crowd unnoticed, which was more than fine with them.

They returned to the office and later met at the nearby Tutwiler Hotel where Jones was staying. Jones's assistant, Amy Gallimore, was fielding calls from *Good Morning America* and other shows that wanted an interview with him.

Fleming suddenly looked up. "Oh my goodness, I better notify headquarters we got a conviction!" He frowned, realizing the only landline phone in the room was in use. Fleming had never embraced technology, never touched a computer, and only carried a beeper. "Yeah, you'd better," Herren said with a wry smile at his absentminded partner. "Remember the last time that happened?" When the grand jury indictments on Blanton and Cherry came down, Fleming had forgotten to notify the FBI director Louie Freeh. Unfortunately, Freeh learned about them on the golf course when someone asked him about it. The director wasn't terribly happy.

Fleming ran out into the hotel lobby to find a pay phone.

33 | DARKEST HOURS

ON MAY 3, 2001, two days after Blanton's conviction, the *New York Times* published a scathing letter from Bill Baxley, the former Alabama attorney general who had obtained a conviction on Robert "Dynamite Bob" Chambliss in 1977. That letter was to plunge Fleming and Herren into one of the darkest moments of their careers.

> This week, a guilty verdict was returned against Thomas Blanton for the dynamite bomb deaths of Denise McNair, Addie Mae Collins, Cynthia Wesley and Carole Robertson on Sept. 15, 1963, in a Birmingham church. In 1977, as Alabama attorney general, I prosecuted Mr. Blanton's associate Robert Chambliss for the same crime. It took a long enough time to bring him to trial—and far too long, unnecessarily long, to do the same with Mr. Blanton. . . .
>
> In 1997, I learned that Doug Jones, the United States attorney in Birmingham, whom I knew to be ethical and highly competent, had opened, once again, investigations of Mr. Blanton and Mr. Cherry. The two men were indicted—and I was astonished to learn that the FBI had tape recordings of Mr. Blanton from the 1960s that incriminated both of them. I was also livid. For more than two decades, Mr. Blanton and Mr. Cherry evaded indictment and prosecution because the FBI held back these recordings. This was evidence we desperately needed in 1977—evidence whose existence FBI officials

had denied. Had it been provided in 1977, we could have convicted all three of these Klansmen.

I held my tongue when I learned of this deception. I did so to prevent lawyers for Mr. Blanton and Mr. Cherry from trumpeting the FBI's dishonesty as a distraction. Mr. Blanton has been convicted—thanks greatly to the new evidence. Mr. Cherry, due to his alleged mental state, may not be tried. There is no longer any reason for me to remain silent.

Why would the FBI aid Klansmen in avoidance of prosecution? I don't know. I consider myself a practical person. I could understand FBI reluctance to share information if it were actively pursuing a case of its own. But all federal statutes of limitation had expired when this deceit took place, and only in state court—Alabama has no statute of limitations for murder—could a case against Mr. Blanton or Mr. Cherry proceed. (Mr. Jones, the federal attorney, prosecuted the Blanton case on Alabama's behalf.) Most of the tape recordings admissible against Mr. Blanton in 2001 were admissible in 1977.

What excuse can the FBI have for allowing Mr. Blanton to go free for 24 years with this smoking gun evidence hidden in its files? How can the FBI justify this to the families of four precious girls? I don't know. I do know that rank-and-file FBI agents working with us were conscientious and championed our cause. The disgust I feel is for those in higher places who did nothing.

FBI Director Louis Freeh agreed the case had taken far too long. It was as if a whirlwind had blown through the FBI field office. Herren was instructed to call Fleming back from a much-needed vacation. They spent hours writing responses and answering questions.

The FBI had been beleaguered by recent scandals: Only a few months earlier, a twenty-year veteran agent, Robert Hanssen, was arrested as a Soviet spy. The day before Baxley's letter was published, the House Committee began hearings on whether the FBI withheld evidence in the 1960s and 1970s regarding the innocence of Joseph Salvati, who had been imprisoned for thirty years for murder. A week after Baxley's letter, the FBI announced it had discovered a failure to turn over a large number of investigative documents to the defense in the Oklahoma City bombing case.

All this intensified the pressure, and Herren and Fleming felt they were illogically being made responsible for something that had happened before they played any part in it. Perhaps it was the timing, only days after their victory, but Herren felt the administration was trashing all their work and effort. He and Fleming were being admonished for doing something wrong, rather than recognized for the hard work and difficult challenges they had overcome.

This feeling was mitigated somewhat when the Birmingham FBI SAC Charlene Thornton asked Baxley to come to the Birmingham office. Baxley assured Fleming and Herren he had nothing but praise for the job they had done; his problem was with those who had refused to cooperate with him in the 1970s. He firmly believed he would have gotten the other convictions had he been given access to the tapes.

Herren was not so sure. Many of the witnesses—Mike Gowins, Bobby Birdwell, and Cherry's daughters and granddaughters—had not been born or were not old enough to have been witnesses in 1977. Also, although technology existed in the 1970s for improving the quality of a tape recording, it did not match the sophistication available with digital techniques in the late 1990s. Even if the tapes could have been enhanced adequately, the information on the Q9 Kitchen Tape—which the jury said made the difference in their determination—would not have been usable to the FBI in the 1960s because the tapes, authorized as intelligence under a national security justification, would not have been allowed as evidence in a criminal investigation or trial. The tapes had been allowed into evidence in Blanton's trial based on US Supreme Court rulings decided in 1984 about exclusionary exceptions. That argument could not have been made in 1977.

When Bob Eddy was researching the files at the Birmingham FBI office, he was given ground rules. He could only ask for case files, not intelligence files, and only if he already knew the name. He could see an informant file only if he found and spoke to the informant on his own, as he had with Elizabeth Cobbs. Even then, after he asked for her file by her cover name, the agent who brought the file and laid it on his desk quietly said, "Bob, you've never seen this file." None of the material he saw mentioned tapes or transcripts from tapes, and, by the rules laid out for him, he couldn't have asked for them, even if someone had whispered in his ear of their existence.

In Herren's mind, as painful as it was to hear it at the time when they should be celebrating, Baxley was right: the fault lay at the top, originally with J. Edgar Hoover who made the decision not to allow Baxley access to the files, and then with his successor who continued that policy decision. By the time Baxley was finally allowed access, the clock was ticking on his term in office, and he did not have time enough as the state attorney general to pursue the other suspects.

Hoover decided originally not to prosecute the case against the strong desires of the local FBI to do so. Did he sabotage the case, or did he truly believe there was not enough evidence or no chance of a fair jury trial in Birmingham, Alabama, at that time? In the 1960s the government's key witnesses—Mary Frances Cunningham, Elizabeth Cobbs, and Kirthus Glenn—all were refusing to testify. Whether the government would have been able to win the case would always remain an open question. In stark contrast, when FBI SAC Rob Langford learned about the possibility his organization might be able to discover something overlooked or obtain new evidence, he just opened the case and invited a partnership with the state.

In the 1970s, the FBI probably did not know there was a "smoking gun" piece of evidence in a dusty cardboard box, although some persons apparently knew tapes existed. J. Edgar Hoover surely did, but regardless, he clearly had an ethical obligation to either give Baxley all the information the Bureau had or assign a federal agent to work with him to give him access. Somewhere, those in power lost sight of their responsibility to justice. It was not a new revelation to history.

Herren kept his thoughts to himself and just answered the questions put to him.

34 | THE BATTLE OVER CHERRY'S MIND

NO ONE ON THE prosecution team believed they would have a shot at Bobby Frank Cherry. Judge Garrett had ruled him incompetent to stand trial based on two expert witnesses' testimonies. One doctor testified Cherry's brain damage was irreversible.

District Attorney David Barber also believed Cherry would never go to trial, so he reassigned Jeff Wallace to family court. That June, James Lay—the man who had seen Blanton and Chambliss at the church two weeks before the bombing—died, illustrating the fragility of all the witnesses . . . and even the remaining suspect. Cherry's health was not good, but the main issue was his mental status. Marsha Allen, a lieutenant with the Jefferson County Sheriff's Department at the time, was temporarily assigned to the jail. She would later recall she came upon Cherry in an obscure section of the jail known as the mental block, and noticed he was having what seemed to be a normal, animated conversation on the pay phone in that section.

Many other people did not believe Cherry's claim of mental incompetence. During the summer of 2001, pressure built in the community to bring Cherry to trial. Almost a thousand people met for a rally at Linn Park, a small park between the old County Courthouse, where Blanton's trial had been held, and city hall. Reverend Abraham Woods, whose confrontational question to SAC Rob Langford had led to the reopening of the case six years earlier, saw the court's ruling about Cherry's incompetence as an affront and denial of justice and called to "chop down that

Cherry tree! . . . If we have to carry him on a stretcher, bring him in to stand trial!" He told reporters, "The world's spotlight was going to be on Birmingham and Alabama—some of us was hoping [*sic*] we were ready to join the twenty-first century. . . . But this verdict makes the statement loud and clear that the justice system is not blind; that there isn't always justice for black folks." Following his fiery speech, the crowd marched to the Sixteenth Street Baptist Church where the orations continued.

In August 2001, in another hearing, the defense presented a motion to dismiss the court's consideration of Cherry's mental state, which would effectively close the door on further prosecution. The prosecution reminded the court it was "obligated to ascertain whether reasonable probability exists that a medical and psychiatric coarse [*sic*] of treatment exists to restore the defendant's competence." They argued neither the Constitution nor Alabama case law required the defendant to be at his "cognitive and intellectual best to come before the bar of justice to stand trial." Judge Garrett ordered Cherry committed to the Taylor Hardin Secure Medial Facility in Tuscaloosa, Alabama, for further evaluation and treatment.

Two months later, in yet another hearing about Cherry's competency, Judge Garrett considered the report from Taylor Hardin, where Cherry had been evaluated and under observation around the clock for sixty days. They had tested him formally and informally in situations where he did not realize he was being tested. He did poorly only when he knew he was being tested, not realizing everyone on the staff, including the aides, were recording his behavior and reactions. Despite his complaint he could not "learn new information or recall anything," his memory problems seemed to disappear when he chatted about sports events he'd seen earlier in the day or found his way around the building or tracked his medications. The staff's general consensus was Cherry was faking his severe memory problems, even in front of his attorneys.

In a test designed to discriminate between *bona fide* memory-impaired patients and malingerers, "Mr. Cherry obtained a score which clearly indicated malingering." Regarding his tendency to change his version of the offense and details around it, the report stated a review of Cherry's statements going back to 1963 "demonstrated a tendency to change facts, deny statements he had previously made, and manipulate

THE BATTLE OVER CHERRY'S MIND | 217

information in a self-serving manner." On January 3, 2002, Garrett ruled Cherry could now adequately assist in his defense and could stand trial.

When the hearing had ended and everyone left the courtroom, they encountered a crowd, still angry and agitated. Cherry's attorneys, Mickey Johnson and Rodger Bass, walked on either side of Cherry, but Herren, even though he was officially no longer a police officer, was uncomfortable at the jeering onlookers who dogged the trio down the sidewalk. Instinctively, he fell behind them and stayed with them until they reached their car.

Later on, Bass told him, "I appreciate you walking us to the car."

Herren shrugged. "It wasn't because it was you or him. I would have done the same thing for anybody being harassed like that."

District Attorney David Barber picked up the phone. The call was from Doug Jones, who had made an unsuccessful run for the US Senate and was now in private practice. "David," Doug said, "as a good Republican, would you call Bill Pryor [the Alabama attorney general] and ask him to appoint me as special prosecutor for Cherry's trial?"

Barber made the call, pointing out to Pryor the importance of the former US attorney's familiarity with the case, and Pryor agreed Jones was the best person to handle the case. Don Cochran, an assistant US attorney, also came on board, saying he was willing to carry water or be a gopher for the opportunity to work on the historic case. Cochran had been a deputy district attorney before coming to the US attorney's office and had tried more than two dozen murder cases. Fascinated with the Blanton trial, he had followed the twists and turns through his friend, Deputy DA Jeff Wallace. One day, Cochran shared his prosecutorial theory about how the Cherry trial could be approached. Impressed, Wallace got him a place on the team.

The prosecution hired specialists to consult in the jury selection process, a critical part of trial preparation. They set up focus groups and presented the evidence to them in a kind of mock trial. Afterward, the participants were split into two groups to deliberate on the evidence. Prosecutors watched them through a one-way glass. One of the surprising conclusions that came from this exercise was that both groups considered a handwritten FBI document signed by Cherry to be a confession. In that document Cherry stated he was at the sign shop with Blanton and Chambliss the Friday night before the bombing. It was unusual for a handwritten document to exist, as FBI rules required interviews to be typed on a 302 form in summary format.

Reactions of the mock jurists were measured and analyzed by age, race, gender, and address. In addition, an extensive phone survey was done. From the information gathered, the consultants developed a questionnaire with one hundred questions, relating not only to views about race, but books, television shows, and radio programs potential jurors preferred.

When the real proceedings began, it took five arduous days of questioning before twelve jurors were selected—six white females, three white males, and three black males.

35 | THE TRIAL OF BOBBY FRANK CHERRY

DEFENSE ATTORNEYS MICKEY L. Johnson and Rodger D. Bass filed a motion for the trial to be moved out of Birmingham because of the intense news media coverage, citing 180 articles in the *Birmingham News* and *Post Herald*; numerous local interviews about Diane McWhorter's book on the civil rights movement, *Carry Me Home*; and recent showings of Spike Lee's film *Four Little Girls*. Prosecutors argued those were not the kinds of things past court rulings set as grounds for changing venue. Only the prejudices of the jurors themselves indicated when a change in venue was appropriate. Judge Garrett ruled against the motion, noting the jurors all stated they were not influenced by the media, and the case stayed in Birmingham.

The same issues dealt with in Blanton's case regarding the delay of trial were brought up and challenged by the prosecution. Garrett repeated his ruling and denied the motions.

On Tuesday, May 14, 2002, the trial began.

Don Cochran gave the opening statements for the prosecution. "Like other Klan activities conducted under a shroud of the hood, this activity was carried out in secret. The bomb was made in secret. . . . But as this trial progresses, I expect that the evidence will remove that shroud." He laid out what he expected the evidence to show, which was that Cherry participated in a conspiracy to commit and cover up the crime. "[Cherry's] own words convict him of this crime. Someone who aids and abets others in a crime, who helps in any way . . . is guilty."

For the defense, Johnson noted, "It is disingenuous that the same government that created the atmosphere that allowed this to happen is now, forty years down the road . . . bringing a man in here and putting him on trial. . . . As a juror, you have to draw a distinction between evidence and proof." Johnson laid out his main proposition—the government's case was built around the story Mary Frances Cunningham told the FBI fifteen months after the bombing. Why did she wait so long? "Because it was a lie." The first thing Fleming did was interview Cherry. "This was not an investigation. This was a target."

After both sides finished with opening statements, the prosecution began calling their witnesses. The prosecution's case was circumstantial, as no physical evidence existed, and they planned the presentation carefully to lay out the story. The first witness was called to make the losses of the girls real to the jury.

Alpha Robertson, the mother of Carole Robertson, recalled that Carole was going to serve as junior usher that Sunday morning and was wearing a white dress with "her first pair of little heels, black pumps." When the bomb went off, "the sound was awful . . . like someone shaking the world."

James Armstrong and his children were participants in 1957 when Reverend Fred Shuttlesworth attempted to integrate Phillips High School to test the 1954 Supreme Court ruling *Brown v. Board of Education*. Armstrong witnessed a handful of white men beating Shuttlesworth and took the children to the hospital. Years later, his two younger boys integrated Graymont Elementary School five days before the church bombing. With prompting from Jones, he recalled the times of 1963: the segregated water fountains and lunch counters; the marches and protests; and the words of Governor George Wallace's fiery inauguration speech, "Segregation now, segregation forever!"

Jimmy Parker, the man who had taken the historic video of the Phillips High School incident with Shuttlesworth, explained how he happened to be at the school and grabbed his camera to record it. He remembered seeing a young man strike Reverend Shuttlesworth and identified that person on the video footage, which was played for the court.

Bobby Birdwell, then a young friend of Tommy, Cherry's son, was in and out of the Cherry house frequently. He often heard Bobby Frank Cherry say, "My kids will never go to school with niggers." Birdwell recalled an afternoon three to five days before the church bombing. He and Tommy were playing outside at Tommy's house and came inside for water. A white Klan robe with cutout eyes was spread out on the living room couch. Birdwell asked Tommy who it belonged to, and Tommy proudly said, "That's my daddy's." On their way out of the kitchen, Birdwell overheard the handful of men at the kitchen table talking, but only caught the words "bomb" and "Sixteenth Street." The only man he knew was Tommy's father, Bobby Frank Cherry. Birdwell watched the film of Shuttlesworth at Phillips High School and identified Bobby Frank Cherry.

Robbins pushed Birdwell about documents showing differing dates of birth for him and asked why Fleming's 302 report mentioned Birdwell's story had changed somewhat from the original phone conversation. Birdwell insisted he didn't know.

Reverend Cross, the pastor of the Sixteenth Street Baptist Church, explained that Sunday, September 15, 1963, was to be the first of monthly Youth Days when the youth would conduct the church services. That information was published in the newspaper and on the exterior bulletin board beside the church.

After the explosion, Cross went outside where Edward Lay, a black civil defense worker, handed him a bullhorn and asked him to help calm people. After Cross did so and said a prayer, he went around to the side of the building and looked into the dust- and debris-filled cavern of the basement. "Let's search . . . for any injured in here." The four men behind him replied, "We're afraid to go in there, Reverend. You better not go in there. Another bomb might go off."

"No," he said, "we have got to go in there . . . if you are afraid, let me go." He started crawling in. After he had made it about five feet inside, he looked back to see all four of them had followed. Inside, they found the blackened bodies buried beneath the debris.

Barbara Cross, who was thirteen at the time of the bombing, was the daughter of Reverend Cross. Recalling the Youth Day Sunday School lesson, she said, "The lesson we talked about was what we would do if somebody did something wrong against us, like punch us. . . . We would say the initials 'WWJD,' which means 'What Would Jesus Do?'" After Sunday school, which was held in the basement, her classmates Cynthia Wesley and Carole Robertson went to the women's lounge to freshen up for the services. Barbara wanted to go, but her teacher gave her an assignment.

"There was the most horrible noise I had ever heard," she said. "I remember things got real black, and I was hit in the head. . . . I heard screams. I thought Russia had bombed Alabama . . . because I remember reading about nuclear weapons back then."

The following morning Cochran questioned Dr. Robert Brissie, the chief coroner and medical examiner for Jefferson County who had examined the autopsy photos and reports. He asked Dr. Brissie to explain how a blast kills a person.

"Well," Dr. Brisse said, "when you have a high-order explosion . . . you have numerous fragments, pieces of wood, stone, brick . . . you get projectiles. If these strike an individual, they may . . . even decapitate."

Once again prosecutors used FBI experts to explain the difference between what they saw at the scene and a natural gas explosion. Richard Harris, a retiree from Alabama Gas Company, explained a distinctive odor was added in 1946 or 1947 when natural gas was first used in Birmingham, and that odor was not detected at the scene.

During a break in proceedings, Herren went to the office the judge had given them for retired agents and some of their other witnesses who needed to stand by. The agents were talking, laughing, and reminiscing about old times. Judge Garrett poked his head in. "Ben, you've got to get them to be a little quieter; I can hear them in the courtroom."

Herren shook his head with a grin. "Judge, just look at 'em. Every one of them's got a cotton-picking hearing aid!"

Garrett laughed. "I understand, I understand."

In preparation for playing one of the tape-recorded conversations, the prosecution put retired FBI special agent Ralph Butler on the stand. Butler testified he had been responsible for installing the tapes in Mitch Burns's car. He turned on the recorder before Burns left, and it stayed on until his return from his night excursions with Thomas Blanton, when Butler would remove the tapes from the car.

On cross-examination, defense attorney Johnson asked if Burns ever appeared drunk when he returned to deliver the tapes.

"As to his sobriety, I have no idea. . . . I would speak to him or say, 'I'm glad to see you back' . . . or some remarks like that. But I did not check him . . . as to his physical condition."

Herren was called to the stand to talk about the tapes. He explained the cassette tapes presented as evidence were made by the FBI lab directly off the original tapes and they had not been enhanced or spliced.

Outside the hearing of the jury, the tapes were once again hotly contested. In Blanton's trial, the legality of the tape had been challenged primarily under his Fourth Amendment right against unlawful search. In this case, however, Cherry had no standing to challenge on that ground, since it was not his home or car that had been bugged.

In general, however, a person cannot testify to hearsay—what he heard from another person about a third person; nor can a written statement or oral statement such as a tape recording made out of court by third parties be introduced. The tapes would normally be considered hearsay, but they played a key role in the prosecution's strategy.

This was where Cochran's approach would come into play. Statements made by one conspirator "during the course of and in furtherance of the conspiracy" are admissible against other conspirators and are an exception to the rule against hearsay. Under Alabama law, this holds true even after the crime has been completed if the conspirators actively try to conceal their part in the crime. Also, in an acknowledgement of the difficulty in proving conspiracy, Alabama law allows conspiracies to conceal to be proven by inference and circumstantial evidence.

Cochran pointed out to the judge, outside the jury's hearing, several instances that illustrated a conspiracy to conceal. "When they [Blanton and Burns] went over to Cherry's house, Cherry said, 'The FBI thinks the bomb was made somewhere else,' and [Cherry] laughs about it.' . . . At another point, Cherry, [who is talking to Burns, Blanton, and Ed Fields with the National States Rights Party] says, 'The FBI gave me a polygraph and I lied all the way through it.' He laughs about it," Cochran repeated. "That is clearly evidence of conspiracy."

This was rebutted by Johnson, who pointed out Burns once asked Blanton if Cherry was a friend of his. Blanton responded, "I don't know if Cherry knows anything at all." It was a confusing response.

Cochran challenged the inference that Blanton and Cherry hardly knew each other. "They are talking about the Klan, about who in the Klan they can trust. They are talking about niggers. These are racists who are Klan buddies."

After hearing all the arguments on both sides, Judge Garrett ruled some of the tapes were too prejudicial and would not be heard, but portions of other tapes could be played in court.

Burns took the stand and explained once again how he had met Blanton through the waitress Marie Aldridge and how Blanton and he became friends and drove around almost every Friday night barhopping. "We would . . . go out and have a party or get some help to get the FBI off of our back. . . . [We] went to just about every honky-tonk between here and Blount County," Burns said. "And then we got tired of that and we went to every one between here and Bessemer." Burns identified Cherry in the courtroom as "the man with the pretty wavy hair."

The courtroom grew silent as the old recording began. The first thing heard was a distant siren, then Blanton laughing and bantering: "Where were you guys when the church blew up?"

Cherry says, "Yeah. We're just trying to make a bomb. . . . [I] was a demolition expert in the Marine Corps."

The conversation wandered into the subject of bombs found in the city that had not exploded. "They said they had the wrong kind of caps on two of them," Cherry remarked.

"What kind of batteries do they use?" Blanton asked.

"Hell, I don't know what kind they used. Hell, a flashlight battery would have set it off. Hell, they have had it in there when a clock, the alarm, or something . . . the motherfucker makes contact, you see."

On other tapes Cherry's voice says, "The FBI came here, and I didn't tell them shit." And, with a laugh, "The FBI thinks the bomb was made somewhere else."

"Careful what you say around this boy right here," Blanton cautioned, referring to Burns. "He doesn't know too much. Let's keep it that way."

As part of their presentation of a conspiracy to conceal, the prosecution introduced several interviews where Cherry made conflicting statements. In one, he said he quit the KKK in August 1963 because he was "against violence."

"That must have been news to Fred Shuttlesworth," Cochran commented.

The prosecution introduced the handwritten five-page statement the mock jury had considered a confession. It was the linchpin for their conspiracy theory. On October 9, 1963, three weeks after the bombing, Special Agents Joseph Ayers and Carl Welton interviewed Cherry, who denied any involvement or knowledge of the bombing. Three days later, on October 12, Cherry said Blanton came by his house to ask what he had told the FBI. Afterward, they walked out to Blanton's car, and Blanton told Cherry not to talk because his car was bugged. When agents asked Cherry where he was Friday, September 13, he said he was at the Modern Sign Company with Blanton and Chambliss, helping to make signs for a planned protest against integrating the schools. Apparently thinking of this as an alibi, he gave details of everyone who came and left the store from 5:30 PM until midnight. The agents wrote out what he said by hand, told Cherry to read it and write below it: "I have read the above statement of this and four other pages and it is true and correct to the best of my knowledge." Cherry signed the statement, "Bobby F. Cherry."

This document, along with the Q9 Kitchen Tape recording where Blanton told Jean he was at the Modern Sign Company that same Friday night making the bomb, linked Cherry to the time and place where Blanton said the bomb was being planned and/or made.

Herren testified to his lengthy interview with Cherry in Texas, glad to have the 302 reports in hand. In the Texas interview Cherry had claimed he had been home with his wife, who was sick with cancer, watching wrestling on television the night of the church bombing. Not only did Cherry's wife not have cancer until August 1965—two years after the bombing—there was no wrestling on TV in Birmingham that night. Virginia Cherry's medical records and TV program listings for that evening were submitted as evidence.

Fleming took the stand for a very long time while the defense attorneys probed details of how they had conducted the investigation and made decisions about identifying the prime suspects.

Willadean Brogdon Cherry, Bobby Frank Cherry's third wife, took the stand. She told the judge, "I have restless legs syndrome, and may have to take some medicine." Indeed, she was constantly squirming and moving around in her seat as she explained that she met Cherry while she drove an eighteen-wheeler carrying explosives in early 1970. She married him by August of that year, but divorced him three years later in April 1973.

Posey asked if she had seen Cherry with any KKK clothing.

"I saw what he said was a Ku Klux Klan robe in a footlocker. It was white with red stripes on the arms and gold on the shoulders."

In response to Posey's questions, Willadean Cherry related several incidents. Once, "his car broke down and I went to get him. And he [Cherry] pointed out the church and said that was the church that he put the bomb under the steps. He said the steps . . . [were] made different then. He said he lit the fuse to it. And he said he regretted that it was children that was killed, but at least they couldn't grow up to have more niggers. . . . Those were his words."

Herren remembered Willadean telling him and Fleming in Montana that Cherry would cry out in his sleep, "The girls! The girls!" Then he would wake up and mumble, ". . . at least they can't breed."

Willadean said Cherry claimed "he was Robert Shelton's [the Imperial Wizard of the Ku Klux Klan] right-hand man, and he said he did everything Robert Shelton wanted him to do."

On one occasion she and Cherry took their children to the zoo in Atlanta and stayed with a friend of Cherry's. Another man named Robert was there. She later identified him from a picture as Robert Chambliss. "He [Cherry] said Robert Chambliss was the best bomb maker . . . and that he was the one that built the bomb. He said they were all together that night when the bomb was built."

When they moved to Calera "after all the kids was [sic] there, he took it [Klan robe] out and danced all around, showing them what he looked like as a Klansperson."

After Cherry started treating her badly, she fled to Chicago, staying with her sister. Cherry followed her and brought her back to Birmingham, stopping along the way at his sister's house to pick up his children. When Cherry stepped out of the car, leaving her and her children inside, Willadean "put her foot on the gas and took off." Until today in the courtroom, she had not seen him again.

Johnson asked Willadean about a kidnapping charge on her record. She explained that while she and Cherry were dating, she sent her children to her sister in Virginia while she [Willadean] had an operation and until school was out. When she went back to get her children, she was told she couldn't see them. She put them in the car and came back to Birmingham. Cherry had her see Art Hanes Sr., who was a Klan attorney and "could get her out of anything." Hanes advised her to go back and straighten it out, which she did. She was arrested in Virginia and charged with kidnapping. The judge told her to write him a letter telling him she had a home for the children, and he advised her to get married. She wrote the letter and married Bobby Cherry. The charge was dismissed, and she regained custody of her children.

On cross-examination, Johnson pushed her about the dates of her marriage and divorce, pointing out inconsistencies in her statements. Irritated, she admonished him, "You should write some of this down."

She repeated what Cherry had told her about placing the bomb at the church and lighting the fuse. "Sometimes he cried," she said.

Johnson jumped on this. "You didn't say anything about Bobby crying to the grand jury. You said he always bragged about that."

"He bragged about it, but he also said he felt sorry for them too."

Johnson asked her about Cherry's statement that he had put the bomb under the steps of the church. She explained that their car had broken down about a block away and Cherry pointed to the church. At that time, the concrete steps where the bomb had been placed no longer existed; the only steps were the front steps, and apparently Willadean assumed those were the steps Cherry was talking about.

"You told them [Herren and Fleming] that Bobby Cherry told you that he lit the fuse?" Johnson asked.

"Yes."

"After putting the dynamite under the steps?"

"No. He said the dynamite was put under the night before. He said he got out of the car and went and put the bomb under the steps the night before."

Johnson pointed out the illogic of him planting a bomb the night before and claiming he had lit the fuse. Willadean said she didn't know—that was just what he said.

———

Willadean's brother Charley Wayne Brogdon had visited with them when they lived in Chicago. He testified Cherry had once shown him a Klan robe.

"What did you talk about?" Cochran asked him.

"Race. The Klan. He used the *N* word. That's all he used."

"Anything else?"

"He told me he made the bomb, the one that killed four kids in the church house. . . . He was remorseful some of the time, then hateful."

On his cross-examination, Johnson challenged, "Did he ever tell you he lit the fuse [to the bomb] . . . planted it anywhere?"

"No," Brogdon said, "he [just said] he made it."

George Ferris, a nephew of Willadean Cherry, testified that Bobby Frank Cherry had once tried to get him to join the KKK. He had refused.

Cochran asked, "He ever make comments about blacks?"

"Just that he . . . hated niggers"

"Any comment about bombings?"

"He said that damn church should have been full of niggers."

Both Fleming and Herren watched worriedly as Michael Wayne Gowins was called. Gowins was dying from the exposure to asbestos in his youth. Testifying in this case had become important to him. Financial reasons had forced him to move several times since his initial interview. On each occasion, he faithfully called Fleming to give his new address. Once, he called to ask if he should get a haircut for the trial. "Would that be OK?" Nervous about testifying, he requested they give him plenty of time to prepare. "Please give me a day or two notice," he asked. Fleming passed the request to the attorneys, but Fleming had to call Gowins at 10 AM to tell him, "We need you at 1 PM today." Fleming knew it had shaken Gowins, and wished the attorneys had agreed to give him more time.

Gowins rolled into the courtroom in a wheelchair with his oxygen tank. He testified in a raspy voice about helping his mother clean apartments in Texas. Bobby Frank Cherry had come in to clean the carpets.

Cochran asked him, "What was being said?"

"Well, he and my mother were talking about Mexicans coming into America, and he said something about them leaving apartments dirty."

"Anything else?"

"About the Klan," Gowins said.

"He said he was in the Klan?"

"Yeah, and they was [sic] talking about the Sixteenth Street church and he said, 'You know, I bombed the church . . .' Well at that time it got real quiet [in the apartment]. And about that time he got through working [cleaning the carpet] and left."

"When did you decide to tell someone about it?"

"About ten years later, I read where the FBI was looking for the church bombers and I called them, the FBI."

Agent John Downey testified to interviews with Cherry in which Cherry made the statement: "The only reason I didn't do the church bombing was maybe because someone beat me to it." He denied wanting to bomb the church, but said if he had something against that particular church he would have "done something to the pastor" and not killed innocent children.

In another interview Cherry told Agent Downey about a visit from Blanton and his wife at Cherry's home. Blanton handed him several petitions that demanded a congressional investigation of the US Department of Justice and asked Cherry to solicit signatures for them.

In that interview, Cherry also gave a detailed description of how to make an acid detonator, including giving Downey a warning about being careful not to get the acid on one's skin because it would burn. Cherry added he had never seen such a thing and had no idea how he knew about it.

The prosecution showed a video of how an acid detonator could be made and used to ignite a fuse.

Special Agent Robert Murphy testified to an interview in which Cherry said if he had wanted to bomb this church he probably would have used two cars and only two men. One man would be the lookout parked somewhere in the immediate vicinity while the other man would drive into the area, park his car, and plant the bomb. Cherry indicated he was in favor of such a plan since he would not want too many people involved.

Remembering how Blanton's attorney had grilled Blanton's girlfriend, Fleming was worried about Teresa Stacy's testimony, even though the judge had ruled the prosecution could not bring up anything about her alleged sexual molestation by her grandfather, Bobby Frank Cherry, or her time as a go-go dancer after fleeing her home.

She testified that she contacted the FBI after seeing Cherry on a televised news conference denying he had bombed the church. When she was between nine and eleven years old, they were on the front porch, and "I heard him say, 'I helped blow up a bunch of niggers back in Birmingham.'"

On both the direct questioning and cross-examination, Stacy spoke in detail about her past life in a matter-of-fact, candid manner, explaining what drugs she had preferred in what time period and what her life had been like. She was a stable, married woman now, and her testimony came across very well. Judge Garrett afterward commented that she had been the most believable of all the witnesses.

Chris McNair, the father of Denise McNair, and Sarah Collins, Addie Mae Collins's sister, testified as they had in Blanton's trial. It was just as emotional as it had been the first time Fleming had heard it. This was a case that pulled at your heart. He was glad he had never taken that resignation from the drawer.

The state rested its case, and the court adjourned for the day.

36 | CHERRY TRIAL: DEFENSE

NEITHER CHAMBLISS NOR BLANTON had taken the stand in their trials, and Bobby Frank Cherry's attorneys (or Cherry himself) chose to follow that same path. The first witness they called was Mary Frances Cunningham. Cunningham was the woman who reported to the FBI that she and her niece Elizabeth Cobbs had disguised themselves and followed the bombers to the church; the woman who later told Bob Eddy she had lied to the FBI and never saw the bombers; the woman who reacted hysterically when Fleming asked her about her law enforcement boyfriend; and the woman who called Herren her angel. Prosecutors had decided not to call her as a witness, but the defense did.

In her original statement to the FBI she identified Chambliss, Blanton, Herman Cash, and Bobby Frank Cherry as being at the church at 2:15 AM the morning of the bombing. She saw one of them walking down the alley toward the east side of the church "carrying something with a handle." On the stand, Cunningham, now seventy-eight years old, denied ever making such a statement to the FBI or knowing anything about the episode.

When Jones cross-examined her, however, she admitted her niece Elizabeth Cobbs had gone with her one time to the FBI, and that would probably have been the December 7, 1964, meeting with the FBI.

Bob Eddy was called to the stand. Even though he had been the investigator in the case against Chambliss, as a defense witness he was only allowed to answer the questions given to him. He said that Cunningham told him she had made up the story—based on things she overheard from the FBI—of being at the church in the wee hours of Sunday morning.

Fleming was also called. The defense questioned why he didn't doubt the credibility of Willadean Brogdon when she claimed Cherry showed her steps at a time they no longer existed. He also pointed out the inconsistency of Willadean Brogdon's statement that Cherry said he "lit the fuse," while her brother reported Cherry said he "made the bomb." Fleming said those things did not cause him to doubt the witnesses.

Although Bill Jackson, the Catholic barber, had been a prosecution witness in both the Chambliss and Blanton trials, now the defense called him to the stand. He stated he had been at the Modern Sign shop on the Saturday night with Blanton making signs for an upcoming rally protesting school integration, but he did not know Cherry and had not met him until that morning.

Cochran's cross-examination was very much like the defense's cross-exam in Blanton's case.

"Mr. Jackson, you were a Klansman, that's right?" Cochran asked.

"No, sir. Never been."

"Just on a fact-finding mission about the Klan?"

"I did some fact-finding."

"Writing a school paper on it or something?" Cochran asked wryly.

"No, sir. I'm just interested."

"Isn't it in fact true that you lied to the FBI, Mr. Jackson?"

"I lied to the FBI once in a jailhouse," Jackson said. "I told them I didn't know Tommy Blanton."

Cochran reminded him of his grand jury statement—"Would it be fair to say that on some occasions you lied to the agents you were talking to?"

Jackson squirmed around the answer, but then admitted, "Yes, I misled people."

"You lied to the FBI?

"They've misled me, too."

"So it's OK for you to lie to the FBI because they've misled you?" Cochran asked.

"It's not OK for them to lie to me as a citizen."

The defense brought two of Cherry's grandsons forward as witnesses to his character. They stated they had never heard their grandfather say he bombed a church and that he referred to African Americans as Negroes.

The pastor of a church in Mabank, Texas, that Cherry attended said the congregation was about half black and half white and Cherry fit right in. When asked if he ever heard Cherry use the *N* word, the pastor said, "Yes, I have."

"Often?"

"Well, yeah." As the pastor attempted to explain he had used the word himself when he was younger, Jones objected, cutting him off, a move that left the jury with a sour impression of both Cherry and his pastor.

In Thomas Blanton's trial, Eddie Mauldin had testified that he observed a Rambler station wagon drive by the church that Sunday morning right before the explosion, and that the car burned rubber driving away. Mauldin died not long after Blanton's trial, but the judge agreed to allow his statement to be read to the court.

Cherry's defense attorneys wanted to bolster their argument that the entire case against their client was based on Mary Frances Cunningham's statement that she saw Cherry at the scene the night of the bombing. Their theory was that the FBI then targeted Cherry (and the other suspects Cunningham placed at the scene) and didn't bother to follow up on other leads. Because Cunningham had retracted her statement, the defense believed this cast doubt on the whole investigation.

Outside the jury's hearing, Johnson asked the judge to allow him to point out that a witness at the church Sunday morning, Carolyn McKinstry, told FBI agents in 1963 she had answered a warning phone call moments before the bomb went off. That statement was not reflected on the agents' report. The defense felt this would bolster their argument that the FBI had been sloppy about their investigation and had not followed up on other leads. The agents who authored the 1963 report, however, were dead, and the judge didn't allow the defense to challenge the veracity of the report.

The judge, however, did allow Carolyn McKinstry to testify as to what she had seen and said. McKinstry, who was now the chair of the Sixteenth Street Baptist Church board of trustees, told the defense attorneys that she didn't know if she would or could testify, and that she had to pray about it. She called Doug Jones, who was a friend, and asked him if she had to appear. He told her if she didn't, she could be arrested, but he promised not to cross-examine her.

According to court records, Johnson told the judge that she said she wasn't coming to court; she had a doctor's appointment the morning she was scheduled to testify. Judge Garrett instructed Johnson to get her in court and, if he had to, bring the doctor with her.

McKinstry did appear. She later related in her book, *While the World Watched*, that she was terrified to relive the traumatic bombing that had killed her friends and to face Bobby Frank Cherry. While she testified, she said his eyes "never stopped shouting out silent death threats." But she told her story, answering the questions put to her as succinctly as possible.

In 1963 she had been fifteen years old and worked as secretary of the Sunday school. The morning of the bombing, she was collecting financial and attendance records and went upstairs when she heard the phone ring in the office. She answered the phone, and a man's voice said simply, "Three minutes." By the time she took fifteen steps into the sanctuary, the bomb exploded. She testified that she related this to the FBI at the time.

Taken together with Mauldin's statement about seeing a car drive by just before the explosion, the defense wanted the jury to believe McKinstry's testimony indicated someone called in the warning because the bombers were on their way to the scene and could have thrown a bomb out of the car just prior to the explosion.

In her autobiography, however, Carolyn McKinstry went into more detail. She said she arrived at the church the morning of September 15, 1963, as Sunday School began and went directly to the church office where she found Ms. Mabel Shorter flustered from answering calls that Shorter said seemed "more threatening than just prankster calls." At the time, McKinstry dismissed the comments because Shorter was "the nervous type." McKinstry did her morning tasks and then went to her own class. Afterward, she stopped to speak to her friends who were in the Ladies Lounge getting ready for services—the four girls who were killed—and then went upstairs, answering the ringing phone with the three-minute warning.

So, the bomb exploded between the end of Sunday School and the beginning of the church services. According to McKinstry's biography, there were previous warning calls an hour or so before the bomb went off.

37 | CHERRY TRIAL: CLOSING ARGUMENTS

"LADIES AND GENTLEMEN," DON Cochran began in closing for the state, "for almost thirty-nine years this defendant has avoided justice. In fact, the evidence shows that for almost thirty-nine years this defendant has mocked justice. Ladies and gentlemen, the time for justice is here. Now, Mr. Johnson has tried from the start of this case . . . [to have] you believe that this investigation started on the seventh of December 1964, because a statement given by Mary Frances Cunningham caused this investigation to jump off on a sidetrack, and ever since that moment, they have wrongly accused this man. In fact, what the evidence shows is that this defendant was a prime suspect from the start. By my count, he was interviewed at least ten times by the FBI *before* December 7, 1964. . . .

"Now you're not going to know everything that happened in Birmingham about this bombing back in September 1963. Juries never know everything. And certainly [in] a case tried this long after it happened, you're not going to know everything. But you will know enough."

Cochran went over Cherry's history of violence and then talked about his motive.

"Well, motive, you always have to sort of think of [that] in a common-sense way. I suppose—" He paused. "I suppose it could be a coincidence that the biggest, the deadliest, the worst bomb of all the bombs in Birmingham just happened to happen five days after the public schools were integrated for the first time. That could be a coincidence, I suppose. But your common sense tells you otherwise."

He referenced Cherry's statement to the FBI that he wished Arthur Shores, a prominent black civil rights attorney, had been killed when his house was bombed, and that "the only reason he didn't do the church bombing was that somebody 'beat me to it.'"

Cochran then referred to Blanton's statement in the Q9 Kitchen Tape where he explained to his wife that "we" met at the Modern Sign Company to "make the bomb." He reminded the jury of the statement Cherry gave the FBI that he had been at the Modern Sign shop that same Friday night. The shop was only three blocks from the church. This, he said, was "aiding and abetting" the crime.

"It makes perfect sense," Cochran said, "that if you're going to arm the biggest bomb that's been used in Birmingham, that you're going to do it somewhere close to the church. Maybe they built the fuse at his [Cherry's] house, and finally put the thing together and armed the fuse there at the Modern Sign Company. They only had to go three blocks to get it to the church. All they had to do was leave it there [at the sign shop] on Friday night, come back and pick it up on Saturday [Sunday AM] and drop it off."

Black-and-white pictures of the girls displayed on the screen in the courtroom. In the last photo eleven-year-old Denise McNair was hugging her Chatty Cathy doll. "She never got to be fourteen years old. Never got to get over being so naive that she didn't even understand that she was supposed to hate that doll because it had different colored skin than she did. Ladies and gentlemen, the time for justice is here. In fact, it's way overdue."

Johnson presented the closing arguments for the defense. His main point was centered on the theory that Mary Frances Cunningham's story was the basis for the case against Cherry, and that the government had made Cherry the scapegoat for the crime. "It seems strange," he said "that the men the FBI go after are the same ones she [Mary Frances Cunningham] names. She told the story back in 1964, but no one in Washington took note because they probably thought it sounded a little phony. Somebody comes up after a year and says, 'I was there.' And you want to go to that person and say, 'Why in hell didn't you say something to save lives?'"

Fleming wondered what the jury would think about this. It sounded reasonable, if you didn't know the whole back story—Cunningham tried to report it to Deputy Hancock. The prosecution had declined to get into all of that, so the jury was unaware of it. He hoped it wasn't a mistake.

Johnson attacked the prosecution's witnesses and the way the FBI made their reports, the 302s, suggesting not only did they base their case on what Cunningham said, but that the jury should also "look at all of these racial slurs. Look what an undesirable person we've got here. This looks like an easy man to prosecute because he's the human equivalent of a cockroach. So let's just go where the light is brightest. Let's focus in on this story."

Johnson blamed the state for allowing hatred to persist during the 1960s. Justice would not be served, he said, by convicting an innocent man. "The memories of those children will survive anything we do here. And they will always be cherished. And they will always be important because of . . . the change that they have made in all of us. Nothing we can do here can add anything to the importance of their memories."

In the state's final closing arguments, Doug Jones said, "This was the most heinous of crimes, an attack on God's house where innocent children were prepared to conduct the first of monthly youth worship services. And it rippled through the world where good and decent people asked—Why? Is nothing sacred in Birmingham, Alabama, where innocent children cannot even go and worship without fear of death or injury?

"Bobby Frank Cherry," he said, "wore the shock like a badge of honor." Jones compared the men "hiding under their hoods" to the forefathers of terrorism.

Referring to the picture of Denise McNair with her doll, he said, "It is an image of hope, the dream that all God's children can live together." Cherry "could not understand that hope is a good thing, and good things never die. I ask you to hold this defendant accountable . . . and when you do . . . justice will truly roll down like a mighty river."

The jury retired and deliberated for a while, and then went back to the hotel where they were sequestered. From the window of the 2121 Building, Herren could look down and see across the street to the criminal justice building. The press and onlookers milled around the outer courtyard, waiting. By lunchtime, Herren was worried. This was taking way too long; Blanton's jury had been so quick.

About an hour after lunch, he happened to look up and saw people running toward the courthouse with cameras and microphones. He turned and said, "I think we got a verdict." On the heels of his comment, the phone rang.

The walk across the street was silent but full of emotions.

It was May 22, 2002. Once again, as the foreman stood to read the verdict, Herren felt it could go either way. Regardless, he told himself, they had given everything they could to bring the case to a jury. If the jury decided they didn't feel it was enough to convict him, well that was what the jury system was for.

Fleming looked at the items sitting on the prosecution's table—Denise McNair's pristine shoes and white purse, the Bible, and the piece of cinder block removed from her head. He would not have wanted the burden of being a juror in either of these trials.

The foreman stood. The verdict was guilty on all counts of first-degree murder.

Both prosecution and defense attorneys often spoke to the jurors after a trial to figure out what had gone right or wrong. In the Blanton trial, jurors told prosecutors it was the tape-recorded conversation of Blanton and his wife—a conversation just over one minute in length—that made the difference in their vote. Jurors from Cherry's trial reported they took their time carefully categorizing the evidence, but their verdict was unanimous on the first vote.

Throughout the trial, Cherry sat in his suit, his wavy gray hair giving him a grandfatherly appearance, his eyes unfocused, staring ahead, a picture of the senile old man who was mentally incompetent to stand trial. The jury told prosecutors that on one occasion when they were getting into the bus, they saw Cherry in the back alley talking animatedly to his attorneys and realized that his demeanor in court had been an act.

Before pronouncing sentence, Judge Garrett asked Cherry if he had anything he wished to say. Cherry turned to face the prosecutors and investigators, dropping his vacant, stare-into-space demeanor. "This whole bunch have lied all through this thing. . . . I've told the truth. I don't know why I'm going to jail for nothing!"

EPILOGUE: REFLECTIONS

◆

HERREN AND FLEMING STOOD on the steps of the courthouse after the last conviction. The crowd swirled around them. Microphones again were pointed at Doug Jones's face.

"Ben, I'm going to send Mike Gowins a couple of those little model cars," Fleming said.

"Yeah, we can do that now."

It was over. They could have their lives back, spend weekends with their families. Go hunting. Photograph the graves of Confederate generals.

Herren looked at the whirl of people. There was excitement here, but he knew the reactions would be mixed. The parents of Denise McNair and Carole Robertson's mother had expressed their gratitude for the work done to bring the case to trial. He knew others who had ached for a long time would be grateful, relieved there was finally some resolution. For some though, it had just stirred up old anger—four innocent girls had their lives cut short while their murderers had almost forty years to live without being bothered. And still others questioned, *Why go after old men for something they had done so long ago?* Herren wondered, Would younger people with no real memory or connection with the bombing, other than a mention in the history books at school, even be touched at all?

Birmingham was still a city torn. *If we keep living our past, we can never move forward*—Herren had heard that too, accompanied by frustration that the words "Birmingham, Alabama," were paired with scenes of dogs and fire hoses from the 1960s in the media, and in the minds of people who had never been here to see and judge for themselves what had grown from the seeds of the past. People wanted to move forward.

But can you move forward without resolving the past? A few hung onto it for the wrong reasons. Fleming had remarked once: "Some people want to keep race as much in the forefront as they can, because they are in the race business." That was the only way they knew.

A retired police officer had asked Herren, "Why now? Why don't you just let it die?"

It would never die, Herren knew, nor should it, at least not in the sense that people should forget. They needed to remember, because the capacity for hatred was built into the human race, as rooted as the capacity for good. You couldn't be a police officer and not understand that.

He took a deep breath. It was hard to believe he had been part of this. Many times over the past five years he'd asked, Why me?, especially when things looked bad and it didn't seem they were going anywhere.

There were many ironies over the past five years. In the beginning, they had guarded the media from the case, afraid it would ruin things. They thought time was their enemy; the case was too old. Yet it was the media exposure that brought witnesses forward, and time itself that solved the cases—time for a person like Rob Langford to work his way to the SAC of the Birmingham FBI and do what seemed right to him, regardless of the failures of the past; time for people like Robert Chambliss's niece to grow into the kind of person who could overcome her fears to tell her tale; time for Mike Gowins to be born and hear Cherry's ranting about what he had done in Birmingham; time for technology to advance so a reel-to-reel tape could be digitized and cleaned of extraneous noise; time for children and grandchildren to be born and hear the bragging tales and have the courage to speak about it; and, perhaps, time for a jury to reflect the diversity of the community and to act on the evidence presented to them.

"You know," Fleming said, "we chase the bank robbers. We chase the kidnappers. It's just another day. But here we—we've *impacted* something."

Herren nodded.

"Ben," Fleming said, a bit of awe in his voice, "we touched history."

Herren turned to him. "Bill, I think it's more like history touched us."

Not more than a few blocks away, the Sixteenth Street Church stood, rebuilt with funds from around the world—a symbol of dark days, but also a symbol of hope—hope that people could change, that justice could come. Martin Luther King had said as much at the funerals. "The innocent blood of these little girls may well serve as the redemptive force that will bring new light to this dark city."

It had taken a long time, and neither the light, nor the justice was perfect . . . but they had come.

POSTSCRIPT

◆

AFTER THE CHURCH BOMBING, one of the most significant pieces of legislation in the civil rights movement passed Congress—the Civil Rights Act of 1964. Many historians credit the church bombing for ensuring its passage and for propelling the movement forward. On a visit to Birmingham, Archbishop Desmond Tutu remarked that the courage of Birmingham's civil rights protesters inspired those who fought against apartheid in South Africa.

During the first years Robert "Dynamite Bob" Chambliss spent in prison, officials hoped he would reveal the other participants, but the Klan's vow of silence was strong, and rumor spread that, should he talk, the Klan's "kiss of death" would fall upon his wife. Chambliss wrote several letters from his cell claiming it was Thomas Rowe (in a CIA conspiracy) and others who bombed the church and that his own lawyers framed him. He wrote to his prosecutor, Bill Baxley, and to the families of the four victims, asking them to put in a good word for him to the governor. His wife Flora "Tee" Chambliss died in 1980. Even after her death, Chambliss never confessed or led investigators to other Klansmen. He died in prison in 1985.

Both Bobby Frank Cherry and Thomas Blanton were given life sentences. Cherry died in prison in 2004. He never renounced his claim to innocence or violated the Klan code of silence.

As of the date of this printing, Blanton remains in Saint Clair Correctional Facility in isolation, more to protect him from other prisoners than because he is considered dangerous. In 1998 he wrote a letter to Congress asking for a reopening of the case, claiming both his and Chambliss's innocence—"Chambliss was no more guilty of this crime than the man in the moon."

The Anti-Defamation League accorded FBI SAC Robert Langford a "Heroes in Blue" award in October of 2000. In 2002 Bill Fleming and Ben Herren were recipients of the Federal Employee of the Year Award. Bill Fleming retired from the FBI in 2002 to enjoy being with his family, pursuing his interest in the Civil War, and volunteering at his church. He volunteered his time to work on the 1946 murder of two black couples in Georgia, which unfortunately was never solved.

Ben Herren continued to work for the FBI until 2012, when he retired to enjoy his family and his neglected woodworking and to go hunting. Bob Eddy still resides on his farm near Montgomery, but continues to work cases when called upon.

The Sanbomb abortion clinic bombing continued as an active case until May 31, 2003, resolved after the fortuitous arrest of Eric Robert Rudolph in North Carolina by a rookie police officer. Fleming remarked that he, along with every other FBI agent and police officer who had worked on the case, would have liked to have been the one making that arrest.

In 2006, Anthony Pellicano, who had enhanced the Q9 Kitchen Tape, was arrested for wire-tapping and convicted on multiple counts of racketeering. Looking back, Herren believed the Los Angeles Police Department might have been trying to give them a warning about Forensic Audio's owner, commenting, "We're not really sure you want to do this." Perhaps they were already working a case on him but couldn't reveal it. That, however, was hindsight, and, at the time, the investigators were focused on their own case.

Both Blanton's and Cherry's cases were appealed. Since these were state cases, the attorney general's office prepared the state's response to the appeals. In Blanton's case, Bill Pryor and his staff added a strong argument, overlooked by the prosecution in 2001, for allowing the Q9 Kitchen Tape. The microphone had been placed on the wall, but had not pierced the wall, although there was a small hole nearby that was already present. This meant there was no trespass involved in obtaining the recording. In 1963, the FBI was operating under a 1928 case *Olmstead v. United States* that made bugs placed without trespass admissible.

Frank Myers filed the Cherry defense appeal brief, making an unusual argument. In addition to the issues of pre-indictment delay and change of venue, Myers asked the appeals court to rule as unconstitutional an

Alabama law that put a cap on payments to attorneys for the indigent. He claimed removing a judge's ability to make an exception for a significant and voluminous case, such as Cherry's, violated Cherry's right of due process. In other words, he was not being paid enough to make an adequate appeal.

Before the appeals were completed, Cherry died in prison. Charles Flowers, a new attorney hired by Cherry's wife, also filed a surprising motion termed "Suggestion of Death and Motion to Remand to Vacate Convictions." In effect, this motion proposed that since Cherry's death occurred while his appeal was still technically in process, the court of appeals should dismiss his appeal and instruct the trial court to vacate the convictions.

Marc Starrett was the attorney in the attorney general's office assigned to write the Cherry appeal briefs. Starrett felt if the court threw out Cherry's convictions, it would be a terrible blow to the community. Starrett took to heart the responsibility and honor of preparing the best legal arguments he could to support the findings of the trial court, and he was not going to overlook any opportunity. This motion was a bombshell, and reporters were waiting for the state's response. Knowing the reporters rarely read more than the first page of a legal brief, he carefully crafted his opening statements, hoping to impress upon the public and the court the importance of this case. Starrett wrote:

> This Court must not allow Cherry to rewrite history from the grave. In life, Cherry murdered Carole Robertson, Cynthia Wesley, Addie Mae Collins, and Carol Denise McNair, when he and others bombed Birmingham's Sixteenth Street Baptist Church on September 15, 1963; he was convicted of these murders on May 22, 2002. In death, Cherry's convictions—a testament to this State's commitment to justice—must stand.

And stand it did. The court of appeals rejected all of the arguments made in both Blanton's and Cherry's appeals. The defense asked for reviews by the Supreme Court, but they were denied.

ACKNOWLEDGMENTS

◆

MANY PEOPLE HAVE CONTRIBUTED to this book, primarily, of course, Ben Herren, Bill Fleming, and Bob Eddy, the investigators who worked on the cases and gave so much of their time and patience to what had to seem like endless questions from me. Without their commitment, this book would not have been possible. To my agent, Jessica Papin with Dystel & Goderich, who is everything a superlative literary agent should be. To Dan Waterman, senior editor at University of Alabama Press for believing in this book and offering his advice and encouragement. To my wonderful and patient editors, Jerome Pohlen and Michelle Schoob, and to Mary Kravenas in marketing and all the great folks at Chicago Review Press.

Also, I'd like to thank the following people for their willingness to share what they remembered and for their insights: Robert "Bob" Langford (retired FBI special agent in charge of the Birmingham office), Bill Baxley (former Alabama attorney general), Jeff Wallace (former assistant Jefferson County district attorney), David Barber (former Jefferson County district attorney), Robert Posey (US assistant attorney), Frank Sikora (retired reporter for the *Birmingham News* and prolific civil rights author), John Ott (chief US magistrate and retired assistant US attorney), Herbert "Bud" Henry (retired assistant US attorney), Caryl Privett (circuit court judge and former US attorney), Neil Shannahan (retired special agent), Charlie Melton (retired Birmingham police lieutenant), James House (retired Birmingham police lieutenant), Mike Wisland (professor of audio in digital media), Marsha Allen (Jefferson County sheriff's office captain), and James Baggett (archivist at the Birmingham Public Library), and his staff, Catherine Oseas and Don Veasey. Thank you Kay Schuffert for providing photos of your father, Bob Eddy, and to Khrissie Masters at Shelby County sheriff's office and Deputy Chief Randy Christian, Captain Marsha Allen, and Sergeant Jack Self at Jefferson County sheriff's office and Deputy Chief Ray Tubbs for your assistance tracking down photos. I'm grateful to the Leadership Birmingham program coordinators who enabled our class (2003, the best class ever) to talk with Fred Shuttlesworth and Ed Lamont, who played important roles in the Birmingham civil rights story.

A special thank you to Julie Carter, court reporter for Jefferson County, who came through with transcripts from Blanton's trial, and Marc Starrett, with the Alabama attorney general's office, who provided transcripts and appellate documents. Without their assistance, I would not have been able to have access to the court trial transcripts. Many thanks to Beth Lefebvre with the FBI who helped get permissions for the FBI photographs included in the book and guided me to further resources. I also appreciate the discussions with Jonathan Horn, who interviewed Thomas Blanton in prison, and Donna Frankavilla who was present as a reporter at the trials.

To those friends and family members who read drafts and gave their encouragement and input, I am most grateful—John Archibald, Jimsey Bailey, Clarence and Sheila Blair, Lee and Fran Godchaux, Debra Goldstein, Robin deMonia, Warren and Sarah Katz, Sally Reilly, Laura Katz Parenteau, and Roger Thorne. There is no way I can put into words my appreciation for my sister Laura's support, encouragement, editing, and ideas, or for my husband's support in so many ways. In addition to reading drafts, editing, and hugs when I needed them, he has never complained about the time my head has been buried in research and writing, time that cost lost hours with him, not to mention his support in little ways that add up to make a huge difference.

SELECTED BIBLIOGRAPHY

◆

Anderson, Willoughby and Schiff Hardin, LLP. "The Past on Trial: The Sixteenth Street Baptist Church Bombing and Civil Rights History." www.theamericanbarassociation.org, 2010.

Birmingham, Alabama, Police Department. Surveillance Files 1947–1980. Birmingham Public Library, Department of Archives and Manuscripts.

Baxley, Bill. "Why Did the F.B.I. Hold Back Evidence?" Opinion. *New York Times*, May 3, 2001. www.nytimes.com/2001/05/03/opinion /why-did-the-fbi-hold-back-evidence.html?ref=robertechambliss.

Bass, S. Jonathan. *Blessed are the Peacemakers: Martin Luther King Jr., Eight White Religious Leaders, and the "Letter from Birmingham Jail."* Baton Rouge: Louisiana State University Press, 2001.

Chambliss, Prince Caesar. *Prince of Peace: A Memoir of an African-American Attorney Who Came of Age in Birmingham during the Civil Rights Movement.* Lulu.com, 2009.

Cobbs, Elizabeth/Smith, Petric. *Long Time Coming: An Insider's Story of the Birmingham Church Bombing that Rocked the World.* Birmingham: Crane Hill Publishers, 1994.

Cochran, Donald Q. "Ghosts of Alabama: The Prosecution of Bobby Frank Cherry for the Bombing of the Sixteenth Street Baptist Church." *Michigan Journal of Race & Law*, 2006.

Colloff, Pamela. "The Sins of the Father." *Texas Monthly*, April 2000. www.useekufind.com/peace/a_sinsofthefather.htm.

Egerton, John. *Speak Now Against the Day: The Generation Before the Civil Rights Movement in the South.* New York: Alfed A. Knopf, 1994.

Eskew, Glen T. *But for Birmingham: The Local and National Movements in the Civil Rights Struggle.* Chapel Hill: University of North Carolina Press, 1997.

Federal Bureau of Investigation. "Birmingham Alabama Sixteenth Street Baptist Church Bombing, September 15, 1963." Freedom of Information and Privacy Acts. http://vault.fbi.gov/search?SearchableText=bapbomb.

Federal Bureau of Investigation. Sixteenth Street Baptist Church Bombing Investigation Files, 1963–1965, 1975–1977, 1980. Birmingham Public Library, Department of Archives and Manuscripts.

Foley, Gary. "J. Edgar Hoover and the American Civil Rights Movement." Koori History Website, April 2001. www.kooriweb.org/foley/essays/essay_14.html.

Hamlin, Christopher. "Reopening Bombing Investigation Opportunity for New Day Dawning." Birmingham News, July 20, 1997.

Hansen, Jeff and John Archibald. "Klansman Still on Suspect List." Birmingham News, August 31, 1997.

Howard, Gene L. The Life and Career of John Patterson, Patterson for Alabama. Tuscaloosa: University of Alabama Press, 2008.

Jones, Doug. "Justice for Four Little Girls: The Bombing of the Sixteenth Street Baptist Church Cases." The Young Lawyer 14, no. 5 (February/March 2010). www.americanbar.org/publications/young_lawyer_home/young_lawyer_archive/yld_tyl_febmar10_justice.html.

Kimerling, Solomon. "Unmasking the Klan: Late 1940s Coalition Against Racial Violence." Weld for Birmingham, July 18, 2012.

King, Pamela Sterne. "The Awful Legacy of Jim Crow." Weld for Birmingham, August 16–23, 2012.

Lee, Helen Shores and Barbara S. Shores with Denise George. The Gentle Giant of Dynamite Hill: The Untold Story of Arthur Shores and His Family's Fight for Civil Rights. Grand Rapids, MI: Zondervan, 2012.

Manis, Andrew M. A Fire You Can't Put Out. Tuscaloosa: University of Alabama Press, 1999: 147–152.

McGriff, William A. "Crowd Forms at Bombed Church." Los Angeles Times, September 16, 1963.

Martin, Douglas. "J.B. Stoner, 81, Fervent Racist and Benchmark for Extremism, Dies." New York Times, April 25, 2005. www.nytimes.com/2005/04/29/national/29stoner.html?_r=1.

McKinstry, Carolyn Maull with Denise George. While the World Watched: A Birmingham Bombing Survivor Comes of Age During the Civil Rights Movement. Carol Stream, IL: Tyndale House Publishers, 2011.

McWhorter, Diane. *Carry Me Home, Birmingham, Alabama: The Climactic Battle of the Civil Rights Revolution.* New York: Simon and Schuster, 2001.

Sack, Kevin. "After '63, Hard Lives for Suspects." *New York Times,* May 20, 2000. www.nytimes.com/2000/05/20/us/after-63-bombing-hard-lives -for-suspects.html?pagewanted=all.

Sikora, Frank. *Until Justice Rolls Down: The Birmingham Church Bombing Case.* Tuscaloosa: University of Alabama Press, 1991.

Temple, Chanda, and Jeff Hansen. "Ministers' Homes, Churches among Bomb Targets." *Birmingham News,* July 16, 2000.

Unknown. *Knights of the Ku Klux Klan Kloran.* Imperial Press, 1968.

Wright, Barnett. *1963: How the Birmingham Civil Rights Movement Changed America and the World.* Birmingham: Birmingham News Company, 2013.

Author Interviews

Conducted from 2009 to 2013

Marsha Allen, captain, Jefferson County Sheriff's Office, interview by author.

David Barber, Jefferson County district attorney (retired), interview by author.

Bill Baxley, Alabama attorney general (former), interview by author.

Bob Eddy, investigator for Alabama attorney general (retired), interviews by author.

William Fleming, FBI special agent (retired), interviews by author.

Herbert H."Bud" Henry III, assistant US attorney (retired), interview by author.

Ben Herren, Birmingham Police sergeant (retired) and FBI analyst (retired), interviews by author.

James House, Birmingham Police Department sergeant (retired), interview by author.

Robert "Bob" Langford, special agent in charge, Birmingham FBI (retired), interview by author.

Joe Lewis, special agent in charge, Birmingham FBI (retired), interview by author.

Charlie Melton, Birmingham Police detective captain (retired), interview by author.

John Ott, US assistant attorney (retired), interview by author.

Robert Posey, assistant US attorney, interview by author.

Caryl Privett, circuit judge and US attorney for Northern District of Alabama (former), interview by author.

Neil Shannahan, special agent FBI (retired), interview by author.

Jeff Wallace, deputy district attorney (former), interview by author.

Court Transcripts

Alabama, State of, v. Robert E. Chambliss, C.C. 1977-01954.

Alabama, State of, v. Thomas E. Blanton, C.C. 2000-2216, 2218, 2219, 2220.

Alabama, State of, v. Robert Frank Cherry, C.C. 2000-2213, 2214, 2215, 2217.

Appellate documents CR 02-0374 and CR 00-1665.

INDEX

Page numbers in italic type indicate illustrations.